TRADIVOX

VOLUME VIII

TRADIVOX

CATHOLIC CATECHISM INDEX

VOLUME VIII

Giuseppe Frassinetti
Pius X

Edited by
Aaron Seng

SOPHIA INSTITUTE PRESS
MANCHESTER, NEW HAMPSHIRE

South Bend, Indiana
www.Tradivox.com

This book is an original derivative work comprised of newly typeset and reformatted editions of the following Catholic catechisms, once issued with ecclesiastical approval and now found in the public domain:

Frassinetti, Giusseppe. *A Dogmatic Catechism*. Revised and edited by the Oblate Fathers of St. Charles. London: R. Washbourne, 1872.

Pius X. *Compendium of Christian Doctrine*. In *A Compendium of Catechetical Instruction*. Translated by John Hagan. Dublin: Browne and Nolan Ltd., 1910.

Scripture references follow the Douay-Rheims Bible, per the imprint of John Murphy Company (Baltimore, 1899).

Cover and interior design by Perceptions Design Studio.

Sophia Institute Press
Box 5284, Manchester, NH 03108
1-800-888-9344

www.SophiaInstitute.com

Sophia Institute Press® is a registered trademark of Sophia Institute.

ISBN 978-1-64413-364-4

Library of Congress Control Number: 2022933546

Dedicated with love and deepest respect
to all the English Martyrs and Confessors.
Orate pro nobis.

CONTENTS

ACKNOWLEDGMENTS

THE publication of this series is due primarily to the generosity of countless volunteers and donors from several countries. Special thanks are owed to Mr. and Mrs. Phil Seng, Mr. and Mrs. Michael Over, Mr. and Mrs. Jim McElwee, Mr. and Mrs. John Brouillette, Mr. and Mrs. Thomas Scheibelhut, Mr. and Mrs. Kyle Barriger, as well the visionary priests and faithful of St. Stanislaus Bishop and Martyr parish in South Bend, Indiana, and St. Patrick's Oratory in Green Bay, Wisconsin. May God richly reward their commitment to handing on the Catholic faith.

FOREWORD

The Catholic faith remains always the same throughout the centuries and millennia until the coming of our Lord at the end of the time, likewise "Jesus Christ is the same yesterday, today and forever" (Heb 13:8). The Catholic faith is "the faith, which was once delivered unto the saints" (Jude 1:3). The Magisterium of the Church teaches us solemnly the same truth in the following words of the First Vatican Council: "The doctrine of the faith which God has revealed, is put forward not as some philosophical discovery capable of being perfected by human intelligence, but as a divine deposit committed to the spouse of Christ to be faithfully protected and infallibly promulgated. Hence, too, that meaning of the sacred dogmas is ever to be maintained, which has once been declared by holy mother Church, and there must never be any abandonment of this sense under the pretext or in the name of a more profound understanding. May understanding, knowledge and wisdom increase as ages and centuries roll along, and greatly and vigorously flourish, in each and all, in the individual and the whole Church: but this only in its own proper kind, that is to say, in the same doctrine, the same sense, and the same understanding (cf. Vincentius Lerinensis, *Commonitorium*, 28)."[1]

An authentically Catholic catechism has the function of learning and teaching the unchanging Catholic faith throughout all generations. The Roman Pontiffs indeed, taught: "There is nothing more effective than catechetical instruction to spread the glory of God and to secure the salvation of souls."[2] Saint Pius X said, that "the great loss of souls is due to ignorance

[1] Vatican I, Dogmatic Constitution *Dei Filius de fide catholica*, Ch. 4

[2] Pope Benedict XIV, Apostolic Constitution *Etsi minime*, n. 13

of divine things."[3] Therefore, the traditional catechisms have enduring value in our own day and age, which is marked by an enormous doctrinal confusion, which reigns in the life of the Church in the past six decades, and which reaches its peak in our days.

I welcome and bless the great project of the "Tradivox" in cataloguing and preserving the hundreds of long-lost Catholic catechisms issued with episcopal approval over the last millennium. This project will convincingly show the essentially unchanging nature of the apostolic doctrine across time and space, and so I invite the faithful of the entire world to support this historic effort, as we seek to restore the perennial catechism of the Church. The project of a catechism restoration on behalf of "Tradivox" will surely be of great benefit not only to many confused and disoriented Catholic faithful, but also to all people who are sincerely seeking the ultimate and authentic truth about God and man, which one can find only in the Catholic and apostolic faith, and which is the only religion and faith willed by God and to which God calls all men.

+Athanasius Schneider, O.R.C.,
Titular Bishop of Celerina
Auxiliary Bishop of the Archdiocese of Saint Mary in Astana

[3] Cf. Pope St. Pius X, Encyclical *Acerbo nimis*, n. 27

SERIES EDITOR'S

PREFACE

SOME are surprised to find that when a given Catholic is asked to "look something up in the catechism," he may well respond: "Which one?" The history of the Catholic Church across the last millennium is in fact filled with the publication of numerous catechisms, issued in every major language on earth; and for centuries, these concise "guidebooks" to Catholic doctrine have served countless men and women seeking a clear and concise presentation of that faith forever entrusted by Jesus Christ to his one, holy, Catholic, and apostolic Church.

Taken together, the many catechisms issued with episcopal approval can offer a kind of "window" on to the universal ordinary magisterium — a glimpse of those truths which have been held and taught in the Church *everywhere, always, and by all.* For, as St. Paul reminds us, the tenets of this Faith do not change from age to age: "Jesus Christ yesterday and today and the same for ever. Be not led away with various and strange doctrines" (Heb 13:8-9).

The catechisms included in our *Tradivox Catholic Catechism Index* are selected for their orthodoxy and historical significance, in the interest of demonstrating to contemporary readers the remarkable continuity of Catholic doctrine across time and space. Long regarded as reliable summaries of Church teaching on matters of faith and morals, we are proud to reproduce these works of centuries past, composed and endorsed by countless priests, bishops, and popes devoted to "giving voice to tradition."

In This Volume

As the preponderance of early catechisms originated in Latin and often from the printers of Rome, the provinces of Italy may justly lay claim to the title: "Patroness of Catechisms." In this volume, we reclaim two of the greatest catechisms to originate on Italian soil, from the time period generally regarded as "the golden century" of the genre, stretching from the mid-1800s to the mid-1900s. Paired here in English for the first time, these two catechisms are renowned for their doctrinal precision no less than for their venerable authorship.

The first is *A Dogmatic Catechism*, first published in 1842 by Ven. Fr. Giuseppe Frassinetti. Born the eldest son of a middle-class Genoese family in 1804, he was observed from infancy to have a highly reflective and intelligent demeanor, leading him to excel in his schooling and show signs of deep devotion and even genius by the time of his first Communion. There was great expectation as he matured, enduring the hardship of his mother's death in 1818 with inspiring faith and care for his four younger siblings—three of whom would become priests, and the other a religious foundress and canonized saint. He assisted his widowed father and aunt with the education of his four siblings at home until being drawn to the seminary, after which he was ordained in 1827 and ordered to the pastorship of San Pietro di Quinto in Genoa while still in his early twenties. Immediately giving himself to intensive apostolic labors within and around the seaside parish, he became a member of the congregation of Evangelical Workers, who devoted themselves to constant preaching and catechesis, as well as of the Urban Missionaries of St. Charles, who ministered to those in prison.

His instruction and solicitous care were sorely needed in the port city, as heretical tenets and moral laxity gained easy inroads among the historically Catholic populace. In the face of this challenge, his reverence and zeal, erudition and charity were no more apparent in the pulpit and confessional than in the highways and byways, which he often traversed to feed a true hunger for souls that characterized his life. A contemporary wrote of him:

> The visitation of the sick, the assistance of the dying, the succor of the poor, the care of those in peril of losing their innocence, the prevention of scandal, the consolation of the afflicted, and the correction, now loving and now severe, as occasion demanded, of the erring, were the matter of his daily thoughts and labors. His parishioners found in him a pastor of power, a master of virtue, meek, patient, and affable, careful in his conversation with women, profuse in giving, sober in his living, poor in apparel, and given to mortification.[1]

His personal holiness and obvious gifts for teaching and preaching soon gained him the reputation of being "the Italian Curé of Ars," and his introduction of perpetual adoration and regular processions of the Blessed Sacrament in the area met with such success, that he would often gather thousands of worshippers at a time.

The remainder of Frassinetti's life showed no decrease in zeal or pastoral projects; instead, they tended to multiply. In 1830 he invited his younger sister Paola to live at his parish, where she served as housekeeper and instructed the local girls. When her chronically poor health prevented her reception in a local religious congregation, her brother helped her to establish a new institute in 1834: the Sisters of Saint Dorothy. She would remain the superior general of the order until her death in 1876, having outlived her brother and seen the Dorothean Sisters spread throughout Italy and abroad. She was later beatified in 1930, and declared a saint by John Paul II in 1984. Before her death, Bl. Pius IX wrote to her with esteem for both her institute and her brother, calling him "a priest outstanding for doctrine and virtue."

Among the other pastoral projects of this outstanding priest were the founding of the Sons of Mary Immaculate in 1860, as well as a remarkable number of tracts and books, the most notable of which were his two compendiums: one of the moral theology of St. Alphonsus Liguori, and the other of dogmatic theology, later retitled *A Dogmatic Catechism*. This catechism met with immediate success throughout the dioceses of Italy, running in six local editions and later translations abroad. Appearing in the leadup

[1] From the original *Notice* of the sixth edition.

to the First Vatican Council, there was already a growing demand for more detailed catechisms for adults; a demand that would only continue when the council failed to realize its plans for a universal catechism for the lay faithful. In such a climate, Frassinetti's single-volume overview of systematic theology was destined to be highly serviceable for multiple generations.

Witnessing the great success of this catechism and Frassinetti's other writings, his friend Father Antonio Ballerini, S.J., observed: "In my poor judgment, they combine solid doctrine with a quality rarely to be found, that of adaptation to the capacities of all. There is in them a union of devotion and spiritual affectionateness with discretion, in no way inferior to the sweet spirit of St. Francis de Sales."[2] We are proud to reclaim here the enlarged sixth Italian edition, rendered in English by the Oblate Fathers of St. Charles (London: Washbourne, 1872). Our only changes to the text have been to recast the section numerations, and to include footnoted citations for several sources that are referenced in the body text. In this edition, Fr. Frassinetti recommends careful attention to a number of fundamental sections on the necessity of religion, revelation, and faith, observing that "the knowledge of these subjects is of especial importance in our days, because of the many errors so daringly scattered abroad," insisting that these chapters "contain observations of great importance, and such as are rarely met with in catechetical works." In this, he shows himself to be one of the first catechists to truly appreciate the rising danger of atheistic secular education, which at that time was just beginning to emerge, even among historically Catholic nations.

Some fifty years after his death in 1868, proceedings began for Fr. Frassinetti's canonization, with his cause being formally introduced in 1939 and the title of Venerable conferred in 1991. Even then, few could have guessed at the continued relevance of his catechism in the second Christian millennium. To those who nowadays content themselves with a life devoid of any organized religion, Frassinetti insists: "It is necessary for men to have a religion; that is to say, that they should offer worship to the supreme being, who is God, from whom they derive existence and all

[2] Ibid.

blessings." To those now claiming that natural scientists posing as philosophers have disproven the existence of God, Frassinetti points out: "No true philosopher, that is to say, no good reasoner, even among pagans, has ever doubted the existence of God." To those now asserting that all religions are essentially the same, albeit worshipping God in different ways, Frassinetti illustrates the need for divine revelation: "Human reason of itself cannot determine by what sacrifices and with what rites man should acknowledge [God's] supreme dominion, and honor him. Moreover, of itself it is not able to determine all the laws of moral rectitude." It is greatly to be hoped that Fr. Frassinetti will soon join his sister in the dignity of the altar, and that his catechism will continue to enjoy a wide readership and renewed attention.

The second catechism in this volume has remained one of the most widely used "short catechisms" among the lay faithful since its first publication at the beginning of the twentieth century: The Catechism of Pius X. The great pontiff who authored this text was the first of nine children entrusted by God to the Sarto family in Riese, a small rural village near Venice. The son of devout parents, little "Bepi" was born in 1835, and by age eleven was already eager for the priesthood. He was sent to a Catholic high school outside of town, and later a seminary in Padua, where he graduated at the head of his class in 1858 and was ordained a priest.

A "farm boy" himself, the good Fr. Sarto served with great care and calm devotion as the assistant pastor in the farming village of Tombolo for nine years. He began several programs of regular catechesis for the villagers, during which time he began taking thought for what would later become his well-known little catechism, written for the basic instruction of the laity. He was named the pastor of St. Bartholomew's in Salzano in 1867, where he remained until 1876. Although at first rather poorly received by the local congregation, who had expected an older and more prominent prelate to be appointed, he soon won the respect and affection of many throughout the region. Humble and quick-witted, he served as headmaster of the town schools, worked to reopen the local health care facilities, and fulfilled his priestly duties with great courage and distinction during the deadly cholera outbreak of 1837. Of particular importance were his regular religious education classes for adults, which were so effective and popular that scores of men and women from nearby parishes began to attend as well. It seems to have been during this period that he first drafted and used his catechism for the laity, as his handwritten notebooks left behind in Salzano bear witness.

His successes did not, however, render him proud or overconfident in his own abilities as a priest, and at heart he always seemed to remain the son of poor laborers from a rural town. When he was at last informed of his designation to become the bishop of Mantua in 1884, his protestations of unworthiness were so extensive that they prompted a handwritten response from Pius IX, consisting of a single word: "Obey!" As bishop, he never lost sight of the gravity of his office, once writing to his mother, who lived to see his later appointment as cardinal: "Mother, you do not realize what it means to be a bishop. I shall lose my soul if I neglect my duty." This same awareness followed him to the chair of Peter in 1903, when he took the name of Pius X and wrote to his fellow bishops:

> It is not necessary to remind you with what tears and warm insistance We exerted Ourselves to ward off this formidable burden of the pontificate. ... Since, however, it has been pleasing to the divine will to raise Our lowliness to such sublimity of power, We take courage in Him Who strengthens Us; and setting Ourselves to work, relying on the power of God, We proclaim that We have no other program in the supreme pontificate but that of restoring all things in Christ.

Instaurare Omnia in Christo became the unofficial motto of his papacy, and he lost little time in implementing it. He reformed the standards for priestly formation, worked for the improvement of liturgical music and homiletics among his priests and bishops, lowered the standard age for first Communion and fostered a universal increase of Eucharistic devotion, which remained so central to his own prayer life that he would be declared "Pope of the Eucharist" by his successor, Pius XII.

Theologically, Pius X is certainly best known for his battle against the heresy of Modernism, "the synthesis of all heresies," which he thoroughly catalogued and condemned in his 1907 encyclical *Pascendi* and accompanying decree *Lamentabili*. Recognizing what by that time had become a cancerous error in the very heart of the Church's institutions, he launched a campaign of stringent pursuit and censorship of the modernists and their tenets, requiring the public profession of the famous Oath against Modernism for clergy and teachers. "That We should act without delay in this matter," wrote the saint, "is made imperative especially by the fact that the partisans of error are to be sought not only among the Church's open enemies; but, what is to be most dreaded and deplored, in her very bosom." Why the Oath was rescinded in 1967 by Pope Paul VI remains a matter of some mystery, although it must be observed that its removal was at least ill-advised. In recognition of its contextual significance, we have reproduced this Oath at the end of the present volume, in English that follows the original Latin more carefully than other translations in common circulation.

When Pius X at last succumbed to a lingering illness in 1914, an Italian press headline read: "Saint is Dead." Despite the outbreak of subsequent wars and other dreadful events, pilgrims continued to flock to his tomb over the years, with those who knew him able to confirm the words engraved there: "Pope Pius X, poor and yet rich, gentle and humble of heart, unconquerable champion of the Catholic faith, whose constant endeavor it was to renew all things in Christ."

Although the character and career of Pope St. Pius X has been the subject of exhaustive study and is rather simple to outline, the explosive popularity of his catechism—particularly after the publication of his encyclical *Acerbo Nimis*, which lent tremendous impetus to greater catechetical efforts and publications—have rendered its origins more difficult to trace among the numerous editions and formats found in every European language. Comparison with the early Salzano notebooks show marked similarities in the text that Pius X ordered to be published for the province of Rome in 1905, called the *Compendium of Christian Doctrine*—a thorough and precise text, which is clearly a modification of the catechism previously in use in the northern Italian provinces. Recognizing the need to reduce the size of this *Compendium* for the sake of children preparing for Communion, Pius X entrusted the composition of a different catechism to a papal commission in 1909, with the final result of two different texts, published in 1912: one was a complete edition, of roughly half the size of the *Compendium*, while the other was a further abridgement for children, sized down to less than 200 questions and similar to the English "penny catechism," albeit in masterful Italian. Given their immediate applicability and the constant emphasis given by the pope to religious education (he was also dubbed the "Pope of the Catechism"), each of these three texts were variously published, translated, and republished as "The Catechism of Saint Pius X," with some editors offering recombinations of each of the three, or even their division into several different booklets.

The original *Compendium*, marked by the Saint's attention to thoroughness and detail suitable to several levels of instruction, appears to have first been translated into English in 1908, by the Vice-Rector of the Irish College in Rome, Msgr. John Hagan, as part of his own monumental *Compendium of Catechetical Instruction* (New York: Benziger Brothers, 1908). Over the years, Hagan's excellent English translation was subjected to various redactions and reprints, often under the (perhaps misleading) title of *Catechism of St. Pius X*. The English versions were still further confused in 1974, with the appearance of Msgr. Kevane's *Catechism of Christian Doctrine; Published by Order of Pope St. Pius X*, which was in fact a heavily edited version of a different catechism that had been based on the original Pius X text. Kevane's version was also "adapted according to the Second Vatican Council," which seems to have required the deletion of several original sections and the removal of valuable expressions, e.g., the description of the confirmand becoming a true "soldier of Christ."

Hoping to remedy some of this confusion, and in an effort to bring the great pontiff's original text of 1905 to English-speaking readers without any diminution or substantial change, this volume recovers the first English translation of his *Compendium of Christian Doctrine*, as found in Hagan's four-volume work of 1908. Our only adjustments have been to add footnoted citations where they are lacking, as well as certain section titles to better highlight the inherent organization of the text. We entrust the fruitful reception of this landmark text to the intercession of its author in heaven.

Editorial Note

Our *Catholic Catechism Index* series generally retains only the doctrinal content of those catechisms it seeks to reproduce, as well as that front matter most essential to establishing the credibility of each work as an authentic expression of the Church's common doctrine, e.g., any episcopal endorsement, *nihil obstat*, or *imprimatur*. However, it should be noted that especially prior to the eighteenth century, a number of catechisms were so immediately and universally received as reliably orthodox texts (often simply by the reputation of the author or publisher), that they received no such "official" approval; or if they did, it was often years later and in subsequent editions. We therefore include both the original printing date in our Table of Contents, and further edition information in the Preface above.

Our primary goal has been to bring these historical texts back into publication in readable English copy. Due to the wide range of time periods, cultures, and unique author styles represented in this series, we have made a number of editorial adjustments to allow for a less fatiguing read, more rapid cross-reference throughout the series, and greater research potential for the future. While not affecting the original content, these adjustments have included adopting a cleaner typesetting and simpler standard for capitalization and annotation, as well as remedying certain anachronisms in spelling or grammar.

Woodcut depicting an early method used in the production of Catholic catechisms, circa 1568.

At the same time, in deepest respect for the venerable age and subject matter of these works, we have been at pains to adhere as closely as possible to the original text: retaining archaisms such as "doth" and "hallowed," and avoiding any alterations that might affect the doctrinal content or authorial voice. We have painstakingly restored original artwork wherever possible, and where the rare explanatory note has been deemed necessary, it is not made in the text itself, but only in a marginal note. In some cases, our editorial refusal to "modernize" the content of these classical works may require a higher degree of attention from today's reader, who we trust will be richly rewarded by the effort.

We pray that our work continues to yield highly readable, faithful reproductions of these time-honored monuments to Catholic religious instruction: catechisms once penned, promulgated, and praised by bishops across the globe. May these texts that once served to guide and shape the faith and lives of millions now do so again; and may the scholars and saints once involved in their first publication now intercede for all who take them up anew. *Tolle lege!*

Sincerely in Christ,
Aaron Seng

TRADIVOX

VOLUME VIII

A

DOGMATIC CATECHISM.

FROM THE ITALIAN OF FRASSINETTI.

REVISED AND EDITED BY

THE OBLATE FATHERS OF ST. CHARLES.

WITH A PREFACE,

BY HIS GRACE

THE ARCHBISHOP OF WESTMINSTER.

LONDON:

R. WASHBOURNE, 18A, PATERNOSTER ROW.

1872.

Original Title Page
(1872)

A

DOGMATIC CATECHISM.

FROM THE ITALIAN OF FRASSINETTI.

REVISED AND EDITED BY

THE OBLATE FATHERS OF ST. CHARLES.

WITH A PREFACE,

BY HIS GRACE

THE ARCHBISHOP OF WESTMINSTER.

LONDON:

R. WASHBOURNE, 18A, PATERNOSTER ROW.

1872.

Approbations

The translation into English of Frassinetti's catechism is highly opportune. The Council of the Vatican most wisely decreed that a Lesser Catechism should be prepared for the use of the faithful. What the Council of Trent provided in the *Catechismus ad Parochos* for the "*Ecclesia Docens*," the Council of the Vatican is providing for the "*Ecclesia Discens*." But, in decreeing that one authoritative text, in the form of a catechism, should be prepared, the council in no way limits either the liberty of bishops to frame catechisms of a fuller and more explicit kind for the use of their dioceses, or that of catechists to deliver such oral explanations as are suited to the capacities and needs of their people.

The bishops of England, in a united pastoral letter, have enjoined the clergy to renewed diligence and punctuality in their office as catechists. No one who knows the condition of this country can fail to see the need we have of expository catechisms, rising from the simple text of the penny catechism to such extensive works as Gaume's *Catechisme de Perseverance*.[1] The rapid development of intelligence in all classes renders the office of the catechist both more necessary and more difficult. It must never be forgotten that a good catechist is a preacher of a very high order. The *traditio Symboli* is not a mere repetition of question and answer, but an elucidation of the doctrines of faith, which affords full scope for the intelligence of a theologian, and for the charity of a pastor.

The catechism of Frassinetti is a good example of what a catechist may do. It is singularly well adapted to the needs of our middle class, for whom, as yet, a sufficient provision has hardly been made. I therefore very heartily recommend the use of this catechism to the clergy and faithful.

+ HENRY EDWARD,
Archbishop of Westminster.
Nativity of Our Lady, 1871.

[1] Editor's note: This is the famous catechism by Msgr. Jean-Joseph Gaume — an extensive, four-volume work, included in Volumes X-XIII of this series.

Prologue: Religion

The Necessity of a Religion

1. **Is it necessary for men to have a religion?**
Taking for granted the certainty of the existence of God, which no one who uses his reason can doubt, it is necessary for men to have a religion; that is to say, that they should offer worship to the supreme being, who is God, from whom they derive existence and all blessings.

2. **Why do you say that no one who uses his reason can doubt the existence of God, for many philosophers have not only doubted, but denied it: and they were men, who, besides being very learned, were most acute critics, and profound reasoners?**
No true philosopher, that is to say, no good reasoner, even among pagans, has ever doubted the existence of God. A few only, who, notwithstanding the acuteness of their intellects, abandoned themselves to every kind of infamy and crime, fearing God's chastisements and not choosing to amend their lives, sought to persuade themselves that there was no God, so as, if possible, to arrive at being impious without fear and remorse. They therefore blasphemously asserted that there is no God. But nonetheless were they persuaded that he exists. In fact, after having in their lifetime blasphemously denied God, in the hour of death, either in penitence or in despair, they confessed that there is a God. As a sick man, to whom the thought of death is grievous, seeks to persuade himself that he will recover from his sickness, however clear the reasons may be which should convince him to the contrary; so did these impious philosophers, to whom the thought of the existence of a God was intensely obnoxious, seek to persuade themselves that there is no God, although they had the clearest evidence of his existence.

3. **Assuming the existence of God, why is it necessary that men should offer worship to this supreme being?**
For the same reason that a son should love his father, that a subject should pay homage to his king, that one who has received benefits should be grateful to his benefactor, etc. This supreme being is our Father, our King, and our sovereign benefactor.

The Necessity of a Revealed Religion

4. **Is natural religion sufficient, that is to say, a worship given to God according to the dictates of mere human reason; or is a determinate worship, manifested to us directly by God, by means of a supernatural revelation, requisite?**
Mere human reason is not sufficient to make known to us all the truths necessary to the right knowledge of God. Human reason of itself cannot determine by what sacrifices and with what rites man should acknowledge his supreme dominion and honor him. Moreover, of itself it is not able to determine all the laws of moral rectitude. Omitting all the other arguments which might be brought forward, it is sufficient to observe that this proposition is an undeniable fact. None of the philosophers who have treated of God and his attributes by the light of natural reason alone attained to giving a just idea of the supreme being; and whilst they all agreed that he was to be honored and adored, they were never able to agree as to the kind of sacrifices and rites which ought to be adopted.[1] The laws of morals, when left in the hands of mere philosophers, ever inclined either on one side or on the other, to what was unjust and base.

[1] What Rousseau himself wrote of deist philosophers may be appropriately quoted here. "If we consider their reasons we shall find that they all tend to destroy—they agree only in mutual contradiction."

The pagan philosophers among the Greeks recognized the necessity of a revelation, and constantly looked for and desired it.[2]

5. **It would seem that, as human reason became perfected, it might attain a point which it had not yet reached; that is to say, a thorough knowledge of the divine attributes, of the most acceptable modes of honoring God, and of all the rules of the moral law; and now that, in consequence of the march of enlightenment, human reason is near this perfection, we shall henceforth no longer stand in need of a supernatural revelation.**
Considering the many centuries during which philosophers have studied how to bring the faculties of the human mind to perfection, were our reason capable of an absolute perfection, it would by this time be perfect, and we should know all things, so to speak, better than the angels; but instead of this, the republic of philosophers (I speak of those only who disdain the light of revelation) does but find itself in greater confusion, and greater darkness; so that there is no doubt but that twenty centuries ago, Plato, Aristotle, and other heathens, taught a philosophy far more reasonable, correct, and moral than that taught by the infidel philosophers of the present day. Man has in his nature a depth of malice and ignorance which is unfathomable; and if he would really perfect his spiritual faculties, he must

[2] Here are Plato's sentiments in the Dialogues with Alcibiades. "SOCRATES: The safest course is to wait patiently, and we certainly must wait until he come who shall instruct us in our duties toward God and toward men. ALCIBIADES: When will that hour come, and who shall instruct us in these things? I ardently desire to behold this teacher! SOCRATES: He of whom we are speaking has care of thy concerns, but, as I think, he acts in regard to us, as Homer relates that Minerva acted with Diomed. Minerva dispelled the mists which darkened the eyes of Diomed, and he then saw the objects which were before him. In like manner it is necessary that a dense mist should be taken away from the eyes of thy understanding, in order that thou shouldest discern good from evil, which at present thou canst not do. ALCIBIADES: Oh! that he would come! Oh! that he would dissipate this darkness! For my part, I would be ready to do whatever he should command, so that I might but become better than I am. SOCRATES: This is what we ought to do, because in our ignorance we know not what sacrifices are pleasing to God and what are displeasing to him. ALCIBIADES: When that day shall arrive, our sacrifices will happily be pleasing to God, and I trust in his goodness that this day cannot be far off." You see how even pagan philosophers desired a revealed religion, and acknowledged its necessity.

join the light of revelation to the light of reason. Moreover, it is not for us to judge of the progress of enlightenment in our own age; future ages will judge of it dispassionately and without self-love. We may believe that it will not be denied its just meed of praise for progress in the industrial sciences; we may doubt whether it will secure equal praise for progress in metaphysical and moral science. Meanwhile, we challenge our infidel philosophers to come to some agreement amongst themselves; for, whilst we are deafened by the confused warfare of a multitude of irreconcilable systems, we cannot even understand what they say to us. Let them agree among themselves, and then we may begin to entertain the supposition that they are capable of perfecting human reason. Whilst the tumultuous chaos of their opinions does but deepen more and more, what can we believe, what can we say? Therefore, the ridiculous hope of the complete perfection of human reason cannot exempt us from acknowledging the necessity of a revealed religion, which may instruct us in the knowledge of God, in the way in which we are to adore him, and in the rules of true morality.

The Marks of the Revealed Religion

6. **Many are the religions in the world, which claim to have been revealed by God; but since they are all opposed one to the other, they cannot all have been revealed; one alone can have been revealed by God, and how are we to distinguish it from the rest?**

Most certainly God, who is the truth, cannot reveal as true, things contrary one to another, each of which supposes the falsehood of the rest; and so, amongst all the so-called revealed religions, one alone can be the offspring of a true revelation. No abstruse researches nor prolix demonstrations are needful to distinguish this one from the rest. As a precious diamond is distinguished amidst the fragments of brittle glass, so is the true revealed religion distinguished from those which are false. The religions which call themselves revealed religions are paganism, Mahometanism, Judaism, and Christianity.

Paganism, which is a huge collection, or, to speak more correctly, a huge chaos of innumerable worships, is repugnant to reason, because, we may say, that of everything it makes a god. So that, according to its dictates, that which in one place is the god to whom victims are to be sacrificed, is in another place the victim which is to be sacrificed to, as a god. In Egypt, sacrifices were offered to the ox; in Greece, it was the ox that was offered in sacrifice. One of the ancients relates that, in a certain place, the very priests disputed among themselves, which of two animals was the victim to be sacrificed, which the god to whom the sacrifice was to be made. This religion has all the marks of folly, and none of divinity.

Nor has Mahometanism anything divine about it; no prophecies verified, no miracles wrought; born in ignorance and nurtured in ignorance, it was established and propagated solely by the power of the sword. Barbarity is its support, uncleanness is its food, and both together, all it hopes for in the life to come; never was there a sage who did not abhor it, and hold it in derision.

But of Judaism we must speak in a different way. Judaism can boast of prophecies fulfilled, and miracles performed; its books are holy, and have impressed on them the character of divinity; therefore, the Jewish religion is a religion revealed by God. But this religion was not intended to endure forever; it was to give place to that religion of which it was but the figure. Its books say clearly that God would make to himself a new people, who should possess a new law, and a new sacrifice; therefore, the Jewish religion was that worship by which God chose once to be honored by men; but it is so no longer. And truly wonderful is the abandonment in which God has left it; without a temple, without a priesthood, without sacrifices, and, more than this, without a country; so that the Jews, dispersed over all the world, are strangers in every land. The Jewish religion therefore, of itself, declares that it is no longer that religion which is pleasing to God, but that Christianity has been substituted in its place.

Christianity is now the one and only religion which has the marks of divinity, and it alone will bear them to the end of the world. All the prophecies of holy scripture confirm its truth. Infinite miracles attest that Christianity is the work of God. The Christian religion is that which gives to men the grandest and most perfect idea of the supreme being, which it is possible for them to have; it teaches a most sublime way in which he is to be adored; it prescribes moral laws, all based on justice and holiness; and so the most ignorant Christian, if he be but instructed in the first rudiments of his faith, is more learned in divinity, in worship, and in morals, than any philosopher whatsoever not a Christian. It suffices but to know the Christian religion, in order to feel compelled to proclaim it to be the true, the only religion which enjoys the marks of divine revelation.

7. **How comes it that, since Christianity bears all the marks of revelation, it should be the most opposed of all religions?**
You must observe from whom the opposition comes; because, from the quality of the enemy, we may recognize the quality of the object of his attack. The Christian religion was always more opposed than any of the other religions which are in the world, but it was always opposed by the impious and the impure. The persecutors of the Christian religion, as history shows us, were always the most lost in vice; and the more fierce among them were always monsters of crime and infamy. What wonder is it that the wicked should hate that which is good, and hate it the more, the greater it is? Meanwhile, this continued opposition, whilst it constitutes the glory of Christianity, furnishes us with another mark of its divinity; for, whilst it has been the most opposed of all religions, it is at the same time the grandest and the most unchangeable. After twenty centuries of strife, it is still the same, full of force and vigor, spreading itself triumphantly over the whole world, and changing its enemies into its children, so soon as it becomes known to them. This fact, over and above the promise of God, assures us of its indefectibility.

8. **But in the Christian religion there are many sects opposed one to another; which of these is the true one?**
Not one of those sects; all are false. The true religion is that which is no sect; that which was founded by the apostles, which has their faith and their customs; that which all sects oppose; that which spreads itself over the whole world, embraces all ages, and therefore calls itself, and is in truth, the Catholic religion. All sects have for their heads men who are deserters from the religion of Christ and the apostles; therefore, they can be called Christian sects only insofar as that they acknowledge Christ

and pretend to honor him after their fashion. But they cannot be called Christian, in the sense of making part of that religion which was truly founded by Christ. Facts demonstrate that they are separated from it, because they fight against it. Of such sects we shall speak in the section, "The Church," below.[3]

[3] The unreasonableness of indifference in the matter of religion will be clear and manifest if we reflect sincerely on the subjects here briefly mentioned. If God ought to be honored by a worship, if he has revealed what that worship is which he wills to receive from us, if in manifesting it to us, he warns us that every other worship is henceforth an abomination to him: this being one of the fundamental truths of the Catholic religion, how is it possible we should believe that God is indifferent as to what kinds of worship there may be on the earth? Can it be reasonable to suppose that God esteems himself honored equally by chaste and pure worship, and by the impure and abominable rites of paganism? Can we imagine that the slaughter of the twenty thousand human victims who were annually sacrificed in idolatrous Mexico, when the breasts of those miserable beings were torn open in order to pluck thence their still living, palpitating hearts, was as pleasing to him as the innocent and pious sacrifice of our altars? Can we suppose that the groans and shrieks of horrible despair which rang through those halls of terror and death, pleased him as much as the peaceful hymns, breathing gratitude and love, which resound in our temples? It seems to me a lesser evil to suppose that God does not exist, than to suppose the existence of a God so stupid and insensate as he would be, who should hold himself equally honored by all and every kind of worship that ever has been, and is now, in the world.

Here we will give the propositions condemned in the Syllabus annexed to the encyclical of the 8th December, 1864, Section 3, in order to make known the errors which they condemn:

> "15. Every man is free to embrace and profess that religion which, by the guidance of the light of reason, he shall judge to be true."
>
> "16. In the exercise of any religion whatsoever, men may find the way of eternal life, and gain eternal salvation."
>
> "17. We may at least entertain a good hope of the eternal salvation of all those who are not in the true Church of Christ."
>
> "18. Protestantism is but a different form of the same true Christian religion, in which equally as in the Catholic Church, men can please God."

The Catholic Christian must believe precisely the contrary of that which these condemned propositions set forth.

The third proposition condemned in the above-mentioned encyclical must also be noted; as in it the following error, or rather errors, are confuted: "Liberty of conscience and of worship is the proper right of every man, and in every well-constituted society it ought to be proclaimed and established by law; every citizen has the right of perfect freedom in manifesting and declaring openly and in public, by word of mouth and in print, or in any other way, his own opinions, whatever they may be, unrestricted by any authority ecclesiastical or civil."

The Sources of Theology

The sources of theology are the springs whence the necessary arguments are taken, both to prove and elucidate the truths of the faith and the principles and rules of morals, and to defend those truths and rules from the sophisms of heretics, or of bad Catholics.

These sources or grounds are ten in number: 1) holy scripture; 2) tradition; 3) the consent of the Church Catholic; 4) councils; 5) the judgments of the Roman pontiff; 6) the authority of the holy fathers; 7) the authority of the doctors and schoolmen; 8) the authority of history; 9) the authority of human reason; 10) the authority of philosophy. This is the common teaching of theologians.

Holy Scripture

9. **What is meant under the name of holy scripture?**
The Holy Bible, which comprises all those divine books to the number of seventy-two, which, by the sacred Council of Trent, are recognized as having been inspired by God to their authors, and written by them with such assistance of the Holy Spirit as that they could not have inserted therein the very smallest error, whether out of malice or from human weakness.[4]

10. **How is holy scripture divided?**
It is divided into the old and new testaments. The old testament contains all the sacred books written before the incarnation of the Son of God, beginning with Genesis, and ending with the second book of Machabees; the new testament contains those which were written after the incarnation, beginning with the gospel of St. Matthew, and ending with the Apocalypse of St. John.

[4] Cf. Council of Trent, Session 4

11. **There cannot, of course, be errors in those books, the authors of which were inspired by God; but there might be errors in the Latin Bible which we make use of, seeing that this is not the original, but is entirely a translation from the Hebrew and Greek texts.**[5]

The Church has made use of this Bible for more than twelve centuries; were it corrupted or changed in any important particular, Jesus Christ could not have permitted his Church so to make use of it, without failing in that assistance which he promised her, and which renders her infallible. The sacred Council of Trent even declares him excommunicated who does not believe any one, or any part of any one of the said sacred books which are contained in our Latin Bible,[6] which is also called the Vulgate of St. Jerome, because that most learned and holy father is the author of the greater part of this version.

12. **But would it not be safer to trust to the ancient original texts, rather than to our Vulgate?**

Whatever may be the state of the original texts at the present day, it is certain that they have not been revised and corrected by the Church in the same way as our Vulgate; therefore, in matters concerning faith and morals, our Vulgate ought really to be preferred to the original texts.

13. **Have the words of holy scripture one meaning, or several meanings?**

Very many words and sentences of holy scripture have two meanings; that is to say, a literal meaning and a mystical meaning. The literal meaning is that which the words present of themselves; the mystical meaning, on the contrary, is that which the things present which are signified by the words. For example: holy scripture narrates that Abraham had two sons—one by Agar, a bond-woman, the other by Sara, a free woman. The literal sense is that Abraham had Ishmael by Agar his servant whom he had taken to wife, and that afterward he had Isaac by Sara, who was also his wife, and who was born of the same particular family from which he himself sprang. The mystical sense is that God, figured in Abraham, had two peoples who

5 Some pretend that the epistle of St. Paul to the Romans was written in Latin.

6 Cf. Council of Trent, Session 4

worshipped him: the one in bondage under the Mosaic law—that is, the Jewish people; the other free under the Gospel law—that is, ourselves, the people of Christ. So the holy fathers explain St. Paul (Galatians 4).

14. **There is still another sense, which is called accommodated. What is that?**
We call that the accommodated sense when a sentence of holy scripture which expresses some determinate truth is made use of to express another to which it may be applied. Thus, the Church uses in praise of most holy Mary, various encomiums applied by scripture to the divine Wisdom; as for example, the following words: "I am the mother of fair love, and of fear, and of knowledge, and of holy hope."[7]

15. **May we trust to our own judgment alone, in the understanding and interpretation of holy scripture?**
The Catholic, apostolic, and Roman Church is the depositary of holy scripture. She alone may judge definitively of the true senses of the sacred books; she desires, however, that in the understanding and interpretation of them we should follow the unanimous judgment of the holy fathers,[8] who are the depositaries of tradition, and who were specially assisted by God in the interpretation and understanding of them. It should be noted that all heresies have sprung from the desire to interpret holy scripture according to the private judgment of individuals. "No heresies have sprung up, save when the scriptures, which are good, were not well understood."[9]

16. **Would it not be well to make translations of the Bible into the vulgar tongue, so that it might be put into the hands of all, even of the laity?**
The Church forbids that the Bible, literally translated into the vulgar tongue, should be given to be read by all persons indifferently. She even forbids absolution of sins to be given to those who choose to read it, or retain possession of it without permission. The proof that it cannot be a good thing to put the Bible into the hands of all persons is that, being full of mysteries, it would

[7] Ecclus 24:24

[8] Cf. Council of Trent, Session 4

[9] Augustine, *On John 18*

injure rather than profit the ignorant; and this is manifest from the zeal with which protestants scatter abroad, everywhere and at great expense, an incredible number of vernacular translations of the Bible. Moreover, the Sacred Congregation of the Index, in a decree dated the 13th June, 1757, prohibits "all translations of the Bible in the vulgar tongue, unless they have been approved by the apostolic see, or edited with notes taken from the fathers of the Church, or from learned and Catholic writers." Further, this decree was renewed in the *monitum* of the Congregation of the Index, fer. v. die 7 Januarii, 1836.

This applies even to translations of the Bible in the vulgar tongue made by Catholic authors, and faithfully following the Vulgate, such as that of Monsignor Martini, printed without notes.[10] Hence we may understand how rigorously prohibited are the translations made by protestants, changed and mutilated as they are, and wanting in whole books. Such are Diodati's Bibles, which are scattered abroad by the Bible Societies, with the hope, but we trust the vain hope, of protestantizing Italy. Those Bibles especially may neither be bought, nor received as a gift, nor read, nor kept possession of, by anyone.

Tradition

17. **What is tradition, properly so called, as constituting one of the sources of theology?**

According to the sense of the holy fathers and the holy Council of Trent, by *tradition* is to be understood those doctrines which the inspired

[10] Translator's note: Of the edition, however, published by Monsignor Martini, with notes, His Holiness Pius VI, in a letter to that prelate, in April, 1778, writes: "You judge exceedingly well that the faithful should be entitled to the reading of the holy scriptures: for these are the most abundant sources, which ought to be left open to everyone, to draw from them purity of morals and of doctrine, and to eradicate the errors which are so widely disseminated in these corrupt times. This you have seasonably effected, as you declare, by publishing the sacred writings in the language of your country, suitable to everyone's capacity; especially when you show and set forth that you have added explanatory notes which, being extracted from the holy fathers, preclude every possible danger of abuse. Thus you have not swerved either from the laws of the Congregation of the Index, or from the Constitution published on this subject by Benedict XIV." As to the Catholic translations in English, they may be read by all the faithful, as appears from the approbations of the bishops prefixed to them.

authors did not originally commit to writing, and which may, or may not, have been since written.[11]

18. **How are the traditions divided?**

Of the traditions of the evangelical law, of which we are now speaking, some are called divino-apostolic traditions; and some, apostolic traditions.

The divino-apostolic traditions are divided into traditions that regard dogma, and into traditions that regard morals. The first comprise the truths taught by Jesus Christ to his apostles, or revealed to them after his ascension into heaven. Among this number may be placed the dogma that there are seven sacraments of the new law, neither more nor less.

The traditions that regard morals, that is, practice, comprise the precepts or commandments given by Jesus Christ to his apostles. Amongst them may be reckoned the rites essential to the administration of the sacraments, and which, if changed as to their substance, would render the sacraments invalid. For instance, in the form of the sacrament of penance, were the priest to say, "I wash thee from thy sins," instead of saying, "I absolve thee." These divino-apostolic traditions, both as regards dogma and practice, are unchangeable, and constitute an irrefragable source of theology.

The simply apostolic traditions comprise the constitutions framed by the apostles, as pastors of the Church, for a sound rule of discipline. Among these may be placed the fast of Lent. Such traditions are changeable; so that the supreme pontiff, as universal pastor, may make changes in them as he deems expedient.

19. **Must the traditions of the Church be necessarily admitted?**

It is a dogma defined by the holy Council of Trent that there are traditions.[12] This must necessarily be admitted; because all that is to be believed and practiced is not found in the books of the Bible. We do not find in the Bible that the sacraments of the new law are seven; therefore, without tradition we could not believe that dogma. In like manner, the forms of the

[11] Cf. Council of Trent, Session 4

[12] Cf. Council of Trent, Session 4, and elsewhere.

different sacraments are not found in the divine books; therefore, without tradition they could not be administered. For this cause St. Paul said: "Hold the traditions"; *Tenete traditiones.*[13] Moreover, all heretics, as Canus points out, reject tradition, because they recognize in it a weapon even more fitted to defeat them than holy scripture itself; for by interpreting scripture according to their own fashion, they twist it to their own meaning, but tradition does not depend upon interpretations.

The Church

20. **How do you define the Church of Christ?**
The true Church of Christ on earth — not to speak of the Church triumphant, which is the union of the blessed in heaven; nor yet of the Church suffering, which is the union of just souls detained in purgatory — the true Church of Christ on earth, that is, the Church militant, is the union of all the faithful, who communicate one with another by profession of the same faith, by the participation of the same sacraments, and who are subject to their own bishops, and in especial to the Roman pontiff, who is the center of all Catholic union. Such is the definition common to theologians.

21. **What persons do not belong to the Church of Christ?**
Those who have not yet received baptism; and therefore, not infidels only, but even catechumens, although they believe all the revealed truths of the holy faith, do not belong to the Church. Heretics, that is to say, those who belong to some sect which does not believe all the dogmas of the faith, do not belong to it.[14] Schismatics, that is to say, those who refuse to submit to their own lawful pastors, and, still more, to the authority of the Roman pontiff, do not belong to it. Excommunicated persons also who are notoriously and publicly declared such, do not belong to it.

[13] 2 Thes 2:14

[14] All protestants are heretics.

22. **Are there then excommunicated persons who do belong to the Church?**
Of right, no excommunicated person belongs to the Church; but by indulgence or permission of the Church herself, such excommunicated persons as are called tolerated, that is, such as are not publicly declared excommunicated, belong to it. In like manner secret heretics, that is, such persons as, without declaring themselves for any sect in particular, secretly gainsay some Catholic dogma, whilst they affect to be united to the Church, and subject to their lawful pastors, belong to it. Such men, however, belong not to the soul, but to the body of the Church, in the same way that a withered member sometimes remains united to the body from which it derives neither vigor nor life.

23. **Has it not been said by some that imperfect Christians do not belong to the Church?**
There were a few heretics who pretended that the Church was composed of perfect Christians only; but this was to destroy and annihilate the Church, for on this earth none were ever found perfect, properly so called, except the most Blessed Virgin, who, preserved from original sin, was also free from every imperfection; other saints are called perfect, not because they really were so, but because they constantly aspired after perfection,[15] and with every possible endeavor, sought to strip themselves of their imperfections.

24. **Are those to be considered as belonging to the Church who are in a state of mortal sin?**
Without doubt, nay! This is an article of the faith, and the contrary error was condemned in various propositions of Quesnel by the bull *Unigenitus*.

25. **Do reprobate Catholics, that is, those whom God foresees will be damned because of their iniquities, belong to the Church?**
It is an article of the faith that they belong to it. The contrary error was also condemned by the said bull *Unigenitus*.

[15] A continual striving after perfection is reputed perfection (St. Bernard).

26. **What are the marks of the Church of Christ?**

They are four, as enumerated in the Niceno-Constantinopolitan Creed. The Church is one, is holy, is catholic, and is apostolic.

27. **Explain to me the first mark.**

The true Church is one, especially by the unity of her head, which is Christ; by the unity of the means which lead her to her end, which is eternal salvation; by the unity of her one and the same spiritual food, which is the body and blood of Jesus Christ; by the unity of one and the same faith, of one and the same hope, of one and the same Spirit who directs and governs her.

28. **Who is the origin and center of this unity which the Church has on earth?**

Following the authority of all the holy fathers, all Catholics are agreed that the origin and center of this unity is the Roman pontiff; that he has a primacy of honor, jurisdiction, and authority over all the various churches of the earth, which all, united under this head constituted by Jesus Christ, form one sole Church. Take away this center of unity, and they would be so many separate churches, and no longer one Church.

29. **Explain to me the second mark.**

The true Church is holy, especially by the holiness of her head, which is Christ; by the holiness of her sacraments, of her faith, and of her morals; by the holiness also of the more excellent of her members, who are the just; and by the holiness of her rites.

30. **Explain to me the third mark.**

The true Church is catholic, that is, universal, because she extends through all times, and will last to the end of the world; because she extends over all places, being spread abroad in all the parts of the earth; and because she gathers all nations within her fold.

31. **Explain to me the fourth mark.**
The true Church is apostolic, because she was founded by the apostles, because she preserves their doctrine, and because their successors are her legitimate pastors.

32. **What are the properties of this Church?**
They are three: she is visible, indefectible, and infallible.

33. **Are those properties necessary to her?**
Their necessity is manifest. The Church of Christ is the only true religion in the world, and those only who belong to her can obtain eternal life; therefore, it is necessary that she be visible, in order that those who are not in this Church may recognize her, and may seek to enter within her fold. It is necessary that she be indefectible, because if the Church could fail, even for a short time, during that time it would be made an impossibility for men to save their souls. It is necessary that she be infallible, because if she could err, she could not securely lead her children to the attainment of their end—of eternal salvation.

34. **In what matters is the Church infallible?**
She is infallible in matters of faith and morals. So that when she declares that any truth appertains to the faith, and when she approves or disapproves of any practice appertaining to morals, it is impossible that she should err.

35. **What renders her infallible?**
The assistance of the Holy Spirit, who by a special providence governs her, and moreover speaks to men by means of her.

36. **To what Church do the foresaid marks and properties belong?**
To the Roman Church; not simply as Roman, that is, as restricted within the limits of the territory of the diocese of Rome; but as she is the universal Church, which has for its head and supreme pastor the Roman pontiff.

For this reason, not now only, but in the first ages of Christianity, to say Roman Christians, and to say Catholics, was one and the selfsame thing.

37. **What must we say, then, of the protestant churches, who also claim to be called holy, Catholic, and apostolic?**
They call themselves so with as much right as Italians would have to call themselves French. When they were united to the Roman Church, they really made part of the holy, Catholic, and apostolic Church; but now they are neither holy, nor Catholic, nor apostolic. They are not holy, because they have no longer Jesus Christ for their head, who is the source of all holiness; and they sometimes authorize dogmas and morals which are not holy. They are not Catholic, because they do not extend throughout all times, and are restricted to some particular province or kingdom. They are not apostolic, because their founders were not the successors of the apostles, but deserters from the Church founded by the apostles, and enemies of their doctrine; and in the same way that Italians, if they chose to call themselves French, would find none, either friends or enemies, to give them that name, so protestants will never find anyone who will give to their churches the names of holy, Catholic, apostolic. They must be content with their own names, and to be called the Lutheran Church, the Calvinist Church, the Zuinglian Church, the Anglican Church, etc.

38. **What must we say of the schismatical Greek Churches?**
Inasmuch as they are schismatical—that is, separated and divided from the holy, Catholic, and apostolic Church—they do not belong to her. Moreover, they are also heretical, because they deny several dogmas of the faith; and, amongst others, that the Holy Spirit proceeds as from the Father, so also from the Son. Observe that although these Churches, separated from Catholic unity, are called by many by the name of Greek or Eastern Churches, they ought to be called simply protestant, because in opposing dogmas defined by the Church, they protest against the Church, as is clearly pointed out by Count De Maistre.

39. **We have seen that the Church is infallible in her decisions regarding faith and morals. Now, supposing some controversy should arise, to whom does the definition belong?**

Observe that in the Church we must distinguish two parts: the teaching Church and the hearing Church. The sovereign pontiff, with the other bishops, forms the teaching Church; the whole of the rest of the Christian people, priests not excepted, forms the hearing Church. It belongs, therefore, to the sovereign pontiff and the bishops to define questions which may arise in regard to faith or morals.

40. **Can any particular bishop define such questions?**

Certainly not; but the body of bishops united with the Roman pontiff can definitively determine such questions; and this agreement is made by means of a general council, or by means of a pontifical bull, accepted by the whole body of bishops. It is not, however, necessary that all the bishops should accept it; it is sufficient that it be received, or not opposed by the majority; and in such case, bishops who should dissent and refuse to submit themselves would become schismatics and heretics. You must carefully note that all this is of faith,[16] as all Catholic theologians agree.

[16] Translator's note: Since the date of the Vatican Council, it is now also certain, by the certainty of Catholic faith, what before and always was certain by certainty of theological demonstration, that the supreme pontiff, apart from the bishops, and by himself, is infallible in his definition of questions of faith and morals. The council teaches and defines: "That the Roman pontiff, when he speaks *ex cathedrda*, that is, when, exercising his office of pastor and teacher of all Christians, in accordance with his supreme apostolic authority, he defines a doctrine as to faith and morals, to be held by the Universal Church, has, through the divine assistance, promised to him in Blessed Peter, that infallibility wherewith the divine Redeemer willed his Church to be endowed in defining doctrine as to faith and morals; and therefore, that such definitions of the Roman pontiff are, of themselves, and not from the consent of the Church, irreformable" (Fourth Session, July 18th, 1870. First Dogmatic Constitution on the Church of Christ, Ch. 4).

41. **How must we answer heretics who maintain that scripture is the judge of all controversies regarding faith and morals?**
You must answer that holy scripture serves as a rule by which errors are condemned and truths defined; but that holy scripture itself neither defines nor condemns. Every state has a body of laws; but would it not be a ridiculous thing to suppress the tribunals, and expect the laws to condemn the guilty and to absolve the innocent? Holy scripture is the code of the Church; but the Church is the tribunal to whom it belongs to define the meaning of her code. It pleases heretics to establish holy scripture as the judge in all controversies; because, by explaining it according to their caprice, they may say that the judgment is in their favor, and they are not afraid that holy scripture should ever summon a council, or issue a bull to condemn them.

42. **They say further that everyone may judge all controversies by his own private judgment, enlightened in the understanding of holy scripture by the Holy Spirit.**
Were it true that the Holy Spirit enlightens the minds of all Christians, so that no one could err in the understanding of holy scripture, there would never have been controversies in such matters; hence we must say that he does not enlighten all, and does not render all infallible. Which, then, are the private judgments illuminated by the Holy Spirit? How shall we distinguish them from those which he has not illuminated? And further, if heretics are illuminated by the Holy Spirit to decide controversies according to their private judgment, they must needs make the Holy Spirit the author of those innumerable contradictions which divide them into a thousand sects, and make a chaos of their faith or religion.

43. **What shall we say of those who give authority to decide controversies to the general multitude of the Christian people?**
This is pure delirium in matters of faith. We may admit it when we see the sheep leading their shepherds to pasture. Jesus Christ said to the apostles, "Teach ye all nations."[17] He did not say this to the multitude.

[17] Mt 28:19

44. **May not the decision of religious controversies be assigned to the temporal sovereign?**

From the very fact that the authority of sovereigns is temporal, it does not extend to religious controversies, which are spiritual. Jesus Christ gave the keys to St. Peter, not to the kings or to the emperors. In a word, be well assured that to give authority to determine religious controversies to any, save only to the Church, and to those who represent her, is an error against the faith which no Catholic would ever take upon himself to defend.

45. **Can the Church make laws which will bind the consciences of the faithful?**

There is no doubt of it; and all the councils and the bulls of the sovereign pontiffs prove it. Both the one and the other are full of laws which are always observed by good Christians. Besides, no society can subsist without laws which shall rule and direct the actions of its members. Now the Church is a society; and so without laws to rule and direct the actions of her members, she could not subsist.

46. **Have the laws of the Church force and vigor without the approbation and sanction of the civil government?**

Undoubtedly the laws of the Church have force and vigor of themselves, independently of any approbation or sanction whatsoever of civil governments. We have new proof of this in the condemnation of the following propositions, proscribed in the encyclical of 8th December, 1864:

"10. The laws of the Church do not bind in conscience, except when they are promulgated by the civil power."

"11. It is necessary that the acts and decrees of the Roman pontiffs concerning religion and the Church should have the approbation and sanction, or at least the assent, of the civil power."

"12. The apostolic constitutions by which secret societies are condemned (whether the oath of secrecy be exacted in them, or be not exacted), and by which their followers and abettors are excommunicated, has no force whatever in those countries where such assemblies are tolerated by the civil government."

"17. The ecclesiastical power is not, of divine right, distinct from and independent of the civil power, nor can such distinction and independence be maintained without invasion and usurpation by the Church of the essential rights of the civil power."

The errors contained in these propositions are reproved, proscribed, and condemned; and the sovereign pontiff wills and commands that they be regarded as such by all the children of the Catholic Church.

47. **Can the Church decree anything which binds the consciences of the faithful in order to the use of temporal things, if those temporal things have regard to spiritual things; as for example, were she to punish the invaders of ecclesiastical property with excommunication?**

It is certain that the Church has such a right and power; of this right and power she has need for her spiritual interests; and although in the abstract these are diverse and distinct from temporal interests, nevertheless, in practice, they are so closely allied with them, that it would be impossible for her to promote the former, if she were hindered her guardianship of the latter. In this world, spiritual things have need of material things, as the soul has need of the body. The sacraments themselves, the very dogmas of the faith, have need of material objects: one sacrament needs water; another, bread and wine; another, oil, etc. The dogmas of faith need paper on which they may be written and by which they may be transmitted unchanged from generation to generation. It is clear that her ministers need food and raiment; that the churches need objects appropriated to worship, etc. It is clear, therefore, that the Church could not promote her spiritual interests if she could not also guard her temporal or material interests. The Church, then, having the right and the power to guard her temporal interests, inasmuch as they are necessary to her spiritual interests, it follows, as a consequence, that she can bind the consciences of the faithful in order to the use of temporal things, where such temporal things have regard to spiritual things. This is proved by the condemnation of the following propositions, which are proscribed by the same encyclical as those abovementioned:

"14. The Church may decree nothing which can bind the consciences of the faithful in order to the use of temporal things."

"13. The excommunication fulminated by the Council of Trent and by the Roman pontiffs against those who invade and usurp the rights and property of the Church is based on the confusion of spiritual with civil and political order, in the sole pursuit of a worldly good."

Councils

48. **How do you define an ecclesiastical council?**
It is an assembly of the prelates of the Church, convoked by their legitimate head, in order to decide questions which may arise concerning the truths of religion, and to reform the morals of the Christian people and ecclesiastical discipline. A council is not always assembled for all these motives at once; it may be convened for one or other of them.

49. **How many kinds of councils are there?**
There are four kinds, viz.: a general council, to which all the bishops of the Catholic world are summoned by the sovereign pontiff. It is not necessary, however, that all should assist at it. A national council, to which all the bishops of a nation or kingdom are summoned by the primate. A provincial council, to which the metropolitan summons all the bishops of the province who are his suffragans, and even such as are exempt, according to the terms of the Council of Trent. A diocesan council, to which the bishop summons those priests of the diocese who have cure of souls, or an ecclesiastical benefice.

50. **Has the Roman pontiff alone the right to convoke a general council?**
All Catholics agree that this right belongs solely to the Roman pontiff. Heretics pretend that this right belongs to the emperor; but this pretense is most foolish, since it would be necessary that all the kingdoms of the world should be subject to the emperor, if he is to exercise in them an act of jurisdiction, by convocation of the bishops; moreover, he must hold the primacy in the Church, if the bishops are to be obliged to assemble at his order. The Roman pontiff alone has supreme power and jurisdiction over all the Christians of the world, and therefore over all bishops. You must observe that if councils have sometimes been convoked by the Roman

emperor, it was done with the consent and by order of the Roman pontiff. All sound theologians and historians are agreed on this point.

51. **To whom does it belong to preside at a general council?**
To the Roman pontiff, as it belongs to the head to preside over the members. He may preside, however, either in person, or by means of his legates. This is the doctrine of all Catholic theologians.

52. **What prelates may assist at a general council?**
Of ordinary right, bishops alone can assist and give decisive votes, as judges of religious controversies. Cardinals, who are not also bishops, assist and give their votes as advisers of the sovereign pontiff; as also abbots and generals of religious orders, by privilege. Temporal sovereigns, or their ambassadors, assist as protectors.

53. **Is a general council of infallible authority?**
No Catholic has ever doubted that it is of infallible authority; it has not, however, such authority, until after the approbation and confirmation of the Roman pontiff.

54. **Are other councils, which are not general councils, infallible?**
Of themselves they are only authoritative and not infallible; for infallibility is promised only to the universal Church, and to him who represents it. We say, "of themselves," because whenever their decisions have been approved by the Roman Church, they become infallible. Further, you must observe that, in matters regarding discipline, they are of obligation only for the places in which they are made; that is, if they are national, for that nation; if they are provincial, for that province; if diocesan, for that diocese.

The Roman Pontiff

55. **Who is the Roman pontiff?**
The Roman pontiff is the bishop who is the successor of St. Peter in the Roman see.

56. **Has the Roman pontiff all the privileges of St. Peter, and all the authority which he had over the Church?**
He has all the privileges and all the authority which St. Peter received from Christ, when he constituted him head of the apostolic college, and of his Church; that is to say, he has the same jurisdiction and authority over all the bishops, and over all the faithful. This is of faith.

57. **Is it then an article of the faith that the Roman pontiff has the primacy over all the Church?**
It is an article of the faith, specially defined in the Council of Florence, with the full consent of both Greeks and Latins.[18]

58. **Is this primacy of the Roman pontiff in the Church necessary?**
A society that had many independent heads, such as bishops, would be without the Roman pontiff, and could not but result in confusion and anarchy. The very heretics themselves acknowledge this when they give jurisdiction to the emperor, or to kings over bishops.

59. **Supposing it were at any time necessary to call the Roman pontiff to account for disorderly or wicked conduct, to whom would belong the right of judging his case?**
God has reserved this right to himself. No one on earth can judge the Roman pontiff. Besides the authorities which might be adduced, a palpable reason is this: the head of a government can never be called to account, save in case of a revolt; but the Church does not admit revolt within her bosom. If a revolt occur in the Church, from the mere fact that it is a revolt, those who promote it, and those who take part in it, are separated and cut off from the Church, at least as schismatics; and therefore, as separated from her, they no longer have any authority in her. The Roman pontiff may be fraternally admonished, but not judged.

[18] Cf. Council of Florence, Session 6 (July 6, 1439)

60. **When the Roman pontiff, as head and master of the whole Church, decides a controversy in matters of faith and morals, or, to use theological terms, when he defines *ex cathedra*, is he infallible in his judgment?**

He is infallible, as might be proved by every sort of authority and reason. It is an established fact that when the Roman pontiffs have defined any question, in their quality of heads and masters of the Church, they have never erred. Contumacious men have ever been found to reclaim against the truth of the pontifical decisions, but the matter has always ended by the whole Church accepting the pontifical decisions, and declaring the recusants to have fallen into heresy.[19]

61. **Is the authority of the Roman pontiff inferior to the authority of a general council?**

The Roman pontiff, by his authority, gives force to a general council, and therefore he is superior, and not inferior to it. The supreme pontiff does not cease to be head of the Church when the Church is assembled in council. Remember that no general council has ever been recognized as infallible by the Church, without the confirmation and approbation of the pope. Remember, moreover, that it is impossible to conceive the idea of a general council without the pope. The pope must convoke it, must preside over it, either in person or by his legates, and finally, as we have said, must confirm it. To conceive a general council without the pope, we must conceive a general council in opposition to the pope; and in that case it would be an unlawful material assembly of bishops, all really disunited, because without a center of unity.

[19] The Nestorians and Eutychians opposed the decisions of St. Leo the Great; the Monothelites, those of St. Martin I; the Lutherans, those of Leo X; the Jansenists, those of Innocent X, Alexander VII, etc. But these and all others, both ancient and modern, who have imitated them in their opposition to the decisions of the Roman pontiffs, are all heretics in the judgment of Catholics. The condemnations of the Roman pontiffs are called, and are, thunderbolts which issue from the throne of God, and there is no shield which they will not shiver in pieces. There is no escape for him who provokes them, unless he submits, and humbly pronounces his own condemnation. It is impossible to repel them. They are like the arrow of Jonathan, of which holy scripture says: "The arrow of Jonathan never turned back" (2 Kgs 1:22).

62. **This would be the case in regard to a pope living at the time a general council was assembled; but would the pope be subject to the decrees of former general councils, lawfully celebrated, and confirmed by the authority of the popes, his predecessors?**

Undoubtedly, in dogmatic decisions, because that which was true, and infallibly true once, will be true to all eternity: moreover, to say that the pope must in this way be subject to councils is the same as to say that the pope must be Catholic; which no one doubts. In decisions, however, which regard discipline, which in the Church is changeable, the pope is superior to councils, and may derogate from their laws when he sees necessity for so doing; and this authority is necessary to him, for otherwise the well-being of the Church would be ill-provided for.

63. **Why would the well-being of the Church be ill-provided for?**

For this reason: as an inferior can in no case derogate from the laws of a superior, so the pope would be unable in any case to dispense or derogate from the canons of councils; therefore, for every dispensation and for every derogation, which a council had not authorized the supreme pontiff or others to make, it would be necessary to convoke a general council. Now we all know how difficult a matter this is, and that many times it would even be an impossibility. Hence on many occasions the Church would lack the means of providing for her own needs.[20]

[20] Translator's note: The infallibility of the supreme pontiff in his dogmatic decisions, and his authority over general councils, are now dogmas, not only divinely revealed, but proposed by the Church, and so binding on the intellects and consciences of all the faithful, under pain, not only of error, but of heresy. See the definition on this point, of the Vatican Council, footnote, p. 22. This council also teaches and declares "that the Roman pontiff is the supreme judge of the faithful; and that, in all causes pertaining to ecclesiastical examination, recourse may be had to his judgment; and that the judgment of the apostolic see, than whose authority there is no greater, can be revised by no man; and that to no one is it lawful to judge its judgment, and that they therefore err from the right way of truth, who affirm that it is lawful to appeal from the judgment of the Roman pontiff to an ecumenical council, as to an authority superior to the Roman pontiff" (Ch. 4). The authorities quoted in the text will serve to show the previous absolute theological certainty of the doctrine, which is now also of Catholic faith.

64. **However it is not a truth defined as of faith that the pope is infallible in his dogmatic decisions, and that he has authority over general councils.**[21]
It is true that this is not in the number of those truths which must be firmly believed, under pain of heresy in him who does not believe them. Still, it is one of the most certain truths which we have in theology next to the dogmas which are of faith. The following proposition was condemned by Alexander VIII, the 7th December, 1690: "The assertion of the authority of the Roman pontiff over an ecumenical council, and his infallibility in determining questions of faith, is futile, and has repeatedly been overthrown." He who should defend such a proposition would incur an excommunication reserved to the pope.

65. **Has the pope authority to declare books to be heretical or scandalous, and to prohibit such?**
Undoubtedly he has, for as universal pastor it is for him to determine what pastures are unwholesome, and to hinder his flock from approaching them.

66. **When the pope declares that a book contains a certain heresy, must we blindly submit our own judgment to his declaration?**
There is no room to doubt it; because in matters of faith the homage of the tongue which submits to keep silence is not sufficient, there is required also the submission of the heart, that is to say, of the will, which is made with submission of the understanding. This truth, which was always recognized in the Church, has in these later times been more clearly illustrated by the fact of the condemnation of the heretical propositions of Jansenius.

The Holy Fathers, the Doctors, and the Schoolmen

67. **Who are the holy fathers?**
The holy fathers are those great men, who, for their great learning, sanctity, and antiquity have, either expressly or tacitly, been declared such by the Church. The last of the holy fathers was St. Bernard.

[21] Translator's note: This divine truth is now of Catholic faith, as defined by the Vatican Council. See footnotes on p. 22 and 30.

68. **Who are the doctors?**
Men famous for learning and sanctity, declared such by the Church, as St. Thomas, St. Bonaventure, etc.

69. **When the holy fathers and the doctors of the Church are unanimous in affirming anything pertaining to faith and morals, may we doubt of its truth?**
We may not doubt of it, for they are the depositaries of the tradition of the Church, and if they are unanimous in affirming any truth in such matters, it is as much as to say that it comes directly from the apostles.

70. **Is it necessary that they be all agreed, without any exception?**
This is not necessary, for no one of the holy fathers, of himself alone, is infallible, and any one of them might be mistaken, and so not agree with the rest: in such case the error of one must not detract from the force of the truth taught by all, or nearly all.

71. **The opinion of one holy father must then be accounted of no weight?**
Not so; on the contrary, it must be accounted of great weight, if it be not opposed to the common opinion of the other fathers; if, however, it be contrary to their judgment, it must not be regarded.

72. **Who are the schoolmen?**
Those who wrote after the doctors of the Church, in defense of truths contradicted by heretics. They were very numerous in the sixteenth century, and opposed the heretics of that age; for this reason, the schoolmen are hated and abused by all protestants even in these days, as well as by persons of doubtful or insincere belief, although they may affect Catholicism and union with holy Church.

73. **What authority have the schoolmen?**
If all are commonly agreed in affirming anything appertaining to faith and morals, their authority is irrefragable, even before such truth is expressly defined by the Church; for we cannot suppose that all the learned men who adorn the Church should be mistaken; or that, if they were mistaken, the

Church would not condemn their error, but suffer it to be thus authorized, and taught by all. If, however, they are not generally agreed, but are divided in their opinions, each one has no further authority than the weight of the reasons which he adduces. This is meant, however, speaking generally; for the schoolmen, who have been specially distinguished for right judgment and profound knowledge of the holy fathers, have a personal authority of great account. Who, for example, would not show consideration for the opinion of Bellarmine, if it were only because he was so judicious and learned in ecclesiastical science?[22] However, the authority of the schoolmen can never be put on a par with that of the holy fathers or of the doctors.

History, Human Reason, and Philosophy

74. **What authority has history?**
History has considerable authority in religious controversies, for it furnishes great light, and supplies many facts for the elucidating and proving of truth, and for the confutation of error. Nevertheless, he who would sincerely make use of the authority of history in matters of religion, must not be content with a mere superficial knowledge, nor with the knowledge of disconnected and isolated facts, for if in regard to all sciences, it is better to be ignorant of them than to have an incorrect knowledge of them, this is especially true in regard to history. I speak of ecclesiastical history, as being the most necessary for theological controversies; profane history, generally, cannot be so useful.

75. **What authority have human reason and philosophy?**
They have considerable authority, when they are held subject to faith, and are used in such theological controversies as admit of the arguments which they furnish. You may easily imagine that if the faith were subject to reason and to philosophy, the faith would be destroyed. They cannot decide in matters which are in no way within their sphere. How, for instance, could the existence of the mystery of the most Holy Trinity be proved from philosophy?

[22] When His Holiness, Clement VIII, elected Bellarmine cardinal, he said of him to the sacred college, "We have chosen this man, because the Church of God has not his equal as to doctrine!"

God: The One and Trine

General Idea of God

76. **Who is God?**

He is a Lord infinitely perfect, the Creator and preserver of heaven and earth, and of all things visible and invisible.

77. **What do those words *infinitely perfect* signify?**

They mean that in God is all good, and that he is infinite goodness.

78. **What does the word *infinite* signify?**

It signifies something that has no end. For example, if there were a sea whose bottom we could never fathom, how deep soever we might dive, whose surface we could never reach, how high soever we might soar, whose shores we could never find, though we might continually pass from side to side; or better still, if there were a bottomless, surfaceless, shoreless sea, and if this sea spread itself on all sides without limit, this would be an infinite sea. Observe, however, that it is impossible that any material thing, such as the sea is, for example, could be infinite.

79. **But supposing such a sea to exist, would it be a figure of the goodness of God?**

Yes. The goodness of God is as great spiritually, as this huge sea would be materially, were its existence possible. The goodness of God has no limit or term; no one can measure it; no one, not even the angels, can comprehend it; God alone, by his infinite wisdom, comprehends his own infinite goodness.

80. **Could we find no creature, either in heaven or on earth, whose goodness might be put in comparison with the goodness of God?**

As there can be no comparison between time and eternity, so there can be no comparison between the goodness of any creature whatsoever and the goodness of God. The ineffable goodness of even the ever Blessed Virgin is not only little, but we might even say, is nothing compared with the infinite goodness of God. Hence it is that not even in paradise can the angels, the saints, or the most Blessed Virgin herself—with all the immense love which they bear to God—approach to loving him as much as he merits to be loved in himself. God alone loves himself, as much as he merits to be loved.

81. **What is meant by this infinite goodness?**
The aggregate, the union of his infinite perfections or attributes; his omnipotence, by which he can make or destroy all things, by an act of his will; his wisdom, by which he clearly sees the past, the present, the future, and all possible things; his justice, with which he rewards the good and chastises the wicked; his mercy, with which he pardons the sins of those who with a true heart repent; his eternity, whereby he has never had any beginning, and whereby likewise he shall have no end; his immensity, by which he is in heaven, on earth, and in every place; his impassibility, by which he who is a most pure and perfect Spirit, cannot suffer or endure any evil whatsoever; and all his other infinite perfections, by which he is truly an infinite good.

82. **What do you mean by saying that God is a "most pure Spirit"?**
I mean that God has not a body as we have, therefore we cannot picture him to ourselves as high or low, or broad or narrow; we cannot touch him with our hands, nor can we see him with the material eyes of our body.

83. **Then he is nothing?**
On the contrary, you should say that he is all things, because he is infinitely rich in every perfection, and in all good. He is not material, such as are the things we see and touch, and therefore he has not the properties of material things, which are large or small, broad or narrow, and which may be seen and touched; but he has all spiritual perfections, by which he is a Spirit infinitely good. Our soul is also a spirit which can neither be seen nor touched, and yet our soul thinks, judges, reasons, gives motion to the whole body, and is a far more noble part of man than his body.

84. **How can you say that God has no body, when holy scripture speaks of the eyes of God, the ears of God, the hands of God, and of other members of his body?**

When holy scripture attributes to God members of the human body, it does so in a figurative sense. If I say that a horse flies rapidly over the plain, I do not mean that the horse has wings and flies like a bird: by the word *fly* I intend to signify the speed with which he traverses the country; so, when holy scripture speaks of the eyes and ears of God, it means to signify his wisdom, whereby he sees and knows all things; when it speaks of his hands, it means to signify his omnipotence, whereby he performs all his works; and so as to the rest. All theologians and interpreters resolve such difficulties in this way. In fact, when scripture speaks literally, it says, "God is a spirit";[23] and this is an article of the faith.

85. **Why do you say that God is a "most simple Spirit"?**

Because there is no composition of diverse substances in God, nor any real distinction of perfections or attributes. The omnipotence of God is God himself. The wisdom of God is God himself; and so we may say of his justice, of his mercy, and of all his other perfections. In man, power, wisdom, and piety are things distinct from the man himself, and therefore a man may exist without power, without wisdom, and without piety. But in God every attribute is God himself, neither more nor less. Thus do all theologians, with St. Bernard, answer those heretics who have imagined that in God there is real distinction between his attributes.

86. **Why then do you say that God has so many attributes, and so many diverse perfections?**

We say so according to our mode of understanding, because the divine nature or substance is omnipotent, wise, just, merciful, etc., although this omnipotence, wisdom, justice, etc., are in reality nothing else than the most simple divine substance itself.

[23] Jn 4:24

87. **Seeing that God is infinitely good, and the author of all things that exist, who produced evil in the world?**
Evil came into the world from the abuse of their liberty, in creatures gifted with free will. God has given this liberty to angels and to men. The abuse which many of the angels made of their liberty, when they sinned by pride, is the origin of all the evils which the devils suffer, and which they produce by their malice. The abuse which man made of his liberty is the origin of all the evils suffered by men. Observe, however, that the holy angels who remained faithful to God cannot now any longer sin, that is, abuse their liberty.

88. **Still there are so many evils in the world which have not been produced by the abuse of liberty in the creature. For instance, hell is a great evil, so are hurtful beasts, pestilence, earthquakes, etc. Is God the author of all these evils?**
All those things, and others like them, are not evils in themselves. They are evils only to those who suffer them, inasmuch as they are afflicted by them: in themselves they are benefits necessary to hinder sin, and for the punishment of sin; they manifest the divine justice, give occasion for the exercise of virtue, etc. They are benefits, because they are ordained by God against the one only true evil, which is sin—that is, against the abuse of liberty. If there were no sin in the world, there would be no afflictions in it, that is, no punishment for sin; in like manner as if there were no criminals in a kingdom, there would be no need of prisons, or of other punishments.

89. **But if God is infinitely good, why has he permitted his creatures to abuse their liberty and commit sin, the cause of so great miseries?**
God has given his creatures liberty, in order that they may merit by making a good use of it, and he gives them, at the same time, the necessary aid that they may use it as he requires; and more we cannot expect from his infinite goodness. Further, he brings forth greater good from the evils that are committed: as, for example, when he has permitted the cruelty of tyrants, in order to exercise the faith and love of innumerable martyrs.

90. **Some have imagined that we ought to recognize two principles—one of good, who would therefore be the good God, and another of evil, who would therefore be the wicked God. They attributed all the good in the world to the first, and all the evil to the second. Is not this opinion plausible?**
This is not an opinion, but a most stupid heresy; for evil is not a reality. Evil is an imperfection, a lack of good, just as darkness is not a reality, but simply lack of light. Hence, a wicked God would be an infinite lack of good, and therefore an infinite nothing. Such an idea is contradictory, and a ridiculous imagination.

The Immensity and Providence of God

91. **How are we to understand that God is immense?**
God is immense, because he is not contained in any place, but, on the contrary, contains all places and the universe itself. He is everywhere by his presence, clearly beholding all things; by his power, preserving the existence of all creatures, and concurring to all their operations; by his essence, because, as we have already said, the wisdom and the power of God are none other than the divine substance itself.

92. **If God concurs to all the operations of creatures, do you mean to say that he concurs also to sin, and that therefore he approves it, and cooperates with it?**
In all free actions there is the material act and the formal of the act. In a murder, the material act is the thrusting a dagger into a body, which, of itself, is an indifferent action; the formal of the act is the evil will, that is, the wickedness of unjustly depriving a man of life. Now, God concurs to the material act, inasmuch as it is an indifferent action, but he does not concur to the formal of the act, that is, to the wickedness; on the contrary, he disapproves, condemns, and punishes it.

93. **What is the providence of God?**
It is the disposition of all created things, in order to the attainment of their last end.

94. **Does God exercise his providence toward all his creatures, without exception?**
This is of faith: "He has equally care of all," as we read in the book of Wisdom.[24]

95. **Many things in the world happen by chance, which would not be the case if the divine providence regulated all things.**
I will show you your error by a comparison of St. Thomas.[25] A master sends one of his servants to the marketplace. Unknown to him, he sends another to the same place, without telling him that he has already sent the first, because he desires that they should both meet there unexpectedly. The two servants, at first meeting one another, would think they had met by chance, while, in fact, their meeting is of premeditated design. You will understand from this that nothing in the world happens by chance. Our ignorance, through which we know not the causes of many things, has made us imagine that they happen by chance; but, instead of this, God rules all things by his providence, and nothing happens without a reason determined by him. For instance, a leaf falls from a tree: Why should it lie straight on the earth rather than the reverse? It is impossible for us to know the reason; but there is a reason for it in the divine providence. Chance and fortune are mere names without reality, nor can they signify aught save our ignorance of the causes of things.

96. **Does the providence of God extend to all the free actions of men, both good and bad?**
Undoubtedly: directing, moreover, the evil actions to some good. The sons of Jacob sold Joseph, because of the envy they cherished against him. God directed and overruled this barbarous sale in order to the advantage of the Egyptians, to the salutary confusion of his envious brethren, to the preservation and glory of the family of Jacob, etc.

[24] Ws 6:8
[25] Cf. *Summa Theologiae*, I, q. 116, a. 1, c.

97. **You mean to say that God is the first cause of all things: But are there not second causes, on which all things in their events depend?**
There are indeed second causes; because, for example, it is water that wets us, it is fire that burns us: but still, you must observe that all second causes act in dependence on the first cause, so that, whatever happens, always excepting the malice of sin, we must recognize as coming from God.

Observe, also, that God does not always make use of secondary causes, for he can act without them. If it be his will to send a pestilence or an earthquake, he can make use of secondary causes, but he can also act immediately by himself, without availing himself of them, that is, without permitting the generating of the poisonous insects which naturally produce pestilence, and without permitting the rarefaction and condensation of subterranean vapors, or that disturbance of the equilibrium of electricity which in the ordinary way occasions earthquakes; but observe carefully, that this is a matter of as much indifference as it would be a matter of indifference whether the king punished a criminal absolutely, by a sentence written with his own hand, or by a sentence caused by him to emanate from his tribunals.

Attend especially to this truth, for it is precisely in these days, by continually crying out in all circumstances of public or private chastisements, that they are the effect of secondary causes, that men seek to extinguish and dissipate that salutary fear of God which might correct sinners. Be it so, that all is the effect of secondary causes; it is God, notwithstanding, who regulates those secondary causes by his providence. He is a king who does not write the sentence with his own hand, but causes it to emanate from his tribunals. He does not execute it with his own hands, but causes it to be executed by his ministers: all the same, the sentence and the punishment come from the king. Above all, therefore, remember, that to reward, to punish, or to do any other act whatever, God has no need of secondary causes; and when he does adopt them, it is always he who rewards, he who punishes, and he who acts, by his providence.

The Will of God; Predestination and Reprobation

98. **What is the will of God?**

The will of God, which is one of his attributes, which we conceive in God as, as it were, faculties, such as his understanding and his omnipotence, is that perfection by which he loves good and hates evil; that perfection by which he is directed in all his operations. Observe, that as there is no real distinction between the perfections of God and God himself, the will of God is none other than the divine substance and essence itself.

99. **Is the will of God free in its operations?**

It is free—not to will evil, because God would not be infinite goodness if it were possible for him to will the very least evil; but it is free in willing good, without being forced to do so by anything whatsoever. For example, God was free to create the world, and free not to create it; and this is the case in regard to all those other operations of his which are called operations *ad extra*.

100. **Which are his operations *ad extra*?**

They are the creation, preservation, and government of all things. They are called *ad extra*, to distinguish them from those which take place in God himself, which are called *ad intra*, and in regard to which the divine will is not free, because they are necessary operations, essential to the divine nature. As we have already said, God might or might not create the world, but the Father was not free not to generate the Son, that is to say, the eternal Word; nor the Holy Ghost free not to proceed from the Father and from the Son, because this generation and this procession are absolutely necessary in the divine substance, according to the idea which the faith gives us of God.

101. **Must we acknowledge love in God?**

God loves himself infinitely, and he also loves his creatures, particularly his intelligent and rational creatures, such as the angels and men.

102. **Must we acknowledge hatred in God?**

God hates sin and sinners. He does not, however, hate sinners in that they are his creatures, but in that they are sinners: when they cease from sin, he no longer hates them.

103. **I wish to know if God wills the eternal salvation of all men.**

God sincerely wills the eternal salvation of all men. This was always the faith of all Catholics in all ages, according to the sense of holy scripture, and the tradition of all the fathers. The contrary error, which is that God wills only the salvation of some men, was solemnly condemned in Calvin, and afterward, in Jansenius.

104. **I can easily understand that God wills the salvation of all the faithful, because he furnishes them with the means necessary to obtain it; but how can you say that he wills the salvation of infidels who have no means whatever of gaining it?**

It is false that infidels have no means whatever of obtaining eternal salvation; God gives many graces to infidels, and if they did not abuse them, he would bring them to the knowledge of the true faith, that so they might be saved; and he would do this, even if it required miracles, as St. Thomas teaches.[26]

105. **At least you must admit that God does not will the salvation of children who die without baptism, and particularly of those who die before coming to the light?**

Holy scripture, the fathers, and the sentiment of the whole Church give us sufficient assurance that God wills the salvation of every soul, and therefore also of the souls of such children; nor must we say the contrary, though it may be difficult for us to understand in what manner he wills it. In our holy religion it is not only what we can understand that is true; we must believe many things without understanding them, and this is one.

[26] Cf. *Summa Theologiae*, III, q. 43, a. 1, rep. 3

106. **What do you say in regard to the predestination and reprobation of men?**
It is an article of the faith that there is true predestination, that is to say, that from all eternity God has determined to give paradise to some men; and that there is true reprobation, that is to say, that from all eternity God has decreed to condemn some men to hell; and hence the number of both the one and the other is determined. The predestinate are all those who die in the grace of God, the reprobate are all those who die in mortal sin.

107. **These answers seem to me too material, could you not speak more profoundly of such mysteries?**
It is enough for me to explain to you what is most necessary to be known: many things which might be added are not necessary for all, nor suited to all. In regard to predestination and reprobation, it is sufficient for you to know that God sincerely wills the eternal salvation of all men; and sincerely willing it, he grants to all means sufficient to obtain it. (When I say "sufficient," I understand means which really suffice, because, if in fact they did not suffice, they would not be sufficient means). These means are his graces, without which we cannot obtain salvation; those who correspond to this grace will certainly be saved, and therefore are predestinate. Observe that it is St. Peter who exhorts you to make sure your election to eternal life by means of your good works,[27] and it will be well if the simple divine word content you, without seeking further. Moreover, the reprobate must not be looked upon as persons to whom God on his part has been wanting, but as persons who merit to be excluded from the kingdom of God for their wickedness.

108. **What do you say about children who die before the use of reason, some baptized and some not, and so, some predestinate and others reprobate?**
Children who are predestinate are so through the merits of Jesus Christ, applied to them by means of holy baptism. That such a lot is theirs is the work of divine mercy. Children who are reprobate are such through original sin, by which they die deprived of sanctifying grace. That such a

[27] Cf. 2 Pt 1:10

misfortune should be theirs is an act of divine justice. But you who read this ought not to penetrate too far into these mysteries; if they present difficulties which the holy fathers could not solve, how much greater must these difficulties be to you? Do you suppose that by force of reasoning you would ever come to know the secrets of an earthly sovereign, if he did not choose to manifest them to you? Certainly not. How much less, then, can you come to know the secrets of the King of heaven if he will not discover them to you?[28] We find mysteries in the conduct of finite men, which we cannot solve, and shall we wonder because we find them in the dispositions of infinite divine wisdom? In whatever way God may predestinate the good, or reprobate the wicked, it is impossible but that his purpose should be most just, and worthy of his infinite goodness.

Let it suffice for you to know that God loves you more than you love yourself; that God wills your salvation more than you desire it yourself; that God will not exclude you from his kingdom unless you refuse it of your own free will. He has already done more for us—redeeming us at so much cost, and calling us into the bosom of his Church; now there remains but the lesser work, which is to give us fitting aids in order that we may profit by his infinite mercies, and this he will do; have this hope and you will not be confounded.

109. **There is yet another difficulty which I cannot pass over in silence. It is impossible that what God has appointed should not come to pass; therefore, if God have predestinated Titius to glory, it is impossible that Titius should be damned; while if he have reprobated Caius, it is impossible that Caius should be saved.**

To avoid perplexing ourselves, we must first of all consider that God never works but by the rules of an infinite wisdom; therefore, although we may not know it, there must always be a most just reason for his predestinating

[28] "To will not to know what the best of masters wills not to teach is a wise ignorance" (Scaliger).

Titius and not Caius.[29] Besides, he predestinates Titius, who will freely do good, by means of which he will merit glory, and he rejects Caius, who will freely do evil, by means of which he will merit damnation, so that we cannot say that Titius will necessarily be saved, and Caius necessarily damned.

110. **But since God foresees that Titius will do good and that Caius will do evil, and since the divine foreknowledge cannot be mistaken, must not this good and this evil be done of necessity? If then God sees that I am in the number of the predestinate, it is impossible that I should be damned; if, on the contrary, he sees that I am in the number of the reprobate, it is impossible that I should be saved.**

You must reflect that God's prevision is none other than his infinite knowledge, to which the past and the future is always present. It is a simple vision of things, which does not deprive free causes of their liberty. For instance, I see one man steal, and I see another man give alms; when I see the former stealing, I do not say that, because I see him, he steals of necessity, but that he is certainly stealing; when I see the latter giving alms, I do not say that, because I see him, he does so of necessity, but that he is certainly doing so; therefore, God, when he foresees our future actions, does not necessitate them. This is the teaching of all true philosophers, along with all theologians, and so, God's seeing you in the number of the predestinate, or of the reprobate, is but his seeing the good or the bad use which you make of your liberty. Hence you may know that this difficulty, which appears to you so serious, means no more than this: if you, dying well, merit paradise, it is impossible that you be damned; if, on the contrary, dying ill, you merit hell,

[29] "He has not mercy on those to whom, by an equity most hidden and far removed from human perceptions, he judges that grace is not to be afforded. This the apostle does not disclose, but marvels at, saying, 'O the height of the riches of God'" (St. Augustine). The same holy father affirms (*Enchiridion*, Ch. 95) that in paradise we shall see such reasons and such causes as are now hidden from us; and similarly, we shall know for what motive God has conferred many of his graces on those whom he foresaw would not profit by them, and has not conferred them on those who would have derived profit from them. St. Bonaventure teaches the same doctrine. Observe, however, that such causes, reasons, and motives cannot be other than most worthy of God, that is to say, of infinite goodness. Our ignorance should humble us, but not discourage us.

it is impossible that you be saved. So that, notwithstanding the dogma of predestination and reprobation, that which the Holy Ghost declares will always come to pass, namely, that life and death is in the hand of man,[30] and that it depends on man himself whether he will be saved or damned.

111. **Then we may not say that God, as absolute master of his creatures, without having regard to future merits or demerits, elects some men for paradise and destines others to hell?**
So Calvin blasphemously maintained. God, it is true, can predestinate men to paradise and give them all opportune and efficacious aids in order that they may attain it, although they have no right to such predestination; but he cannot destine his creatures to eternal misery, without foreseeing their demerits. The reason is that the liberality, which confers gifts on those who have no right to pretend to them, is a perfection, and therefore is in God; on the contrary, the cruelty and injustice, which would destine men to punishment without presupposing sin in them, are repulsive vices which destroy the idea not only of infinite, but even of ordinary goodness.

The Beatific Vision

112. **Do the saints in heaven see God?**
They see him intuitively, that is to say, they see him in himself, really as he is.

113. **Does not holy scripture say that God is invisible, and that no one has ever seen him?**
It says that God is invisible, and that no one ever saw him in this life. On this account, the most probable opinion among the interpreters of scripture is that not even Moses saw him intuitively, but that it was an angel who appeared to him, and gave him orders and commands in God's name; they assert therefore that, when he says that he saw God, he means to say that he saw an angel who spoke to him in the person of God. But it is a

30 Cf. Ecclus 15:18

truth of the faith that in the other life we shall see God, and we shall "see him as he is," according to the expression of scripture.[31]

114. **After the resurrection, shall we see God with the eyes of our body?**
We shall never see God with our bodily eyes, because God is a pure Spirit. Our bodily eyes are material, and will be material, even after our resurrection; and it is certain that material eyes cannot see spiritual things. But we shall see God with our intellect, illuminated by the light of glory.

115. **What is this light of glory?**
It is a supernatural habit, by which the mind, whether of men or angels, is perfectly disposed to see God.

116. **Could we not see God, even in heaven, without this light of glory?**
It is certain that we could not see him any more than, with our bodily eyes however strong, we could see a mountain, however near it might be to us, without the aid of light.

117. **What shall we see in God?**
We shall see: his divine substance with his divine perfections, which are in reality but the same most simple divine substance;[32] the mystery of the most Holy Trinity; and we shall also see creatures, as effects in their cause.

118. **I wish to know whether, when we see God clearly in heaven, we shall comprehend him.**
To comprehend God, it is not sufficient to see God clearly. To comprehend him it would be necessary to know him with that perfection wherewith God, by his infinite knowledge, knows himself; and this is impossible for any creature. And so, not even the most holy soul of Jesus Christ, which is hypostatically united to his divinity, can arrive at comprehending God, that is to say, knowing him with that perfection with which God knows himself.

[31] 1 Jn 3:2

[32] As we have already shown in the answer to Question 85, above.

119. **In heaven shall we understand all the mysteries of the faith, which now we must blindly believe?**

No one has ever doubted that in heaven is seen clearly all that we believe on earth; and so the saints in heaven have not the virtue of faith, whereby we believe what we do not see.

120. **Will all the saints in heaven see God equally?**

It is an article of the faith that the beatific vision in heaven will not be alike for all, but proportioned to the greater or less merits of each. (So the Councils of Florence and Trent.)[33] This diversity arises from the greater or less light of glory which the saints will enjoy, and which is measured by the greater or less charity with which they will be inflamed in heaven.

121. **Will not such diversity be displeasing to the saints?**

They are no longer capable of envy; but rejoice in the good of others as in their own, and the felicity of those who are among the least in the kingdom of heaven is so great, and so commensurate to the capacity which they have for enjoyment, that there remains nothing for them to desire. The following comparison will explain the truth of this. A man and a child, both thirsty, reach the banks of a great river. The man drinks, and so does the child. Do you suppose that the child, who must needs drink less on account of the capacity of his stomach, envies the greater quantity which the man drinks? The child is content with being able to drink as much as he wants, and as much as he can.

122. **Are we to believe that God grants the vision of himself to the holy souls in paradise before the resurrection of the body and the general judgment?**

It is an article of the faith, as appears from the definition of faith of the Council of Florence, 25th September, that souls, fully purged from all sin, and released from all punishment due to sin, are admitted at once to the clear vision of God in paradise.[34]

[33] Cf. Council of Florence, Session 6 (July 6, 1439); Council of Trent, Session 6, Can. 32

[34] Cf. Council of Florence, Session 6 (July 6, 1439)

123. **What is to be said in regard to the opinion which teaches that, after the resurrection, the saints together with Christ will reign here upon earth for a thousand years?**
This is a heresy of the Apollinarians, condemned by the First Council of Constantinople.[35] The reign of the blessed and of Christ will be in heaven, and not upon earth, and it will be eternal.

The Mystery of the Most Holy Trinity

124. **I wish that in speaking to me of this mystery, so sublime and difficult, you would use the strictest terms of the schools, in order to my more certain and exact understanding of it.**
I intend so to speak to you of this mystery that every word may be available for teaching the catechism to children, therefore it is not my intention to make rigorous use of the terms of the schools, which would not be understood, and would require too prolix explanations. You must be content that I explain such things as are most necessary for you to know, with the utmost brevity, and in the clearest and most intelligible terms.

125. **How do you define the mystery of the most Holy Trinity?**
One God subsisting in three Persons.

126. **How is it possible that God, being one and most simple, subsists in three Persons?**
There are two truths, equally of faith: that God is one and most simple in his divine substance, and trine in Persons, who are called the Father, the Son, and the Holy Ghost. This is a mystery however, which, while on earth, we must adore, and which we shall not understand till we can contemplate it in paradise.

[35] Cf. First Council of Constantinople, Can. 1

127. **It seems to me, however, to be a contradiction that he who is three should be one, or that he who is one should be three.**
There is no contradiction in it, because these three divine Persons have one and the same divine nature and substance. It would be a contradiction if they had three diverse substances, because three substances would be three gods, and could not be one only God.

128. **We may say then that the Father is God, that the Son is God, and that the Holy Ghost is God?**
You not only may, but you must say so. It is an article of the faith; for the Father has the divine substance, the Son has the divine substance, the Holy Ghost has the divine substance, which is one only, and so there is one only God.

129. **Is the Father eternal, the Son eternal, and the Holy Ghost eternal?**
Most certainly: but they are not three eternals, but one eternal, because one only God.

130. **Is the Father Almighty, the Son Almighty, and the Holy Ghost Almighty?**
Undoubtedly: but they are not three almighties, but only one Almighty; and so it is in regard to the other attributes of God, which are the same one and indivisible substance of God, as we have already said.[36]

131. **Have the Persons of the most Holy Trinity the same perfections, the same understanding, and the same will?**
They have the same wisdom and the same goodness. They live with the same life, know with the same understanding, will with the same will, and work with the same power. The reason of this is always the same, that they have the same divine nature and substance.

[36] See the answer to Question 85, above. See also the Athanasian Creed. Editor's note: The Athanasian Creed, also known as *Quicumque Vult*, may be found in Volume VI of this series.

132. **May we then say that the Person of the Father is the Person of the Son, and the Person of the Holy Ghost?**
You must not say so, for it is an article of the faith that they are three Persons, really distinct (Athanasian Creed); and therefore, the Person of the Father is not the Person of the Son, nor of the Holy Ghost; the Person of the Son is not the Person of the Father, nor of the Holy Ghost; the Person of the Holy Ghost is not the Person of the Father, nor of the Son. They are three Persons really distinct one from another, although they have the same substance.

133. **Can we say that God is distinct in three Persons?**
The expression that God is distinct in three Persons is condemned by the dogmatic bull *Auctorem Fidei*; hence you must say that in God there are three distinct Persons, and not that God is distinct in three Persons.

134. **May we not say, in any sense whatever, that there are three gods?**
No, in no sense whatever; whoever should say so would be a heretic.

135. **May we say that God is Father, Son, and Holy Ghost?**
You should say so, as appears from the definition of the Fourth Lateran Council.[37]

136. **Give me some comparison which may render this less obscure to me.**
Picture to yourself three persons called Peter, Paul, and John, who, nevertheless, had one and the same soul, and one and the same body. We should call them three persons, because one would be Peter, the other Paul, and the third John; they would, however, be one man only, and not three men, not having three bodies or three souls, but only one body and one soul. This would be impossible amongst men, because man's substance is little and limited, and therefore cannot be one and the same in more than one person; but the substance of God, that is, the divinity, is infinite, and

[37] "We believe and confess that there is one supreme, incomprehensible, and ineffable reality, which is truly Father, Son, and Holy Ghost, three Persons together, and each of them distinct" (Const. 1).

therefore can be found, and in fact is found, in several Persons. The substance, therefore, that is to say, the divinity of the Father, is found also in the Son and in the Holy Ghost.

137. **Why is the Father called the first Person of the most Holy Trinity?**
Because the Father is without a principle; that is to say, he has not his origin from, nor is produced by anyone; but he is the principle from which the other Persons proceed, and by whom they are produced.

138. **Why is he called the Father?**
Because from all eternity he produces or generates a Person like to and equal with himself, of the selfsame substance and nature, that is to say, the Son.

139. **Then if the Son proceeded from the Father, the Father was the first to exist?**
I have told you that the Father generates the Son from all eternity; therefore the Father, who was from all eternity, from all eternity generated the Son, and ever generates him eternal as himself.

140. **Why is the second Person called the Son, and how is he generated?**
He is called the Son because he is generated by the Father; and this generation is by way of understanding and knowledge. The Father from all eternity contemplates in himself his infinite perfections, and, like a most clear mirror, produces a living and most perfect image of himself, which has his same divine substance, and is called the Son, and also the eternal Word of God.

141. **Why is the third Person called the Holy Ghost?**
Because he proceeds from the Father and from the Son by way of will and love, and is, as it were, a spiritual Breath; and because he is the love of God, he is essentially holy.

142. **How are we to understand his proceeding from the Father and from the Son, by way of will and love?**
The Father and the Son, loving one another perfectly from all eternity, produce the Holy Ghost, who is the mutual love of the Father and the Son, and has the same divine substance. Observe here, that it is an article of the faith that the Father proceeds from none, that the Son proceeds from the Father, and that the Holy Ghost proceeds from the Father and the Son.

143. **Then the Father is the greatest of the Persons of the most Holy Trinity, the Son is less than the Father, and the Holy Ghost less than the Father and the Son?**
Fix thoroughly in your mind what has been so often said—that the Persons of the most Holy Trinity have the same divine nature and substance, and therefore are all three equal, and equally perfect. Among the Persons of the most Holy Trinity, there is neither greater nor less, but a perfect equality of goodness and perfection.

God: The Creator

The Creation of the World in General

144. **What is the meaning of the word *create*?**
To create means "to bring out of nothing"; so that when we say that God created the world, we mean to say that God, by his omnipotence, drew the world out of nothing. Creating differs from making, inasmuch as in making anything, we use materials which already exist; whereas, in creating, existence itself is given to things.

145. **What end did God propose to himself in the creation of the world?**
In the creation of the world, Almighty God proposed to himself two ends, one primary, the other secondary. The primary end was the manifestation

of his own perfections; the secondary end was the felicity of intelligent creatures, both men and angels.

146. **Creatures, then, manifest the infinite perfections of God?**
It is evident that they manifest them, because from creatures we know the creator, his omnipotence, his wisdom, etc. They manifest them, however, in a limited degree, because creatures, being circumscribed and finite, cannot manifest the infinite perfections of God in their real extent. Observe that God could have created a world, which, considered in itself, would have been more perfect than that which he has created, that is to say, which would have manifested in a more sublime degree his divine perfections. Nevertheless, this world is perfect of its own kind, manifesting in the best mode the divine perfections, in the degree in which it has pleased the infinite wisdom of God to manifest them. The wisdom of God requires that he should choose the means most fitted to the attainment of his end; his omnipotence demands that he should be able to do always more than he has done.

147. **God attains the primary end for which he created the world, which is the manifestation of his infinite perfections, in the exact degree which he has determined; but he does not attain the secondary end, for many intelligent creatures are not happy—men, for instance, on this earth, and the damned and the demons in hell.**
God has given to all his intelligent creatures the necessary means of happiness; therefore, on his part, he has attained the end for which he created them, which was conditional—that is, the rendering those intelligent creatures happy, who should will to be happy by making a good use of their liberty. If many intelligent creatures are not happy, it is because, abusing their own liberty, they have refused the happiness offered them, and become unhappy by their own fault. When I give alms, my end is to relieve the misery of my indigent neighbors: on my part, I attain my end, which is conditional, to relieve him, if he wills to be relieved; it is the fault of the poor man himself, if, abusing the liberty he has to make use of my alms, he throws it away, and so remains unrelieved.

The Angels

148. **How do you define the angels?**

They are created, spiritual, complete, and intelligent substances. They are called created substances, because in the creation of the world they were drawn out of nothing. They are called spiritual, because they have no bodies, not even a most subtle body of air or light, as some of the ancients supposed. No Catholic can now have any doubt on this head, the Fourth Lateran Council having expressly declared in favor of the entire spirituality of the angels.[38] They are called complete, as differing from the human soul, which is designed, not by itself alone, but in union with a body, to form a whole—that is, the person of man. They are called intelligent, because they have great force and subtlety of understanding; so that they are called simply intelligences.

149. **What does the name *angel* signify?**

Angel means "messenger"; therefore, the name angel is given to the celestial intelligences, not as the proper name of their nature, but as the proper name of their office, when they are sent by God to discharge some embassy, or to give some counsel.

150. **Is it an article of the faith that angels exist?**

Undoubtedly it is, as is apparent from innumerable passages of holy scripture, and from the Chapter *Firmiter*, of the Fourth Lateran Council.[39]

151. **Is the nature of angels superior to human nature?**

It is superior, as appears from scripture and the holy fathers.

152. **Do the angels know our thoughts and the secrets of our hearts?**

They conjecture them from signs and indications which we give, even without reflection; they have not, however, a certain knowledge of them. They

[38] Cf. Fourth Lateran Council, Const. 1

[39] Cf. Ibid.

have certain knowledge of them, when we will that they should know our thoughts and the secrets of our hearts; and also, when God, for his own ends, reveals these to them, even without our willing it.

153. **How can you affirm that the angels have not bodies, since they have often appeared in visible forms?**
On such occasions they adapted to themselves a body which was not their own; they assumed it when needful, and laid it aside as soon as they had executed the commissions which God sent them to accomplish among men.

154. **Have the angels power over material things?**
They have greater power over them than men have; with their most subtle intelligence and strength they can produce wonderful effects even in material things, such as no man is capable of. They can move the winds, cause storms, produce earthquakes and pestilences, and heal diseases, humanly speaking, incurable.

155. **May we not believe that all these things proceed immediately from natural causes, as philosophers teach?**
We do not say that every wind that blows, that every storm that rages, and that every destroying pestilence comes immediately from the action of some angel; such things happen ordinarily by the immediate concourse of natural causes, subject to the government of God, as we have already said;[40] but philosophers will never be able to prove that at times angels do not cooperate in such things. Moreover, it is apparent from many passages of holy scripture, from the tradition of the holy fathers, and from the sentiment of the entire Catholic Church that they do concur in them; hence, sound philosophers do not refuse to attribute this power over material things to the angels.

[40] See the section, "The Immensity and Providence of God," on p. 38-40, above.

156. **Were the angels created in a state of grace?**
Certainly; they did not however enjoy the vision of God, and it was in their own power to preserve or to lose grace, according to the good or bad use they made of their liberty.

157. **Did they all preserve themselves in a state of grace?**
Many preserved themselves in grace; but a great part speedily fell into the sin of pride, were excluded from the kingdom of God, and condemned to hell. I say speedily, because when Adam sinned, the angels had already sinned, and had been transformed into demons. Meanwhile, the good angels who remained humble, were admitted to the clear vision of God, and became impeccable.

158. **Who was the chief of the bad angels, whom we now call demons?**
Lucifer, who in this way is the chief or prince of all the proud.

159. **What punishments followed on the sin of the angels?**
Four: 1) blindness of mind in regard to supernatural things; for a great knowledge of natural things they retain; 2) obstinacy of the will in evil; 3) privation of paradise; 4) and the torment of eternal fire.

160. **Can the evil angels induce us to evil?**
They can tempt us in various ways, but they cannot do violence to our will.

161. **Is it true that enchantments and sorcery can be wrought by the power of demons, and by their power over natural things?**
It is most true, as appears from many passages of holy scripture, as many undeniable facts demonstrate, and as is manifest from the sentiment of the Church in all ages. It is rash and ridiculous to venture to deny such a truth, which, moreover, in our days is made even more manifest and palpable by the wonders of table turning and spirit rapping, and by magnetism, the abuse of which has been condemned by the Church in two decrees, emanating from the supreme holy Roman and Universal Inquisition, of the 28th July, 1847, and the 30th July, 1856. Hence, we may consider it certain

that the devil, by permission of Almighty God, has power in many ways over the persons of men, and over natural causes.

162. **Are there any obsessed by evil spirits?**

Although more than once impostors have pretended to be obsessed by evil spirits, it is most certain that, even after the death of Christ, persons have been obsessed by the devil; this has been proved by incontrovertible evidence, and cannot be denied without accusing the Catholic Church of prejudice and ignorance; for she uses exorcisms over obsessed persons, and confers an ecclesiastical order and consecrates ministers for this purpose.

163. **Still in our days many doubt it.**

St. Thomas, speaking of those who in his time doubted these things, feared not to assert that this doubt sprang from a principle of unbelief.[41] What forbids our saying the same of those who doubt them in our own days? We add, moreover, that such men are lacking in logic, in criticism, and in erudition.

164. **How many orders of angels are there?**

There are nine, which constitute three hierarchies or choirs; the highest containing the seraphim, the cherubim, and the thrones; the next, the dominations, the virtues, and the powers; the last, the principalities, the archangels, and the angels.

165. **Does God destine the angels to be the guardians of men?**

It is a truth, clearly expressed in holy scripture, that men are guarded by the angels; but we cannot say that it is absolutely of faith that each individual has his guardian angel: such, however, is the sentiment of all the holy fathers, and of all the faithful, in opposition to the heretic Calvin. Moreover, theologians agree that there are angels deputed to be the guardians of the various kingdoms of the earth, and of the different churches or dioceses which constitute the

[41] "It proceeds from a root of unbelief or incredulity, that they believe that demons exist only in the estimation of the vulgar" (*Summa Theologiae*, III-Sup., q. 58, a. 2, c.). Even Cudworth does not hesitate to assert, that only the impious, and men suspected of atheism, doubt of such matters.

Catholic Church. The archangel St. Michael, who formerly was the guardian angel of the synagogue, is now the guardian of the universal Church.

166. **What is the office of the angel guardians in regard to the men confided to them by God?**
They guard them from perils and imminent evils; they hinder the demons from injuring them; suggest holy thoughts, pray for them, and offer their prayers to God; console the souls in purgatory, and, when they are fully purged, conduct them to paradise.

Man

167. **Of what does man consist?**
Of soul and body.

168. **What are the principal properties of the soul of man?**
It is simple, it is free, and it is immortal.

169. **What do you mean by man's soul being simple?**
The soul of man is a spirit, not composed of parts, and therefore like to the angels. It is neither high nor low, neither broad nor narrow; it has neither right nor left, it can neither be seen with the eyes of the body, nor touched with the hands; it is in the body, and gives life to the body, but it has not any of the qualities which the body has.

170. **What do you mean by the soul being free?**
The soul knows good and evil, and has the power of applying itself to the one or the other as it pleases. When it does good, it is in its power not to do it, and when it does evil, it is equally in its power not to do it.

171. **What do you mean by its being immortal?**
Not only does the soul survive the death of the body, but uniting itself again to the body in the day of the general resurrection, it will share with the body a life which shall never end; eternally happy or unhappy according

to its merits or demerits, that is to say, according to the good or bad use it shall have made of its liberty.

172. **Could not God cause the death of the soul of man; that is to say, could he not reduce it to nothing?**
He could do so of absolute power. Moreover, should he for a single moment cease to preserve it, it would be immediately reduced to nothing, as would be the case with every other creature; but having decreed to preserve man's soul in life forever, and his decree being immutable, he cannot reduce it to nothing.

173. **Is it an article of the faith that the body of man will rise again after death, and that it will be united anew to the soul?**
It is an article of the faith, expressed in the Creed.

174. **Who was the first man created by God?**
Adam was the first man created by God. He then took one of his ribs, and of it formed Eve, who was the first woman.

175. **Relying on the chronology of holy scripture, we reckon about six thousand years from Adam to us; but many learned men, skilled in the antiquity of monuments, are of opinion that some of these are ten or twelve thousand years old. If this be true, it is as much as to say that Adam was not the first man created by God, but that other men existed before him.**
There is no occasion for me to point out to you that those learned men, whom you call skilled in the antiquity of monuments, are either[42] impostors

[42] Translator's note: The author here condemns those men only who endeavor to undermine the facts, and cast discredit on the truths of divine revelation, as contained in holy scripture and tradition, and as proposed by the Catholic Church, on the ground that they are in contradiction to the conclusions of modern philosophy and the progress of science—as, for instance, the Pre-Adamites and Co-Adamites, who maintain that Adam was not the first man, and that the human race has not sprung from one man and one woman, created and made in the beginning, immediately by God himself; both of which are facts divinely revealed, and so for which we have a certainty greater than that of all human science—an infallible and divine certainty. He does not condemn the opinion that the six days of creation were not so many natural days, but epochs, or periods of years.

or ignorant. It is sufficient for you to know that they attribute ten thousand years or more to certain ancient monuments, particularly Egyptian monuments, in order to bring into discredit the sacred scriptures, and so to shake the foundations of our most holy religion. Adam was the first man created by God. He is as old as heaven and earth, within five days, having been created on the sixth day of creation; and all the buildings or monuments which are in the world are less ancient than Adam.

176. **Did God create Adam and Eve in a state of grace?**
When God created Adam and Eve, he adorned them with sanctifying grace.

177. **In the estate of innocence in which they were, could it be said that this sanctifying grace was natural in them, that is to say, due to nature?**
No; this grace was a supernatural and gratuitous gift in Adam and Eve, therefore not due to their nature; and this truth is apparent, especially from the condemnation of the 22nd, 23rd, and 79th propositions of Baius, condemned by the supreme pontiffs, St. Pius V, Gregory XIII, and Urban VIII, as well as from the condemnation of the 34th and 35th propositions of Quesnel, made by His Holiness Clement XI.

178. **Were Adam and Eve created immortal?**
Certainly; and if they had persevered in good, they would have passed to the possession of eternal glory without dying. Observe, however, that even this immortality and destination to the glory of paradise were supernatural gifts.

179. **If sanctifying grace, immortality, immunity from concupiscence, and destination to the glory of paradise were supernatural gifts, it is as much as to say that God might have created man in the same state in which he is now born since the fall.**
Certainly; sin always excepted, God might have created man in the state in which he is now born, without detracting from his justice or his goodness.

180. **Were they perfectly happy in respect both of soul and body?**
There is no doubt of it, because all misery began from sin; therefore, had they remained obedient in the terrestrial paradise, where God placed them, they would never have suffered the least affliction nor adversity.

181. **What was Adam's sin?**
The sin of pride, which is the origin of disobedience, and from which, as holy scripture tells us, every sin has its beginning.[43]

182. **What were the punishments of original sin?**
Expulsion from the terrestrial paradise, the death of the body, all the infirmities and miseries of this life, and the loss of all the other supernatural gifts of which we have spoken. Being deprived of sanctifying grace, they stood deprived also of the right which they formerly had to eternal glory, and condemned to eternal death.

183. **Is Adam's sin inherited by all his descendants?**
It is an article of the faith. Not only was Adam, by his sin, subjected to the said punishments, but also all his descendants, with the exception of the Blessed Virgin Mary.

184. **Why is the Blessed Virgin excepted?**
Because this pious belief always obtained in the Church; and it is now defined as an irrefragable dogma, by the bull *Ineffabilis Deus* of His Holiness Pius IX; for which cause, should anyone now deny, or cast any doubt on the immunity of the Blessed Virgin from original sin, he would be a heretic.

185. **But has the pope, by himself, authority to define dogma?**
The pope has, by himself alone, authority to define dogma.[44] Observe, however, that this definition was preceded by the vote of all the bishops of the Catholic world, and was accepted not only with submission, but

[43] Cf. Ecclus 10:14

[44] See the section, "The Roman Pontiff," on p. 27-31, above.

also with exultation by all the churches of the world, who, together with the Church of Rome, form the Catholic or universal Church. Hence, no one, without being manifestly heretical, can deny or even doubt that the Blessed Virgin Mary was immaculate in her conception.

186. **How can it be that Adam's descendants should be justly subjected to suffer the penalty of a sin which they had not personally committed?**
This is somewhat of a mystery. It is enough for us to know that God is just, and that he cannot punish save the guilty. It would be necessary to know clearly the nature of, or what constitutes original sin, in order to be able to see how just it is that we should bear the punishment of it. If you know little of the nature of a crime which the sovereign punishes, you will, perhaps, be tempted to say that his rigor is excessive; but you would not have had this suspicion had you seen and examined the trial of the criminal. We believe by faith that God cannot exceed in rigor, and this is enough for us. Original sin is transmitted to us through carnal generation; how this transmission comes to pass, how it is imputed to us, has not yet been defined by the Church; but this obscurity in which we find ourselves can give us no right to doubt a truth which is of faith. Can you say that a thing is not because you do not know or understand how it is?

187. **Then children who die without baptism are therefore condemned to eternal death?**
We cannot doubt it; not, however, in the same way in which Adam and Eve would have suffered eternal death, had they not repented. In them this sin was a sin committed by the malice of their own will; not so with us their descendants. Hence, theologians almost universally believe that such children suffer no other pain than that of being deprived of the vision of God; and St. Thomas is of opinion that they will not be sensible even of this pain.[45] This opinion of St. Thomas is embraced by most grave and sound authors, and is therefore very probable. According to this opinion, eternal death for those children would consist in the simple deprivation of

[45] Cf. *Summa Theologiae*, III-Sup., app. 2, a. 2; q. 75, a. 2, rep. 2

eternal life, without sorrow or suffering. Observe, moreover, that there being no necessity why God should reveal to us how he punishes original sin in such children, we ought not to marvel that he has not revealed it to us.

Paradise, Purgatory, and Hell

188. **Is it an article of the faith that there is a paradise?**
It is an article of the faith, expressed in the Creed, under the name of eternal life.

189. **Where is paradise?**
Paradise is in heaven: "Be glad and rejoice, for your reward is very great in heaven";[46] and it is a place of so great beauty, riches, and magnificence, that in this world we can form no adequate idea of it. Every shadow of evil is completely excluded from paradise, and every kind of good is found there.

190. **What do the saints enjoy in paradise?**
Their essential beatitude consists in seeing and loving God. In contemplating his infinite beauty, clearly manifested to their intellects as it is in itself, and in loving his infinite goodness, with a love which causes them to taste it in its own proper sweetness, consists that blessedness which, as St. Paul says, "Eye hath not seen, nor ear heard, neither hath it entered into the heart of man" to conceive.[47]

191. **Why do you say "essential beatitude"?**
Because this beatitude is so great and complete that, with it alone, the saints are so blessed that they cannot desire anything else. They enjoy, moreover, the material beauty of heaven, the society of the saints their companions, and that of the angels, the presence of Mary, the Queen of heaven, and, above all, of the sacred humanity of Jesus Christ: but this joy being in no way necessary to perfect beatitude, it may be called accidental, or accessory

[46] Mt 5:12
[47] 1 Cor 2:9

joy. In heaven, moreover, are given certain accidental rewards, which are called *aureoles*, that is to say, coronets, as distinct from the *aurea*, or crown of eternal glory common to all the blessed. St. Thomas defines these *aureoles* as "a joy, or accidental reward, added to the essential reward, or joy, for some extraordinary victory."[48] He says further that there are three kinds of aureoles: the first, those of virgins, who, overcoming the flesh, live the lives of angels in human bodies; the second, those of martyrs, who overcome the world with all its terrors, and all human respect; the third, those of doctors, who overcome the devil, discovering his frauds, and driving him from men's souls.[49] Observe that these *aureoles* are called coronets, not because they are small in themselves, for their splendor and value are immense; but they are called coronets, or small, in comparison with the *aurea*, that is to say, in comparison with the essential beatitude which is common to all the blessed. In the same way, we should call the greatest treasure in the world small, compared to a high mountain of gold, or to a seashore composed of gems. The glory of those crowns, although it will be specially in the souls of the blessed, will also redound to their glorified bodies after the resurrection, as the same St. Thomas affirms.[50]

192. **Will the blessed be secure of not losing paradise for all eternity?**
They will be perfectly secure; and it is this certainty which makes their beatitude complete, knowing that whatever they then enjoy they will enjoy forever.

193. **Is it an article of the faith that there is a purgatory?**
It is an article of the faith, always acknowledged as such by all Catholics, and finally declared to be so by the most holy Council of Trent.[51] In purgatory, satisfaction is made for every debt of temporal punishment which we owe to the divine justice for venial sins, and also for mortal sins already pardoned as far as regards their guilt and the eternal punishment which

[48] *Summa Theologiae*, III-Sup., q. 96, a. 1, c.
[49] Cf. *Summa Theologiae*, III-Sup., q. 96, a. 11
[50] Cf. *Summa Theologiae*, III-Sup., q. 96, a. 10, c.
[51] Cf. Council of Trent, Session 25, "Decree Concerning Purgatory"

they have merited. We shall see afterward, in its proper place, how mortal sins, which are pardoned so far as regards their guilt and the eternal punishment due to them, must still be satisfied for by some temporal punishment, either by good works and indulgences in this life, or else in purgatory.

194. **What kind of pain do the holy souls suffer in purgatory?**
The pain of fire, which will be most fierce, for as St. Augustine says (on Psalm 37), the fire of purgatory is sharper than any pain that can be experienced on earth;[52] they suffer also the still greater pain of seeing themselves deprived of the vision of God, after which souls separated from the body ardently aspire.

195. **Is it an article of the faith that in purgatory there is material fire?**
It is not an article of the faith, and some have thought that purgatory is a place of darkness, full of sadness, but without fire; but the common opinion of theologians, as Bellarmine proves, is contrary to this opinion, and therefore, as we have said in the section, "The Holy Fathers, the Doctors, and the Schoolmen," above, we must hold it as a certain and undeniable fact that there is in purgatory true material fire.

196. **Do the souls in purgatory remain there for a long time?**
The time is proportioned to the temporal punishments for which they are debtors to the divine justice; hence, some souls remain there for a longer, some for a shorter time. The Church desires that pious bequests for the souls of the departed should still be fulfilled, even for centuries after their death, and thus makes known to us her belief that there are some souls in purgatory who must there remain suffering for an immense time. Observe that, at the day of the universal judgment, purgatory will be at an end, and should there then be some souls who ought to remain a yet longer time, in order to satisfy for their debts, God will cause that in a shorter time they

[52] Editor's note: Aquinas quotes Augustine saying as much in *Summa Theologiae*, III-Sup., app. 1, a. 3, s.c.

shall suffer more intense pains, and so be more quickly purged; in order that all the elect may, on that day, ascend glorious and blessed into heaven.

197. **Are the souls in purgatory certain of their eternal salvation?**
They are most certain of it. Luther taught the contrary error; but it was condemned, with his other errors, by Pope Leo X.

198. **Are the souls in purgatory resigned to the divine will, in so much pain?**
They are perfectly resigned; and although they suffer most grievous pain, they sleep the sleep of peace, being perfectly conformed to the divine will, loving God and his adorable dispensations with the intense affection of charity.

199. **Where is purgatory?**
It is the common opinion of the doctors of the Church that purgatory is in the bowels of the earth.

200. **Can the living afford relief to the souls in purgatory?**
This is an article of the faith, as declared by the most holy Council of Trent. The means by which they can afford them relief are works of mortification, prayers made in their behalf, and the application of such indulgences as are applicable to them; but above all, the souls of purgatory are succored by the Holy Sacrifice of the Mass, as the Council of Trent declares.[53]

201. **Is it an article of the faith that there is a hell?**
It is an article of the faith, as declared by several general councils. By *hell* is meant a place of torment, where the devils, and sinners who die stained with mortal sin, are punished. This place of torment will never have an end, nor can the devils or the damned be ever liberated from it.

[53] Cf. Council of Trent, Session 25, "Decree Concerning Purgatory"

202. **Is it also an article of the faith that the pains of the devils and of the damned will never come to an end?**
It is as much an article of the faith as the existence of hell; and is affirmed by the same general councils.

203. **What are the principal pains of hell?**
Fire, privation of the vision of God, and eternal despair; the damned being most certain that their pains will never end.

204. **Will the damned all suffer equal pain?**
No; it would be contrary to the justice of God. As in heaven, the blessed have diverse degrees of glory according to the diversity of their merits, so in hell, the damned have diverse degrees of pain, according to the diversity of their demerits. Although all who are in hell are most miserable, still the pain they suffer is more or less intense, according to the number and gravity of their sins.

205. **Do the devils and the damned ever come out of hell?**
It is the opinion of theologians that some devils, by the permission of God, inhabit the regions of the air; founding on the authority of St. Paul who calls them: *Rectores tenebrarum harum...in coelestibus*; "The rulers of the world of this darkness, the spirits of wickedness in the high places";[54] but the permanent place assigned to them is hell, from which they, as well as the souls of the damned, can issue, for some just cause permitted by God. Observe, however, that when they do come out of hell, they are not freed from the pains which they suffer there, and which accompany them in every place. Further it is certain that, after the general judgment, they will never more be able to quit hell. It is an undeniable fact, from many facts related in history, that devils and souls of the damned do sometimes come out of hell.

[54] Eph 6:12

The Consummation of the World

206. **When will the consummation of the world arrive?**

It is most uncertain, nor is there any argument to prove with certainty whether it will happen shortly, or after many ages. Moreover, such an enquiry appears useless, Jesus Christ having said that the angels know nothing of that day and that hour in which the world shall come to an end; nay! that in regard to his humanity not even he himself knows it;[55] knowing it only, as St. Gregory the Great says, by reason of his divinity, and not choosing to manifest it. Hence it is not to be wondered at, if various ancient authors, famous for learning and sanctity, wishing to fix the epoch of the consummation of the world were deceived. Wisely, therefore, did St. Thomas set himself to combat every conjecture made by men on this point;[56] and St. Alphonsus Liguori in the work from which we have already quoted,[57] concludes thus: "What is certain is what Jesus Christ said: *De die autem illa, et hora nemo scit*; 'Of that day, and of that hour no man knoweth.'" Moreover, Leo X, in the Lateran Council, expresses himself as follows: *Tempus quoque praefixum futurorum malorum, vel Antichristi adventum, aut certam diem Judicii praedicare, vel asserere quis nequaquam praesumat*; "Let no man presume to lay down, or set forth the time appointed of the coming evils, or the advent of Antichrist, or the certain day of the judgment."[58]

207. **Will Antichrist precede the end of the world?**

It is the teaching of all the holy fathers, and the sentiment of the faithful in all ages, that Antichrist will certainly precede the end of the world. Holy scripture also speaks clearly on this point, in several passages.

208. **Who will Antichrist be?**

Antichrist will be a most wicked man, who will have commerce with the devil, will work false prodigies, will seek to make himself adored as God,

[55] Cf. Mk 13:32
[56] Cf. *Summa Theologiae*, III-Sup., q. 88, a. 3
[57] Alphonsus Liguori, DISS. v.
[58] Fifth Lateran Council, Session 11

will persecute Catholics more cruelly than they have ever yet been persecuted, and who will have a great number of followers. He will be the author of great devastation and ruin; and in his time the public celebration of the divine mysteries, particularly of the Holy Mass, will cease.

209. **Who will come to preach against him?**
Enoch and Elijah, who, according to the common opinion of Catholics, are yet living. They will preserve many Catholics from error, and will convert many infidels, especially Jews, who before the end of the world will detest their obstinate perfidy, and acknowledge Jesus Christ. Enoch and Elijah will crown their preaching at last by martyrdom.

210. **Will other signs precede the end of the world?**
Many terrible signs described in the holy gospels, such as tempests, earthquakes, famines, pestilences, disturbance of the seasons, etc., will precede the end of the world.

211. **What will be the end of the world?**
It will end by a prodigious fire, which will consume everything on this earth, and by which even the heavens being on fire shall be dissolved, as St. Peter says.[59]

212. **Is it an article of the faith that the bodies of men will rise again at the end of the world?**
It is an article of the faith, as expressed in the Creed by the words: "The resurrection of the flesh."

213. **Will all men rise again, without exception?**
We must except the most Blessed Virgin Mary, who rose again soon after her death; a truth most certain on the authority of the holy fathers and doctors, as well as by the sentiment of the whole Catholic Church, which celebrates with the greatest solemnity her glorious assumption into heaven.

[59] Cf. 2 Pt 3:10, 12-13

We must also except Enoch and Elijah, who will rise again three days and a half after their martyrdom, as we read in the Apocalypse.[60] St. Thomas and Maldonatus except also the saints who rose again at the time of our Lord's death.[61] With these exceptions, there is no doubt that all men will rise again, for all men must die, and afterward present themselves with their bodies at the universal judgment.

214. **But if all men must die before they present themselves at the judgment, why is Jesus Christ called the "judge of the living and the dead"?**[62]
St. Thomas answers that by *the living* are meant those who will remain alive up to the last day of the world. Nevertheless, they too will die, because of the condemnation pronounced by God against all the children of Adam. But, being alive a few hours before the universal judgment, their death is scarcely considered, and it is said that they will go, as it were, alive, to judgment, because they have remained in life up to the extremity of time, which ends with the judgment.[63]

215. **Since all men will rise again, will they rise with the same bodies which they had formerly?**
This is an article of the faith. Were they to rise again with other bodies, how could it be said that the flesh, or the bodies which were dead, rose again? The bodies of the damned will rise horrible and frightful, although in their natural form. The bodies of the blessed will also rise in their natural form, but most beautiful and glorious, endowed, moreover, with the four qualities which belong to glorified bodies: brightness, impassibility, agility, and subtility.

216. **Explain to me those qualities.**
Brightness signifies a splendor, of most vivid light, with which they will shine as suns; impassibility will tender them immortal and incapable of

[60] Cf. Apoc 11:11-12
[61] Cf. Mt 27:52; *Summa Theologiae*, III-Sup., q. 77, a. 1, rep. 3
[62] Acts 10:42
[63] Cf. *Summa Theologiae*, I-II, q. 81, a. 3, rep. 1

suffering the least pain or inconvenience; agility will render them most prompt in corresponding with the desires of the soul, for the bodies of the blessed being without weight or heaviness, they will transport themselves from one place to another with the most rapid motion. By the gift of subtility, they will be freed from all density, as St. Alphonsus expresses it, in such sort that the soul will govern the body as if it were a spirit, not because it will become a spirit or an ethereal body, but because the body will be perfectly obedient to the soul.

217. **What will be the stature of the rising bodies?**
St. Thomas says that men will rise with the stature which they had, or would have had, at the natural termination of the increase of the body. Those, however, who were, or might have been, of defective stature, from being immoderately tall or short, will by the divine omnipotence have these defects supplied, that they may rise again of an ordinary stature.[64]

218. **In what place will the universal judgment be held?**
The general opinion of the doctors teaches that the universal judgment will take place in the Valley of Jehoshaphat. There the elect will be placed on the right, and the reprobate on the left.

219. **What will be the sign of the Son of Man which will appear, according to the prediction in the gospel of St. Matthew 24:30?**
According to the common opinion of the holy fathers and doctors, this sign will be the resplendent cross of our Lord Jesus Christ, that is to say, either the very same cross on which he died, or, as is more probable, an image of his cross.

220. **Will Jesus Christ descend in human form to judge men?**
It is certain and undoubted that, as in human form he ascended into heaven, so he will descend thence in human form, and that with great power and majesty, as is revealed in the holy gospels.

[64] Cf. *Summa Theologiae*, III-Sup., q. 81, a. 2

221. **How will the judgment proceed?**

Jesus Christ will cause all the good works of the just, and all the evil deeds of the damned to be made manifest; so that each one will know clearly his own merits or demerits, and in like manner will see the merits or demerits of others. In that day the admirable conduct of the divine justice in regard to all men will be seen.

222. **How will the sentence be given?**

After all things shall have been thus made known, Jesus Christ will invite all the elect to paradise, and will condemn all the reprobate to hell. Then shall the elect, as in a most glorious triumph, ascend into heaven, there to rest forever; whilst the earth opening under the feet of the reprobate, they shall be engulfed by hell, from whence neither the damned nor the devils shall ever anymore issue forth.

223. **Will there then be the consummation of the world?**

Such will be the end of this world, that is to say, the series of vicissitudes amidst which the children of Adam live. Oh! that whilst we are in time, we might know the vanity of all transitory, and the importance of all eternal things, so that, in that great day, we might receive a favorable sentence from Christ the judge.

224. **Will our earth, the sun, and stars cease to exist?**

The earth cannot cease to exist since it contains in its bosom hell, which will never end; neither will the sun and stars cease to exist, but they will shine with a more beautiful and brilliant light. St. John, in the Apocalypse, saw a new heaven and a new earth.[65] All will therefore be renewed in a better form by the omnipotence of God.

[65] Cf. Apoc 21:1

225. **But what will be the use of the surface of the earth, and of the sun and stars, when all the elect will be in paradise, and all the reprobate in hell?**
Holy scripture tells us nothing on this head; nor can we imagine anything probable about it. Therefore, let us turn all our curiosity to the search after those means, whereby we may secure to ourselves the possession of heaven. There we shall see all things; and in all things, and for all things we shall give to God eternal praise.

The Incarnation of the Son of God

Notion of the Mystery

226. **How do you define the mystery of the incarnation?**
It is a primary mystery of the Christian religion, whereby the eternal Word assumed inseparably, in the unity of his Person, a true and entire human nature, in order to appease Almighty God by his sufferings, and to reconcile him with the human race.

227. **Why do you call it a primary mystery?**
Because it is the foundation of the Christian religion, and the basis of all our hopes.

228. **Why do you say that the eternal Word did this?**
To express that a divine Person became incarnate, and that therefore Christ is not a mere man, but true man and true God; and further, to denote that the second Person of the Blessed Trinity alone became incarnate, and not the Father, nor the Holy Ghost.

229. **Then, the incarnation of the Son of God is not the work of all the Persons of the Blessed Trinity? The Father and the Holy Ghost did not concur to it?**
The incarnation of the Son of God is the work of the divine omnipotence; and so is the work of the Blessed Trinity. Therefore, the Father and the Holy Ghost did concur to it; but the union with a human nature was made only by the second Person: the Son alone took and assumed human flesh. To make use of a material comparison, suppose that Peter is dressing himself, whilst James and John are assisting him. Peter alone puts on the dress, but James and John cooperate and concur in the dressing of Peter.

230. **Why do you employ the word *inseparably*?**
Because the Word, having assumed human nature, united it to himself, so as nevermore to separate himself from it: therefore, when Christ died upon the cross, the soul of Christ was separated from his body, but the eternal Word was not separated either from the body which remained in the sepulchre, nor from the soul which descended into hell; and throughout all eternity Jesus Christ will ever be true man and true God.

231. **Why do you say that he assumed human nature, and not that he assumed man? Could you not say that he united man to himself?**
You must understand that God did not create a soul and a body, and form a man of them, and then unite himself with that man in the incarnation; but he created a soul and formed a body, and assumed or united both to his divine Person; therefore, the eternal Word did not take a human person, but a human nature. And anyone who should say that in Christ there are two persons, a human and a divine, would be a heretic: in Christ there are two natures, the divine nature and the human nature, but not two persons. Christ is one only Person, that is, the second Person of the Blessed Trinity.

232. **Why would it be heresy to say that in Christ there are two persons, a human and a divine?**
Because the Church has condemned this error in Nestorius. Nestorius maintained that Christ consisted of two persons, a human and a divine, united together by the bond of charity; and so, he would not have the

Blessed Virgin called the Mother of God, because, according to his error, she was mother only of the human person of Christ.

233. **Mary, then, is the true Mother of God?**
This is an article of the faith, because in the womb of Mary there became incarnate, and of her there was born, a divine Person, Jesus Christ.

234. **Admitting that in Jesus Christ there is one Person alone, might we not also say that in him there is one nature alone?**
This would be the heresy condemned in Eutyches. The Church has defined, as an article of the faith, that in Christ there are two natures, a human and a divine, and only one divine Person, as we have already said; and this is what we must firmly believe and profess.

235. **What consequences follow from these truths?**
That in Christ we must admit what is called by theologians a *communicatio idiomatum*, by which the properties and attributes which belong to the human nature, as well as those which belong to the divine nature, are attributed to Jesus Christ. And so, we say that Jesus Christ was born, and we say that he is eternal: he was born, because his humanity had its beginning in the womb of the Virgin Mary; he is eternal, because his divinity has existed from all eternity. We say that he is limited, and we say that he is immense: he is limited, because his humanity is limited; he is immense, because his divinity is immense; and so of the other properties of the two natures.

236. **Can we say, then, that the humanity of Christ is immense, and that his divinity is limited?**
No. Speaking absolutely of Christ, who is one only divine Person, and has two distinct natures, we may speak of him inasmuch as he is God, and inasmuch as he is man; but when we speak of his divinity or of his humanity, separately, then we may not admit this reciprocal communication; and so we must say that the humanity of Christ is limited, and that his divinity is immense; that his humanity had its beginning in time, and that his divinity is eternal, etc.

237. **What other consequences follow from these truths?**

That Christ must be called the Son of God by nature, and not the Son of God by adoption, not even inasmuch as he is man; and so the Church has defined, in opposition to certain heretics, that Christ is to be adored with the supreme worship of *latria*, and not with the worship of *dulia*, or *hyperdulia*, with which we adore the saints, and the Blessed Virgin, respectively; that the actions of Christ had an infinite merit; that the Virgin Mary is true Mother of God; and other consequences, which you will find in theological writers.

238. **If the Blessed Virgin Mary is to be called the Mother of God, because in her womb the Son of God became incarnate, we must call the Holy Ghost the Father of God, because it was by his operation that the Son of God became incarnate in the womb of the Virgin Mary.**

That one be called father, it is necessary that he contribute of his substance to his son; now the Holy Ghost did not contribute the substance for the formation of the body of the incarnate Word. The Blessed Virgin alone ministered this substance, and from her most pure blood, by virtue of the Holy Ghost, was formed the body of Jesus Christ.

239. **Why do you say further that Christ took a true and entire human nature?**

In order to avoid the error of those heretics who taught that Christ took a body which was ethereal and in appearance only, and so did not take true human flesh. Also to indicate that he took a true, rational human soul, in opposition to the error of those other heretics, who imagined that Christ had taken only a body; or, admitting that he had taken a soul, imagined that it was not a human, that is a rational soul—but that in Christ the eternal Word took the place of a soul.

240. **Finally, for what reason do you say, "in order to appease God by his sufferings, and to reconcile him with the human race"?**

These words show the end of the incarnation, which was to free men from sin, and from the punishment which sin merits; they show also the means which Christ adopted to attain this end, to wit, his passion and death, by which the divine justice was appeased in regard to us.

241. **Did Christ suffer really, that is to say, did he really feel those interior and exterior pains, which he appeared to suffer?**

It is as much an article of the faith that Christ really suffered, as that he took true human flesh. The eternal Word took a human body, subject to hunger and weariness, to wounds and pain, passible and mortal; and he truly suffered all that the holy evangelists relate of his sufferings. He took, moreover, a human soul, which was capable of sadness, heaviness, and affliction, like the souls of other men; with this difference, that we suffer sadness, heaviness, and afflictions which very often we can neither alleviate nor remove by our own will; whereas the soul of Christ ruled as Lord over these passions, and suffered them only in that degree which he willed.

242. **Is it of faith that Christ has merited for us the pardon of our sins, the graces necessary for salvation, and that he has restored to us the right to eternal life, which we had lost?**

These are truths of the faith. Jesus Christ, by his humiliations and sufferings, has not only merited for himself, as St. Paul says,[66] the glory of his body and the exaltation of his name, but he has also merited for us every supernatural grace; and he has merited them, not only for those who have lived since the time of his incarnation, but also for those who lived before that time; so that all the supernatural graces bestowed upon men, even before his incarnation, were merited for them by Jesus Christ; that is to say, they obtained them in regard of the merits of Jesus Christ, who was to come, in order to make satisfaction for the sins of the whole world, and to obtain for men every good availing to eternal life.

243. **If he has merited eternal life for all men, do you mean to say that all men will be saved?**

He has merited eternal life for all men, but he requires the cooperation of men in order to their obtaining the same. He has not merited for men so that they should be compelled to save themselves, but he has so merited for them, that by the help of his grace, they, willing it, may be able to save

[66] Cf. Phil 2

themselves. Hence, notwithstanding his superabundant merits, which are capable of saving innumerable men, more than ever existed, now exist, or shall hereafter exist, he who chooses to damn himself is damned, as we see is the case with the greater part of men, who, abusing their own liberty, are lost.

244. **Could not God have saved men in some other way, without becoming man?**
He could have saved us, of his absolute power, in other ways, but he chose this way, in order to receive an adequate satisfaction for the injury which sin had done him. Observe that God, of his absolute power, could have pardoned sin, without exacting any satisfaction, or by accepting the satisfaction which might have been offered him by some holy creature, as, for instance, by an angel; but this satisfaction would not have been proportionate to the injury received.

245. **For what reason, then, did God choose this mode, rather than any other?**
We must not seek to know the reason of God's operations; nevertheless, we may say that he chose this mode, because it was the most fitting; his divine justice being in this way most fully satisfied, and his other attributes, such as his clemency, his wisdom, his omnipotence, etc., being made manifest in an incomparable degree. Moreover, this was the most efficacious mode to gain our love. For, that a God should become man, and subject himself to sufferings and to death, in order to save men, is such an excess of love as to oblige even the hardest hearts to love this God.

246. **Was God obliged to provide a remedy of some kind for the ruin into which sin had plunged us?**
He might justly have abandoned us in our sin, and to the consequences of our sin; it was the work of his infinite mercy to provide a remedy for our evils.

247. **Was the incarnation of the Son of God foretold before it was effected?**
It was foretold immediately after Adam's fall, and the prophets all spoke of it. Hence Jesus Christ was expected by the Jews; and even the Gentiles, as we gather from profane history, were in expectation of a Savior.

248. **For what reason would the Jewish people not acknowledge him when he came?**
Because of their pride, and the obstinacy of their prejudices. The Jews were absolutely without excuse, for they had the prophecies which spoke clearly of him; and those prophecies they saw verified in Jesus Christ.

The Body and Soul of Christ

249. **Can we say that the body of Jesus Christ consists of human flesh; and that therefore he became a son of Adam?**
We have already declared it to be a Catholic truth, that Christ took true and real human flesh, like that of other men, with this difference—that he did not take it by the operation of man, but by the operation of the Holy Ghost; therefore, having taken true and real human flesh, he became a son of Adam.

250. **Was not St. Joseph, the husband of Mary, the father of Jesus?**
St. Joseph was the husband of Mary; but he remained ever a virgin, and left the Blessed Mary ever a Virgin. It would be heresy to say that St. Joseph was the true father of Jesus Christ; he was only the reputed father, that is, believed to be such by persons who, knowing that he had espoused and lived with Mary, and seeing that she had a son, thought that she had had him by Joseph. On the contrary, however, St. Joseph always lived with Mary as if he had been her brother, and nothing more.

251. **How could the Blessed Mary have had a son, whilst she remained a Virgin?**
This is a miracle of the omnipotence of God; and so great a miracle that none has ever taken place like it. The Holy Ghost, as we have already mentioned, formed the body of Jesus Christ, of the most pure blood of Mary; in due time

Mary brought him forth in the stable of Bethlehem, remaining even then a Virgin as before; and so she brought him forth without pain or sorrow, and without any injury or violation of her virginal integrity. Observe that it is an article of the faith, that Mary was a Virgin before childbirth, in childbirth, and after childbirth, as defined by the General Council of Chalcedon.

252. **In the holy gospel mention is made of the "brethren" of Jesus Christ; does it mean that the Blessed Mary had other children?**
The Blessed Mary had no other children. The Jews called other relations by the name of brethren; these, therefore, were relations of Jesus Christ, but not his true brothers.

253. **How did the death of Jesus Christ occur?**
His soul was separated from his body, as happens when men die; his divinity, that is, the eternal Word, however, remaining united, as we have already said, both to his body and to his soul.

254. **During the time that the body of Christ remained in the sepulchre, did it begin to corrupt as do other dead bodies?**
The body of Jesus Christ suffered no corruption in the sepulchre, as the prophet David had foretold.[67]

255. **For how long did the body of Christ remain in the sepulchre?**
Part of Friday, the whole of Saturday, and part of Sunday. On the morning of Sunday his soul was reunited to his body, which rose glorious, immortal, and impassible. Thus risen, he appeared several times to his disciples, and forty days after his resurrection he ascended into heaven.

256. **When the eternal Word became man, did he take a soul of the same nature as our soul?**
It is an article of the faith, as we have already shown, that the eternal Word took a human soul, and therefore of the same nature as ours.

[67] Cf. Ps 15

257. **Are we to acknowledge a human will in Christ, besides the divine will?**
It is an article of the faith that we are to acknowledge a human will in Christ, which, although free like ours, was nevertheless always conformed to the divine will, the soul of Christ never having willed other than was willed by the eternal Word. The Church defined this article of the faith, in opposition to an ancient sect of heretics—the Monothelites.

258. **Must we acknowledge human operations in Christ, besides the divine operations?**
Christ being not only true God but also true man, we must certainly acknowledge human operations in him. In fact, when we read in the holy gospels that Christ suffered hunger and weariness, that he wept, that he was sorrowful, etc., we at once understand that these are human operations. Moreover, the human operations of Christ have an infinite merit, because, by virtue of the hypostatic union, they were the actions of a divine Person.

259. **Was the soul of Christ endowed with knowledge?**
The soul of Christ, from the first moment of its creation, had a full and most perfect knowledge of all things; and although, as Christ grew in age, he appeared, as the gospel observes, to grow in wisdom, it was not really so, since he had always possessed the fullness of wisdom. Moreover, the soul of Christ enjoyed the intuitive vision of God, even as the saints enjoy it in paradise, beholding clearly the Person of the eternal Word, with which it was hypostatically united, and, necessarily, along with the Person of the eternal Word, it beheld the Person of the Father, and the Person of the Holy Ghost.

260. **If the soul of Christ beheld God clearly, it must have been blessed and incapable of suffering. How then can the Catholic dogma, that Christ really suffered in his passion and death, consist with this vision of God attributed to Christ?**
It is true that the beatific vision of God renders the soul incapable of suffering; but, by a great miracle of the divine omnipotence, the joy which the vision of God occasioned in the superior, that is, in the intellectual part

of his soul, was held in check and restrained, so to speak, in order that it might not be communicated to the inferior, that is, to the sensitive part of his soul, and that so it might be capable of suffering. Hence, he truly suffered both interior and exterior pains, as the gospel teaches us.

261. **Can you explain this to me better by some example?**
Observe what happens on very high mountains. Sometimes the clouds thicken and tempests gather half way up the mountain, whilst the sun shines on the summit. Thus, he who is on the summit of the mountain enjoys a serene sky, whilst he who is on its sides is enveloped in clouds and tossed by the tempest. According to our mode of understanding, the same thing took place in the soul of Christ; the superior, that is, the intellectual part, enjoyed the clear vision of God, the inferior, that is, the sensitive part, suffered every kind of sorrow and pain.

262. **The soul of Christ beheld and knew God more clearly than any other creature whatsoever can know him; was it able therefore to comprehend, that is, to know God, as he comprehends and knows himself?**
We have already shown[68] that, God being incomprehensible, no creature can comprehend him; and as, although the soul of Christ had a more clear knowledge of him than any other creature, yet it did not comprehend, that is, did not know God with that fullness of knowledge with which God knows himself.

263. **Was the soul of Christ endowed with liberty?**
Undoubtedly; otherwise its operations would not have been human actions; and it would have been diverse in nature from the nature of our souls.

264. **Could he sin?**
Being hypostatically united with the eternal Word, he could not sin; on the contrary, he had a grace, called the grace of union, or substantial grace, whereby he was holy substantially.

[68] See the section, "The Beatific Vision," on p. 46-49, above.

265. **Had he sanctifying grace?**

He had it in its highest degree, which, without comparison, exceeded the grace of all the angels, of all the saints, and of the Blessed Virgin herself.

266. **Were all the virtues in Christ?**

Undoubtedly, except those which presuppose sin, or other imperfection. He could not therefore possess the virtue of penance, for there was in him nothing of which he could repent; nor the virtues of faith and hope, because these virtues cannot be present in a soul which enjoys the intuitive vision of God.

267. **When Christ died on the cross, and his soul was separated from his body, did it descend into hell?**

This is an article of the faith, and expressed in the Creed. Observe, however, that here, under the name of hell, is not meant the hell destined for the devils and the damned, but the subterranean regions, commonly called *limbus*, where the holy souls of all the just who had died before the coming of Christ reposed, and there waited till the gates of paradise should be opened to them, by the completion of the work of redemption.

268. **Then the just, who died before the period of the death of Christ, did not enjoy the vision of God in heaven?**

They did not; but they reposed, in the most perfect peace and tranquility, in *limbus*. Thither the soul of Christ descended, and freed them from this prison, in order to conduct them to heaven.

The Various Titles Which Belong to Christ; the Worship Due to Him, and That Which Belongs to His Saints

269. **What titles belong to Christ?**

1. He is the Son of God by nature; not even considering him as man, can he be called the Son of God by adoption.
2. He is a King, not only according to his divinity, but according to his humanity.

3. He is the head of men and of angels.
4. He is a lawgiver.
5. He is a judge.
6. He is a priest, and a priest forever.
7. He is the mediator or reconciler between God and men, having fully, nay, superabundantly made satisfaction to the divine justice for them.

270. **Does Christ pray for us to his Father?**

St. Augustine says that Christ, as man, prays for us, and that as God, he, along with the divine Father, hears our prayer; *Christus homo pro nobis est orator; ut Deus est cum Patre exauditor*; "Christ as man prays for us; and, as God, he, with the Father, hears our prayers."

271. **What worship is due to Christ?**

Observe that there are three kinds of worship. The first is that of *latria*, which is the supreme and absolute adoration wherewith we adore God, by reason of his uncreated and infinite excellence. The second is the worship of *dulia*, which is the adoration with which we venerate certain creatures, for their supernatural, but not supremely, or singularly excellent dignity. The third is the worship of *hyperdulia*, which is the adoration with which we honor a creature for her supernatural, and singularly excellent dignity. Observe this: it is of faith that Christ, God and man, is to be adored with the adoration of *latria*; and that, with the same adoration of *latria*, his humanity is also to be adored, not by reason of itself, but by reason of the uncreated and infinite excellence of the eternal Word, with which it is personally and substantially united.

272. **To whom is the worship of *dulia* due?**

It is due to the angels and saints, who possess a supernatural dignity, but not in a singular degree of excellence.

273. **To whom is the worship of *hyperdulia* due?**
This pertains to the Blessed Virgin Mary alone, who enjoys a supernatural dignity in a singular degree of excellence, she being, as we have already said, the true Mother of God.

274. **Is it meet that we venerate the saints, the angels, and the Blessed Virgin?**
It is most meet, as it is always most meet to honor the friends, the ministers, and much more, the Mother of the sovereign. Earthly sovereigns, when they see their friends, ministers, or mothers honored, reckon this honor as if paid to themselves. In like manner, God is honored by the honor rendered to the saints, to the angels, and to the Blessed Virgin Mary.

275. **Is it useful to have recourse to the intercession of the saints, the angels, and the Blessed Virgin Mary?**
It is most useful; for they hear our prayers, they are most zealous for our welfare, and they obtain for us the graces which we need. Above all, it is most useful to have recourse to the intercession of Mary, for her prayers are so powerful with her divine Son that one prayer of hers is of more value than the prayers of all the angels and saints in paradise combined. The Church has always promoted, with singular earnestness, devotion to the Blessed Virgin, and this devotion consists in venerating her, and in praying to her to intercede for us.

The saints who have been most eminent for knowledge and piety were ever distinguished by a most special devotion to Mary. The authors who enjoy the reputation of the soundest and most stainless doctrine have ever written great things of devotion to Mary; her worship is disapproved only by heretics; and those who have little devotion to her are those only who are not good Christians.

I ask pardon of Mary, I ask pardon of her devout clients when I say merely that devotion to her is most "useful"; for more than this might be said without fear of error.

276. **Do those who say that Mary bestows graces express themselves correctly?**
They express themselves well, because the Church asks Mary to bestow graces, *Solve vincla reis, profer lumen coecis*, etc.; "Break the bonds of the captive, give light to the darkened," etc. Understand, however, that Mary impetrates these graces for us, it being certain that the author of all grace, as the author of all good, is God alone.

277. **What points are expressly defined as of faith, in regard to the worship of the saints?**
The sacred Council of Trent, in the twenty-fifth session, declares it to be of faith that the saints pray for us before God; and that it is a good and a useful thing suppliantly to invoke them. Hence, he who should deny this truth would be a heretic.

278. **Are the images of the saints to be venerated?**
It is of the faith, as defined in the Second Council of Nice, and in the Council of Trent, that holy images are to be venerated, referring however the worship which is rendered to them either to Christ, or to the Blessed Virgin, or to the saints whom they represent.[69]

279. **Are the relics of the saints to be venerated?**
The sacred Council of Trent expressly defines that veneration and honor are due to the relics of the saints.[70] Observe, moreover, that among all relics, the wood of the true cross of Christ merits a special veneration, as the most precious relic which remains to us of our Savior.

[69] Cf. Council of Trent, Session 25, "On the Invocation, Veneration, and Relics, of Saints, and on Sacred Images"

[70] Cf. Ibid.

The Grace of God

The Notions of the Different Kinds of Grace, and Particularly, of Actual Grace

280. **What do you mean by the grace of Christ?**

A supernatural gift of God which, in regard of the merits of Jesus Christ, is conferred upon man gratuitously, in order that he may attain to his supernatural end, which is eternal salvation. From this definition you will perceive that under the name of the grace of Christ we do not intend to speak of natural graces, such, for example, as health, or a good understanding; nor yet of the grace bestowed upon the first man in the estate of innocence, and upon the angels; but of the medicinal grace of the Savior, which is bestowed upon man since his fall by original sin, in regard of the merits of the same Savior.

281. **How is this grace divided?**

It is divided into external grace, internal grace, and grace *gratis data*. External graces are the example of Christ, the preaching of the holy gospel, etc. Internal graces are good inspirations, the gifts of the Holy Ghost, etc. Graces *gratis datae* are those which are given to a man, not so much for his own personal advantage, as for the benefit of others; such as the gifts of prophecy, discerning of spirits, miracles, etc. But the grace of which we would more particularly speak at present is that which is called in the schools *gratia interna gratum faciens* (internal grace making gracious), which is a supernatural gift particularly directed to the spiritual well-being of him on whom it is bestowed. This is divided into actual grace and sanctifying, or habitual grace.

282. **What is actual grace?**

By actual grace we mean those aids called transient in the schools, or, as we should say, passing, transitory, momentary aids, with which God, from time to time, aids our weakness, so that we may do good and avoid evil, in order to the salvation of our souls.

283. **What is sanctifying or habitual grace?**

Sanctifying grace is a supernatural gift of God, which is permanent and inherent in our souls, by way of a habit, and by means of which a man becomes just and the friend of God, and so a son of God by adoption, an adopted brother of Jesus Christ, and an heir of paradise.

284. **Could you, by some comparison, explain to me more clearly the difference which exists between actual grace and sanctifying grace?**

Picture to yourself a little child who has fallen down in the mire. This child has not the power to get up again of himself, and he has need of dry, clean clothes, because his clothes are all wet and soiled with mud. His mother hastens to his assistance, and first gives him her hand to help him up, and then dresses him again, as there is need. Here you have a twofold aid from the mother corresponding to the twofold necessity of the child; but the first is a passing, transitory, momentary aid, since when the mother helps him up, she does nothing which remains on him, to use a material expression; the second, however, is a permanent aid, since the fresh clothes, with which she covers him, remain on the child. In the help which the mother gives her child to get up again, you have a similitude of actual grace; in the clothes which she puts upon him, you have a similitude of habitual grace. The first is transitory; the second is permanent, remaining with a man.

285. **Is actual grace necessary to man?**

It is a dogma of the faith, that, without the supernatural grace of God, man can do no good work contributing to eternal life. We must therefore say that actual grace is most necessary, since we cannot do the very least good action contributing to the salvation of our souls, unless this grace moves us, that is, unless it excites us in the beginning, and accompanies us in the course of our actions, and even to the end. It is necessary, not only for sinners, but also for the just, that is, for those who possess sanctifying grace. St. Augustine says that however sound the eye may be, it cannot see without light, and however just a man may be, he cannot do good without grace moving him, and accompanying him in his good and saving works.

286. **Can we not overcome temptations without grace?**
Without supernatural grace we cannot overcome any temptation, from a supernatural motive, either from the love of God, or from the fear of God; for he who overcomes temptation from either of these motives does a good in itself, saving and meritorious of eternal life. Certain temptations, however, and particularly slight temptations, may be overcome from other motives, and in such case do not require grace. For example, I may vanquish the temptation to steal, from fear of the punishment which the civil law inflicts; in like manner I may vanquish the temptation to tell lies, from fear of the shame which would come upon me were my falsehood made known; such temptations would be overcome from natural motives, and would in no way be meritorious of eternal life; in this way infidels and the most hardened sinners overcome many temptations. In general, however, we affirm that temptations are not overcome without grace, since there is an infinite number of even grave temptations, to which we might consent without fear of temporal evils; and without this fear we might always consent, at least by complacency and in desire.

287. **Cannot we observe all the precepts of the natural law without grace?**
We cannot observe all, particularly those against which the temptations are strongest and most frequent; hence it follows that without grace we cannot avoid all sins.

288. **Is it necessary that the just should have a special grace in order to enable them, in this life, to avoid all and every venial sin?**
It is a truth defined by the holy Council of Trent that not even the just can, during the whole course of their life, avoid all, even venial sins, without a special privilege from God;[71] and it is not certain that this privilege was ever granted to anyone, except to the Blessed Virgin Mary, who was never

[71] Cf. Council of Trent, Session 6, Can. 23

stained with the least shadow of sin. This refers to venial sins which we commit without full advertence; for everyone who wills can avoid all sins to which he fully adverts.

289. **Is the grace of persevering till death in the friendship of God—that is to say, is the grace of final perseverance a special gift of God?**
Undoubtedly it is a special gift, for the holy Council of Trent calls it the great gift.[72]

290. **How is actual grace divided?**
It is divided into efficacious grace and sufficient grace.

291. **What is efficacious grace?**
That which obtains its effect. For example, God gives me grace, in order that I may be sincerely converted to him; I do not resist this grace—on the contrary, I cooperate with it with my free will, and therefore am really converted. Here is efficacious grace—that is, grace which obtains its effect.

292. **What is sufficient grace?**
That which gives to a man sufficient strength to do good and avoid evil, but which, being resisted by man's evil will, does not obtain its effect.

293. **Can you explain the efficacy and sufficiency of grace in any other way?**
Theologians have framed various systems, and have explained, some in one way, some in another, the efficacy and sufficiency of grace; but, in this most difficult matter, it will suffice for us to know what is certain and beyond possibility of doubt. It is certain that there are efficacious graces—that is to say, graces which obtain their effect. It is certain that there are graces which are only sufficient, and which, being resisted, do not obtain their effect. This is a truth of the faith, defined against Jansenius. This sufficient grace must be capable of obtaining—that is, sufficient to obtain the effect for which it is given. If it did not suffice to its end, it would be insufficient,

[72] Cf. Council of Trent, Session 6, "Decree on Justification," Can. 16

and sufficient grace which is not enough—that is to say, which is not sufficient—is a contradiction.

It is certain that God sincerely wills the salvation of all men; it is certain that without his interior and actual grace no adults can be saved; it is certain that God will not allow them to want the true aids of grace, as means absolutely necessary for the attainment of their end—that is, of their salvation; and so we all have grace sufficient to save us, and, if we cooperate with this grace, our salvation is secure. "To everyone is given light and grace, that, doing what is in him, he may save himself by giving only his consent." This is the doctrine, and these are the words of St. Catherine of Genoa, whose authority, as all know, is certainly as good as that of a theologian. Precisely, and in the full rigor of the expression, this is the belief of the whole Christian people: I confess, however, that I prefer the beautiful words of the Council of Trent before all the systems: "God does not command what is impossible; but commanding, he warns thee to do what thou art able, and to ask for what thou art not able to do. In the meanwhile, he helps thee in order that thou mayest be able. His commandments are not grievous, his yoke is sweet, his burden is light... Those whom he has once justified he does not abandon, unless they first abandon Him."[73] This is the consoling doctrine of the Holy Spirit, and all the more consoling because it is infallible.

294. **Is necessitating grace given—that is to say, grace which compels man of necessity to operate?**

This would be not grace, but violence. It is an article of the faith that grace does not take away, and does not hinder the use of man's liberty; therefore, all that is done with grace is entirely free. St. Paul says, "I can do all things in him who strengtheneth me"[74]—he does not say, "in him who forces me." It is as much of faith that grace has part in our good works, as it is of faith that our free will has part in them.

[73] Council of Trent, Session 6, "Decree on Justification," Ch. 11

[74] Phil 4:13

295. **Does God ever impart any grace to hardened and obstinate sinners?**
Even the most hardened and obstinate sinners are never without some graces—at least remote graces, to enable them to pray and obtain mercy. If they availed themselves of these graces, the grace of conversion would not be wanting to them. It is not in accordance with the common sentiment of the faithful that God should ever wholly abandon anyone in this life, and therefore we should never despair of the salvation of anyone, as long as he lives. Moreover, this accords with the teaching of St. Paul, who, speaking to hardened and impenitent sinners, instructs them that the benignity of God invites them to penance.[75]

296. **What do you say with regard to infidels who have no knowledge of the true faith, because it has never been proclaimed to them?**
Even these have some graces, by means of which they could observe the natural law; and if they availed themselves of these graces, doing what was possible to their natural powers, aided by these graces, God would certainly, either by ordinary or extraordinary means, bring them to the knowledge of the true faith, in order that they might be saved, as St. Thomas teaches.[76]

297. **Are actual graces given to man's merits?**
This would be a heresy clearly condemned by holy scripture, and by the decisions of the Church. Graces are gratuitous gifts, which God grants to whom he wills, and when he wills.[77]

298. **You mean to say, then, that the good have no foundation for hoping that God exercises toward them a special providence of graces?**
This would be another error, because, although graces cannot be merited, God nevertheless, in holy scripture, promises a special assistance to the good:

[75] Cf. Rom 2

[76] He says further, that it arises from our negligence that grace is wanting to us: "The primary cause of lack of grace is from ourselves. It is from his own negligence that a man has not grace" (cf. *Summa Theologiae*, I-II, q. 76, a. 2, rep. 2; q. 112, a. 3, rep. 2).

[77] Cf. Council of Trent, Session 6, "Decree on Justification," Ch. 7-8

"The eyes of the Lord are upon the just, and his ears unto their prayers."[78] Therefore, although God is not obliged to confer graces either upon the just or upon sinners, nevertheless he who loves them that love him[79] ordinarily abounds in greater graces to those who show themselves faithful to him. I say "ordinarily," because sometimes, in order more wonderfully to manifest his mercy, he confers great grace even upon great sinners. Such graces he bestowed upon David, the Magdalen, the good thief, etc.

Sanctifying Grace

299. **What is it that justifies a man?**
Sanctifying grace, the definition of which we have already given in the answer to the fourth question of the previous section.[80]

300. **When is sanctifying grace acquired?**
It is acquired in holy baptism.

301. **Once acquired can it be lost?**
It is lost by every mortal sin, because by every mortal sin we lose charity.

302. **Once lost can it be reacquired?**
It can be regained by means of the sacrament of penance, which was expressly instituted for the remission of sins committed after baptism; and even by means of charity, which includes the intention or desire of this sacrament, as we shall explain in the following chapter.

303. **This sanctifying grace is perhaps the justice of Jesus Christ, imputed to us?**
To say that sanctifying grace is the identical justice of Jesus Christ, imputed to us, is a heresy condemned by the Council of Trent.[81] This grace consists in a supernatural gift, not imputed, but really conferred on, and

[78] Ps 33:16
[79] Cf. Prv 8:17
[80] Editor's note: See the answer to Question 283, above.
[81] Cf. Council of Trent, Session 6, Can. 11

made intrinsic to our souls, and by which we are truly justified, and truly cleansed from sin.

304. **Could we not say that sanctifying grace serves as a garment to the soul, covering it, and concealing the deformity of sin?**
To say so would be a heresy condemned by the same council.[82] Sanctifying grace is not extrinsic to the soul, as a garment is extrinsic to the body which it covers; and by the infusion of this grace sins are not concealed or covered, but absolutely taken away and canceled, so that their stains no longer exist. In the same way as when a filthy garment is washed, the stains which were in it are not covered over, but taken away, so that they no longer exist, God, when he justifies a man by infusion of his grace, takes away sin from his soul.

305. **Would not faith alone be sufficient for the justification of the soul?**
This would be a heretical doctrine, in like manner condemned by the holy Council of Trent.[83] Faith is only the root and foundation of justification, as the council defines;[84] otherwise, all the faithful would be in a state of grace, and mortal sin would not be found, save in infidels. For the justification of a man, good works are requisite as well as faith. "Faith without works is dead," as St. James says.[85]

306. **Some have thought that those only were justified, and so that those only had sanctifying grace, who firmly believed that they had that grace, in the same way as we must firmly believe the dogmas of the faith. What do you say as to this doctrine?**
This is also a heretical doctrine, condemned by the Council of Trent. On the contrary, observe that no one can firmly believe that he has this grace, without a special revelation from God.[86]

[82] Cf. Ibid.
[83] Cf. Council of Trent, Session 6, "Decree on Justification," Ch. 9, 11; Can. 9, 14, 29
[84] Cf. Council of Trent, Session 6, "Decree on Justification," Ch. 8
[85] Jas 2:20
[86] Cf. Council of Trent, Session 6, "Decree on Justification," Ch. 9, 12; Can. 14

307. **No one then can be certain of having sanctifying grace?**

The Christian who is not conscious to himself of mortal sin, either because he knows not that he has ever committed it, or because, after having fallen into sin, he has rightly confessed and detested it, may be certain of having sanctifying grace. This certainty, however, cannot be firm and certain, as is the infallible certainty with which we believe the verities of the faith; and the reason of this is that God has revealed the verities of the faith, and, therefore, as to them there can be no deception; but to no one has it been revealed that he has never committed a mortal sin, or that, having committed it, he has sufficiently confessed and detested it, so as to obtain pardon. So that, in regard to the certainty of being in a state of grace, it is possible for a man to deceive himself.

308. **For what reason does God leave us in this state of uncertainty?**

In order that fear may be a continual spur, stimulating us to secure more and more the possession of his grace, by the exercise of the Christian virtues, and so to increase our merits for life eternal. We may, however, be certain of having sanctifying grace, not indeed with infallible and divine certainty, but with moral and human certainty. Moreover, we must guard against excessive fear in this particular, for it would diminish our confidence in God and our love of him.

309. **What is the strongest argument we can have of our being in a state of grace?**

Listen to St Francis of Sales, quoted by St. Alphonsus Liguori, both of whom were great theologians: "The greatest security which we can have in this world of being in the grace of God does not consist in the feeling of love we may have for him, but in the entire and irrevocable abandonment of all our affections into his hands, and in a firm resolution never to consent to any sin, whether great or small." Let us, then, resign ourselves wholly into God's hands; let us resolve to suffer, no matter what, rather than knowingly to offend him in the very smallest matter, and we shall have the strongest argument which upon this earth we can have, of possessing the great treasure of sanctifying grace.

310. **Can there be augmentation of sanctifying grace in the soul of a just man?**
This is a truth of the faith, defined by the holy Council of Trent, and this augmentation is acquired by means of good works.[87]

311. **You mean to say, then, that sanctifying grace can be merited?**
The grace of justification cannot be merited, it being the free gift of God; and this is of faith. No one who is in sin can merit that God should pardon him, and enrich him with sanctifying grace; but, on the other hand, the just—that is, those who already possess sanctifying grace—can, by their good works (as we shall explain in the following section), really merit an increase of this grace.

312. **Is sanctifying grace necessary to good works?**
It is necessary, in order that good works be meritorious of eternal life; still, even without sanctifying grace, we can do works which are good in the sight of God. God accepted the alms of the centurion, who was an infidel, and Daniel counseled Nebuchadnezzar to give alms, etc.[88] Hence sinners should endeavor to do good works, which, although they cannot merit for them eternal life, may yet serve to impetrate for them the mercy of God.

313. **Some say that all the works of infidels and sinners are sins.**
This detestable error was condemned in the twenty-fifth and thirty-fifth propositions of Baius by the sovereign pontiffs St. Pius V, Gregory XIII, and Urban VIII. I call it a detestable error, because it casts sinners into despair, and deprives them of the use of those means—that is to say, of good works—whereby they might obtain God's mercy and the grace of conversion.

314. **Is sanctifying grace the same thing as charity?**
The most probable opinion is that it is the same thing; others, however, suppose it to be a gift distinct from charity. However this may be, it is

[87] Cf. Council of Trent, Session 6, "Decree on Justification," Ch. 10; Can. 24, 32
[88] Cf. Acts 10:1-4; Dn 4:24

certain that he who has charity has sanctifying grace, and he who has sanctifying grace has also charity.

The Merit of Good Works

315. **Are good works meritorious?**
It is a truth of the faith, defined by the holy Council of Trent, that by good works, done in a state of grace, we truly merit an increase of the same grace, that is, of sanctifying grace and eternal life.[89]

316. **Now is it possible that by good works, which, however many and great they may be, can bear no proportion to the pricelessness of an eternal reward, we can truly merit paradise?**
You must consider that by our good works, regarded in themselves alone, we could not merit eternal life, because there would be no proportion between these works and the reward which is given them. But we must look upon our good works as ennobled by the infinite merits of Jesus Christ, and raised to so great a dignity and value by his merits that there is a most true proportion between them and eternal life.

Further, we must presuppose the divine promise, whereby God has bound himself to reward them in this manner; the divine promise which, in a wide sense, obliges Almighty God, in regard of us, to recompense us with this reward. I say "in a wide sense," because God cannot be bound, in regard of us, by a rigorous debt, but he is bound by his own infinite fidelity which demands that he fail not in his promises. And so, you see that eternal life is a true grace, inasmuch as all our merits spring from the grace of God; and it is by a simple act of his divine goodness that our good works are raised to so great a value as to merit paradise, which also was promised to them by a simple act of his divine goodness.

Paradise is, moreover, at the same time a true reward, because in virtue of the supernatural excellence and dignity of our good works, and in virtue of the divine promise whereby God has bound himself to reward them, this

[89] Cf. Council of Trent, Session 6, "Decree on Justification," Ch. 10; Can. 24, 32

reward is truly due to them. Therefore, as is defined against the heretics, by good works performed in a state of grace, we truly merit not only increase of the same grace, but also eternal life.

317. **What conditions must good works have in order that they may be meritorious?**

The first condition is that the good works be done by men who are wayfarers, that is to say, during this life; for the saints in heaven, who are no longer wayfarers, but have finished their journey and attained their end, can no longer merit. The second is that they be free; for, in order to merit, it is necessary that a man know what he does, and that he can do or not do what he does. The third condition is that they be done by a just man, that is, by one in a state of grace, as we have already shown. The fourth is that they be good works, good by a supernatural goodness, either in themselves, such as the receiving of the holy sacraments, or by reason of their end, such as the making a pilgrimage to some sanctuary in order to venerate a devout image of the Blessed Virgin. Those four conditions, besides the divine promise, which we take for granted, are the conditions which necessarily and undoubtedly are required in all good works, in order that they may be truly meritorious. This is the teaching of all theologians.

318. **For what reason does the council say that increase of grace may be merited?**[90]

Because, as the same council defines, the first sanctifying grace cannot be truly merited. The sinner, who is deprived of grace, may impetrate it by his prayers and good works, but truly merit it he cannot, his prayers and good works not being of sufficient value to do so.[91] When, however, he obtains sanctifying grace, and is therefore justified, then by the good works which he thereafter performs, he truly merits the increase of this grace.

[90] Cf. Ibid.
[91] Cf. Council of Trent, Session 6, "Decree on Justification," Ch. 8

319. **Explain to me more clearly the second condition, which requires that good works be free.**

Freedom is essential in man, in order to his merits or demerits before God, that is, in the performing good works which shall be worthy of recompense, as well as in the committing sins which shall be worthy of punishment; and this freedom demands knowledge and determination, not forced or necessitated by any cause, whether external or internal. It demands knowledge; and so, if I bestow a gift on a poor man, believing him to be rich, my gift has not the merit of an alms; in like manner, were I to give poison to someone, believing that I was giving him a wholesome drink, I should not incur the guilt of murder. It requires determination, without compulsion from any external cause; therefore, for example, should anyone by main force compel me to prostrate myself before the Blessed Sacrament, I should not have the merit of that adoration; and if I were forced to prostrate myself before an idol, I should not incur the guilt of idolatry. It is necessary, moreover, that there be no violence or compulsion proceeding from any internal cause; and therefore, were the grace of God to force our will, as Calvin imagined, or draw it irresistibly, as Jansenius taught, there could be no merit in good works; so likewise, if concupiscence forced or irresistibly drew our will, there would be no demerit in wicked works.

And in truth ought we to suppose that possible in God which we could not suppose possible in men, without doing them grievous wrong? If a sovereign were to reward good actions performed by one who could do no less than perform them, and to punish wicked actions committed by one who could do no other than commit them, should we not say that in the first case he was a fool, in the second that he was a tyrant? From this you will easily understand why we say that for a man to merit, by his good works, it is necessary that he should know what he is doing, and that it should be in his power to do, or not to do, what he does.

That free will remained to man after original sin is a truth of the faith defined by the holy Council of Trent.[92] Perfect freedom, exempt not only from all violence, but also from all necessity, in order to man's merits or

[92] Cf. Council of Trent, Session 6, "Decree on Justification," Ch. 1; Can. 5

demerits, is a truth of the faith, as defined in the condemnation of the third proposition of Jansenius. Before Jansenius, Baius had blasphemously maintained that "man sins and merits punishment, even in those things which he does of necessity."

The Theological Virtues

Explanation of the Theological Virtues in General

320. **How many theological virtues are there?**
There are three: faith, hope, and charity.

321. **Why are they called theological?**
Because God is the object of these virtues. By faith, we believe God, and we believe in God. By hope, we hope for God, that is, for the possession of him in paradise; and we hope in God, that is, in his aid. By charity, we love God, and we also love our neighbor for God, that is, for the love of God.

322. **Are these virtues supernatural?**
They are supernatural; and this means that by our natural strength we could not acquire them, but God infuses them into our souls when we receive holy baptism.

323. **Do you mean to say then that children just baptized possess these virtues; and are we also to affirm that, before the use of reason, such children believe, hope, and love?**
It is certain that children, who are just baptized, do possess these virtues; that is to say, they have the habits of them, but they do not exercise them by actually believing, hoping, and loving, because they are hindered from doing so by not having the use of reason. We say they have the habits of them, meaning thereby a prompt disposition actually to believe, to hope,

and to love when they attain the use of reason. I will explain this by a comparison. A child, to whom his father at his death has left great wealth, is, in point of fact, rich whilst he is under the care of guardians, but he cannot dispose of his riches, he cannot spend them till the appointed time. So, before the use of reason, children have the habits of the theological virtues, but cannot then exercise them.

324. **By making acts of faith, hope, and charity, do these virtues grow in us?**
By exercising the acts of any virtue whatsoever, virtues grow in us and attain greater perfection; and so, the oftener we make acts of faith, the more lively will our faith become; the more frequently we make acts of hope, the firmer will our hope be; and the more we multiply acts of charity, the more ardent will be our love.

325. **Can these virtues be lost?**
Faith is lost by the sin of infidelity, which is committed when anyone does not will to believe, or advertently doubts some truth taught by holy Church; for instance, he who would not believe, or should doubt, that there are seven sacraments, would lose it. Hope is lost when one despairs of the divine mercy, that is, if he should think that God will no more pardon his sins. Charity is lost by any mortal sin whatever; therefore, if we lose faith or hope, we also always lose charity.

326. **If these virtues are lost, can they be regained?**
They can be regained by due repentance of the sin which caused their loss.

327. **Have the saints in heaven the theological virtues?**
The saints have charity only; for, as is clear, all that they believed they now see in God, and what is an object of sight is no longer an object of faith. What they formerly hoped for they now possess, since they enjoy God; and what is actually obtained is no longer an object of hope. Faith and hope, therefore, must accompany us to paradise, but they will not enter with us.

328. **Is there an obligation to make acts of faith, hope, and charity?**
There is an express obligation to do so, as might be proved by numberless testimonies of holy scripture and of the holy fathers. The contrary error was condemned by Alexander VII. Therefore, make these acts frequently, and more particularly make frequent acts of charity.

The Virtue of Faith

329. **What is the virtue of faith?**
It is a theological virtue infused by God into our souls, by which we firmly believe, from the motive of the divine veracity, all those things which God has revealed, and which the Church proposes to be believed.

330. **Why do you say "from the motive of the divine veracity"?**
Because we firmly believe all those things which holy Church proposes to us to believe, on the ground that God who has revealed them is infallible truth, and can neither deceive nor be deceived. The certainty of our faith rests, therefore, on the divine veracity.

331. **Why do you say all those things which God has revealed?**
Because he who should fail to believe even one would be an infidel; and as much wrong is done to infinite truth by doubting its veracity on one point as on many.

332. **Why do you say that the Church proposes them to us to believe?**
Because God revealed truths immediately to the inspired writers, such as Moses, David, etc. In like manner, truths were revealed by Christ to his apostles; but now we cannot expect particular revelations as the protestants do, who pretend that the Holy Spirit manifests directly to the understanding of each individual the truths which he is to believe. On the contrary, there is the Catholic Church who is the supreme mistress of the truth, and teaches infallibly to her children all those truths which they are to believe. She speaks by means of general councils, and by means of the definitions of the sovereign pontiffs. For example, she taught, by means of

the holy Council of Trent, in opposition to the errors of the protestants, that there are seven sacraments.[93] She taught, by means of definitions of the supreme pontiffs, in opposition to the errors of the Jansenists, that Christ did not die only for the elect. And he who should say that there are not seven sacraments would be as much a heretic as he who should say that Christ died on the cross only for the predestinate.[94]

333. **When can we give the name of heretic to anyone?**
When he pertinaciously asserts an error which is contrary to some truth of the faith. I say pertinaciously, because if anyone asserts an error out of ignorance, even culpable ignorance, he is not to be called a heretic. For example, a man neglecting to instruct himself may not know that the Church has defined that there are seven sacraments; if he says that there are only three, he says what is heresy, but he is not a heretic, because he utters this heresy from ignorance.

334. **In what respect does heresy differ from infidelity?**
In this: that infidelity is the privation or lack of faith in one who has never embraced it; and in this way idolaters, Turks, and Jews are infidels; heresy, on the contrary, is lack of faith in one who has once embraced it as a baptized person, or at least as a catechumen. Further, heresy is a partial want of faith, that is to say, when one or more dogmas, and not all, are disbelieved; because if anyone should deny all the dogmas of the faith, and so absolutely renounce the Christian religion, his sin would be apostacy. A Christian, therefore, who should renounce his belief in Christ and in his Church, to become a Turk, would not be called a heretic, but an apostate. This is meant, speaking with the precision of the schools, because the name of infidels can be given even to heretics, inasmuch as, sinning against the faith, they lose the virtue of faith. The sin, therefore, of not believing, or of doubting any article of the faith, is called the sin of infidelity.

[93] Cf. Council of Trent, Session 7, "On the Sacraments in General," Can. 1
[94] See the section, "The Church," on p. 17-26, above.

335. **How many kinds of infidelity are there, properly so called?**
There are two kinds, negative infidelity and positive infidelity. Negative infidelity is found in those who do not believe, because they have never heard, and never could have heard, the truths of the faith announced to them; and this is not sin. Positive infidelity is found in those who have heard the truths of the faith preached to them and will not believe, or who might have heard them preached and would not give ear to them; and this is sin.

336. **Will infidels who have never heard the truths of faith announced to them, and who have never had the opportunity of hearing them, be saved?**
Without faith it is impossible that anyone should be saved, for St. Paul says that "without faith it is impossible to please God."[95] Nevertheless, if those infidels should observe the natural law, the Lord would supply their necessity either by ordinary or by extraordinary means, even sending an angel to instruct them, were it necessary, as St. Thomas says, and as we have already shown. If those infidels sin against the natural law, they are damned for such sins, and not for the sin of infidelity, which in them is not voluntary.

337. **How many kinds of acts of faith are there?**
There are two kinds, internal and external.

338. **How do you define an internal act of faith?**
It is the firm consent of our mind to believe revealed truths.

339. **How is an internal act of faith subdivided?**
Into implicit and explicit. It is an implicit act of faith when, without regard had to one dogma more than to another, we believe generally all that the holy Catholic Church teaches. It is explicit when we believe expressly one or more determinate articles of the faith. For example, if I say, "I firmly believe all the truths which the Church teaches"; or, if

[95] Heb 11:6

not knowing what the holy Council of Trent has defined concerning the doctrine of justification, I say: "In regard to justification, I believe all that the Church teaches," it is an implicit act of faith. But if, on the other hand, I say, "I believe that there are seven sacraments"; or, "I believe that, without the grace of God, I can do nothing that shall avail for eternal life," it is an explicit act of faith.

340. **Is implicit faith sufficient for salvation, that is to say, does it suffice to believe all that the Church teaches, without knowing what she teaches?** This faith does not suffice, because it is necessary to believe explicitly the principal truths of our holy religion, that is, we must know them. The principal truths are: that God is just, and therefore that he rewards the good and punishes the wicked; that God is one in three Persons, that is to say, the mystery of the Blessed Trinity; that the second Person of the Blessed Trinity, that is, the Son, was made man, and as man suffered and died for our salvation. Whoever does not believe these truths expressly is not capable of receiving the holy sacraments, and cannot be saved. Moreover, we must believe expressly all the other truths which are in the Apostles' Creed; though anyone who should not know them without fault on his part, that is to say, because he was not able to learn them, might be saved. The first must be known by necessity of means; the second by necessity of precept.

In regard to many other truths which holy Church has defined, it is not necessary that all Christians should know them, but each one must instruct himself according to his own state and capacity. We must resort to instructions, and if we cannot attain to a distinct knowledge of some articles of the faith, it will suffice that we believe them implicitly, intending to believe all that holy Church teaches. Observe also, by the way, that besides the Creed, it is necessary to know the *Pater Noster*, the *Ave Maria*, the commandments of the law of God and of the Church, all that is necessary for the worthy reception of those sacraments, to which we must approach, and the duties of our own state.

341. **During the time of the law of nature, that is, before God gave the written law to Moses, and during the time of this written law, until the coming of our Savior, what faith was necessary for men in order that they might obtain eternal life?**

Besides believing that God punishes the wicked and rewards the good, it was necessary for them to have an implicit faith in the Savior of the world; that is to say, to have some knowledge of the promised Savior. And so, all the just of the old testament were saved, not only through the merits of Jesus Christ, but through faith in the same Christ.

342. **When are we obliged to make internal acts of faith?**

I have already shown that we ought to make them frequently, and in particular at the commencement of the use of reason, and at the hour of death. Some have said that it suffices to make one single act of faith during our whole life, but this mistake was condemned by the holy pontiff Innocent XI.

343. **I should like to know whether an internal act of faith can consist with doubt of the truth of the things believed?**

In defining faith, we have said that it is a virtue by which we believe firmly, therefore it cannot consist with doubt of the truth of the things believed. Faith excludes all doubt, and includes certainty that the thing cannot be otherwise.

344. **What can we say then of certain Catholics, who, listening to errors against the faith, as for example, against the eternity of the pains of hell, against purgatory, against the virginity of the Blessed Virgin Mary, against the supremacy of the pope, profess themselves Catholics, but still think that the protestants who teach these errors may probably, or at least possibly, be right?**

If they admit doubt, that is to say, if they admit the probability, or even the possibility, that the Church may err in teaching the contrary truths, they have lost the faith, and if they profess still to be Catholics, they profess to be what they are not. He who does not believe firmly, absolutely, does not believe with that divine faith which is necessary for salvation.

345. **A Catholic Christian, however, may examine if the things which the Church teaches him are really true?**

If a Catholic Christian examines the truths which the Church teaches him, in order to know if they are really true, and therefore doubts whether they may not be false, he shows by so doing that he has already lost the faith, which is destroyed in every case whatsoever, by every doubt, if such doubt be adverted and consented to.

346. **But then we must believe without reason, or even against reason, however unanswerable may be the arguments against those things which the Church teaches.**

There is no doubt that we must believe under any circumstances; because if divine faith, from any motive, ceases to be firm and unshaken, by that very fact it is destroyed. Besides, divine faith can never be without, or against, reason, for it rests on the infallible authority of God revealing; and if the things which holy Church teaches appear to us to be without reason, or contrary to reason, this proceeds from our ignorance and limited understanding, which cannot arrive at comprehension of the truth of the divine mysteries; just as many physical and mathematical truths which are evident to philosophers appear to an ignorant man to be without reason, or contrary to reason. We must be firmly persuaded that whatever argument we may find against truths revealed by God, however strange and unanswerable it may seem to be, can only be a false reason and a sophism.

347. **And yet we exhort protestants and other unbelievers to examine the truths which the faith teaches, in order that they may be convinced in regard to them. Now if they may examine them, why may not we also examine them?**

Observe the difference there is between them and us Catholics. They have not as yet divine faith, and therefore cannot lose it by doubt, and it is needful that by study they should convince themselves of the truth, and dispose themselves to obtain this gift from God; we, on the contrary, have this gift already, hence, whilst we cannot acquire it, we might lose it by admitting doubt. Nevertheless, we may examine the truths of the faith, in order the better to know their reasonableness, and to put ourselves in a position to convince others. We must make this examination, however, with firm belief, without admitting even the shadow of a doubt.

348. **Why do you say that protestants have not divine faith? They believe many revealed truths as well as we do, therefore, in regard to those truths, have they not the faith that we have?**
Divine faith is a supernatural gift, which only those who are members of holy Church can possess; therefore protestants, who are outside the Church, are deprived of this gift, and if they believe some truths of the faith, they believe them with human faith, that is to say, from the conviction produced in their minds, by the reasons which militate in favor of these truths. For example, we believe that Christ is the Savior, and that Plato was a philosopher; we believe the first of those truths by a virtue, or supernatural force, which operates on our minds, and inclines us to believe it; we believe the second by force of the arguments with which history presents us; and so we believe the first with divine faith, the second with human faith. Protestants who believe both these truths with us, believe both by the power exercised on their minds by the reasons which militate in favor of both the one and the other, without that supernatural aid which inclines us Catholics to believe the first; therefore, when they believe that Christ is the Savior, they believe it not with divine faith, but with mere human faith.

349. **When do we make an external act of faith?**
When we manifest our internal faith in a visible or sensible manner. If I say that I am a Christian, if I prostrate myself before the Blessed Sacrament, etc., these are external acts of faith.

350. **Is it necessary to make external acts of faith?**
It is most necessary, and St. Paul says so expressly;[96] therefore, it is not enough to have faith only in our heads, we must manifest it in our words and actions.

351. **But when, by manifesting our faith, we might be threatened with some grave injury, might we not feign that we are not Christians, or might we not outwardly renounce our faith, retaining it in our hearts?**
This would be a very great sin. Like the holy martyrs, we should be ready to suffer any kind of death rather than renounce our holy faith, or feign not to be Christians.

352. **But will not God, who sees the heart, be content with the homage of the heart, particularly if we could not manifest our faith without serious injury?**
God, who is sovereign Lord of the whole man, which consists of soul and body, requires, by every right, the homage of the whole man, that is, both internal and spiritual homage, and external and material homage. To disguise and hide our faith, in order to make men believe that we are without it, or to make pretense of renouncing our faith, is abominable cowardice and ingratitude toward God, whose gift it is. He made himself man, and sacrificed his infinitely precious life for us; is it not just then that we should show ourselves ready to sacrifice our lives, which are of so little value, for his honor? Moreover, if he permits our faith to be tempted, he gives us powerful aid to resist every trial. Therefore, however serious may be the consequences, we must, when needful, after the example of the holy martyrs, manifest our faith to the world.

353. **In theology, are those things only certain which the Church has already defined and declared to be of faith?**
It would be a grave error to say that those things only are certain which the Church has already defined and declared to be of faith, which is easily proved if you only consider the definition of the dogma of the immaculate

[96] Cf. Rom 10

conception of the Blessed Virgin Mary. In point of fact, this truth was not a defined dogma and declared to be of faith before the 8th of December of the year 1854; nevertheless, it was a most certain truth, a truth such that the Church had threatened with excommunication not only whoever should deny it in express terms, but also anyone who should dare to allege any objections against it, without at the same time confuting them by sufficient arguments.

It does not follow that, because a truth has not been defined and declared to be of faith, it may be denied with impunity, or at least looked upon as doubtful, but only that he who does not believe it, or doubts it, is not guilty of the sin of heresy, though he may be guilty of the most grievous rashness. Before the Council of Trent, certain truths were not defined and declared to be of faith, which in that Council were defined and declared to be so, against the novelties of the protestants; and yet those truths were commonly believed and recognized as certain by holy Church, and it would have been grave temerity to deny or cast doubt upon them, as Luther and Calvin did.

If it were necessary that a truth should be defined and declared to be of faith in order to be certain, it would not be certain that Christ walked upon earth with his feet, such fact having never been defined and declared to be of faith.

Hence, we clearly perceive that it would be a perverse and unreasonable mode of reasoning for a theologian to argue thus: it is not defined and declared to be of faith that in hell there is material fire, that the diaconate is a sacrament, that the contracting parties are the ministers of the sacrament of matrimony, that the pope is infallible when he speaks *ex cathedra* and is superior to a general council;[97] therefore all these things may be denied or regarded as doubtful. A theologian who should reason in this manner would err grievously, for although these truths have not been defined and declared as of faith, they are commonly believed and recognized as certain by the Church.

[97] Translator's note: This cannot now, since the date of the Vatican Council, be adduced as an example. See footnote on p. 22.

The Virtue of Hope

354. **What is the virtue of hope?**

It is a theological virtue by which, with certain confidence, we expect eternal happiness and the means to attain thereto, through the divine aid, and according to the promise which God has made us in regard of the merits of Jesus Christ.

355. **Why do you say "with certain confidence"?**

Because our hope rests on the infinite merits of Jesus Christ, and on his promise that he will give us paradise in reward for our good works, and that he will give us the necessary means to attain it, therefore our hope is certain and secure. Hence St. Paul calls it, "an anchor of the soul, sure and firm."[98]

356. **You mean to say then that we cannot fear being lost?**

Observe that I say "certain confidence," and not "sure certainty"; because confidence of attaining any good always presupposes the peril of losing it. Now on God's part our hope is most certain, because nothing that is necessary for our salvation can be wanting to us on his part; but on our part the necessary correspondence to his grace may be wanting, and therefore we cannot say that we are certain that we shall infallibly be saved. Looking therefore at the certainty of the divine promise on the one side, and at our weakness on the other, our hope cannot be an absolute certainty, but only a certain confidence.

357. **Ought we, in short, to feel most confidence in regard to the certainty there is on God's part, or most fear in regard to the danger arising from our own weakness?**

We ought to feel most confidence in regard to the certainty there is on God's part, because the goodness of God is infinitely greater than our wickedness; therefore, our confidence in God ought to be greater than our fear of ourselves.

[98] Heb 6:19

358. **Can, then, the fear of hell subsist with the hope of paradise?**
You must distinguish between different kinds of fear. There is the fear called filial fear, whereby we fear hell, as we fear an offense against God, which alone can confine souls in hell, and we fear it as an injury done to infinite goodness; such fear is not fear of our own injury, as it is our own injury, but fear of injury to the object beloved, that is, to God. Again, there is the fear called servile fear, whereby we fear hell as an injury to ourselves, but without affection to sin, by which we merit hell. Again, there is the fear called servilely servile fear, with which we fear hell on account of the injury to ourselves, but with affection to sin, so that it is not sin, but hell which displeases us, and we would wish, in a way, that there were no hell, in order to be able to sin without fear. The first, as is clearly evident, is a most holy fear; the second also is good, as the holy Council of Trent defined against the heretics;[99] so that both the first and second kinds of fear can well subsist with Christian hope. The third kind is the fear of the wicked, and most unworthy of Christians.

359. **Is it not an interested and defective service to serve God with the hope of reward?**
Some false mystics of these later times have thought so, but their errors have been condemned by the sovereign pontiffs. The Holy Spirit, as we learn from the scriptures, would have us hope for paradise, and this hope has animated the greatest saints to do great things for God; hence, when we serve our Lord, hoping that he will recompense our service with an eternal reward, we do not commit any defect, but exercise the most necessary virtue of hope. Observe that the Council of Trent excommunicated anyone who should say that the just sin when they perform good works in order to gain an eternal reward.[100]

360. **Can we say, then, that sinners commit sin when they perform works in order to gain this reward?**
If sinners should perform good works in order to gain paradise, but with the intention of not being converted to God, they would most certainly

[99] Cf. Council of Trent, Session 6, Can. 8; Session 14, "Doctrine on the Sacrament of Penance," Ch. 4

[100] Cf. Council of Trent, Session 6, "Decree on Justification," Ch. 11; Can. 31

commit sin; because it is the worst kind of presumption to expect salvation without having the will to forsake sin; but, if sinners perform good works in order to attain God's mercy, to reconcile themselves to him, and hence to attain salvation, they do that which is good and holy; in fact, this is what God commands, and what he would have them do.

361. **Ought we to hope for paradise only for our own good?**
We ought to refer all our good to God, and therefore we ought to hope for and to seek the blessedness of heaven, in order that it may redound to the eternal glory of God. In one word, we ought to endeavor to become saints in order that God may be glorified by our sanctity. This is taken from the holy Council of Trent.[101]

362. **You said a little while ago that our hope rests on the infinite merits of Jesus Christ: What do you mean by that?**
Jesus Christ is our Savior: he offered the infinite merits of his incarnation, passion, and death for us; and by the value of his merits, we have been made capable of meriting heaven.

363. **You added that our hope rests on the promise of God to give us heaven in reward of our good works: What do you mean by that?**
We have seen above, in the section, "The Merit of Good Works," that we could not merit heaven without that promise; therefore, all our hope rests on it. This divine promise is the motive through which we hope for heaven.

364. **When we exercise acts of hope, must we have the intention of performing good works?**
Without such intention, our hope would become presumption, because heaven is promised to the merit of good works; and we can only have a

[101] Cf. Council of Trent, Session 6, "Decree of Justification," Ch. 7. The council declares those to be heretics who hold that in all their works the just sin, if in them they excite their indolences and are moved to running the race by this: that in the first place God be glorified, but also in view of an eternal reward (cf. Council of Trent, Session 6, "Decree on Justification," Ch. 11; Can. 25, 31).

solid foundation for our hope of salvation, when we have the intention to do the good that is required of us in order to attain thereto.

The Virtue of Charity

365. **What is the virtue of charity?**
It is a theological virtue, infused by God into our souls, by which we love God above all things, because he is the infinite good, and love our neighbor for the love of God.

366. **What do you mean by saying that we love God because he is the infinite good?**
God ought to be loved for his infinite goodness. Everything is loved in proportion to the goodness contained in it; therefore, we love a thing because it is good, and, the better it is, the more we love it. Hence, we love God because he is good, and we love him above all things, because there is no goodness which can be put in comparison with his.

367. **In how many ways can we love God above all things?**
In two ways, appreciatively and intensely. God is loved above all things appreciatively when the will is so united to God that it is ready to suffer anything whatever, rather than offend him by any mortal sin; he is loved intensely above all things when to the firmness and attachment of the will is united a lively transport and ardent affection, so that nothing makes so great impression on the feelings of our heart as the pleasure or displeasure of Almighty God.

368. **In which of these two ways are we obliged to love God?**
In the first, that is to say, appreciatively; and he who should be without this love could not be saved.

369. **Does this appreciative love oblige us only to abstain from mortal sin?**
Appreciative love obliges us to prefer Almighty God and his good pleasure before all things, and therefore, to abstain even from venial sin; nevertheless, since venial sin does not extinguish charity in us, appreciative love

would suffice for our salvation, although it might not attain to making us avoid venial sin.

370. **For what reason are we not obliged to love God intensely above all things?**
Because this intense love is not in our own power; it is an extraordinary gift of God, most precious and greatly to be desired. The purest souls possess it, generally speaking, even in this life; still, even they have not the fullness of the intensity of the divine love, this fullness of love being reserved for the saints in heaven.

371. **How can it be that a soul should prefer God and his good pleasure before all things, whilst some other object may make greater impression on the feelings of the heart?**
The act of giving preference to one thing before all others is an act of the will, which is free; feeling the impression of one thing more than another belongs to the sensitive faculty, which in us is not free, but of necessity. For example, I may determine to give preference to bitter food instead of sweet, but I cannot prevent myself feeling the bitterness when I eat it. From the same sensitive faculty, it arises that even pious mothers feel more lively joy in seeing their children restored to health after a dangerous illness, than in seeing them penitent after the commission of some sin; and yet their will would prefer rather to see them sick than sinners.

372. **When a man prefers God before all things because he is an infinite good, and would lose anything whatever rather than offend him grievously, has he the perfect love of God?**
It is certain that such a one then possesses the perfect love of God; perfect in its nature, though capable of becoming more and more perfect, as is clearly seen in the case of a man who would be ready to lose anything whatever rather than offend God by even a venial sin.

373. **Can love, or perfect charity, subsist in a soul together with mortal sin?**
Baius taught that perfect charity might be found in a soul together with mortal sin, but the Church has condemned this doctrine. Hence it is

certain that the perfect love of God cannot be found in any soul together with mortal sin, any more than light can be in a room at the same time with darkness.

374. **But suppose the case that a person guilty of some mortal sin should make an act of perfect love of God, should we not then find in the same soul mortal sin and the perfect love of God?**
This could never happen, because that act of perfect love of God would immediately expel mortal sin from the soul, just as a lighted taper when carried into a dark room at once expels the darkness.

375. **But is not sacramental confession required in order to take away sin from the soul?**
Sacramental confession is requisite, either in effect or in intention. It is requisite in effect, when there is only attrition; and in that case it is necessary for a Christian to confess and receive sacramental absolution in order to expel sin from his soul. But when there is perfect charity, then the intention to confess at the usual time suffices. He who has charity or the perfect love of God has contrition implicitly, that is to say, sorrow for having offended God, it being impossible that anyone should love God above all things and not abhor sin above all things; he has also the intention of confessing at the usual time, because it is equally impossible that anyone should love God above all things and not have the intention of obeying his commands; therefore, if a sinner makes an act of perfect love of God, he is immediately justified. Nevertheless, he is obliged to confess his mortal sins at the proper time, that is to say, when he has to fulfill the precept of confession, or, even when he does confess apart from precept, as is clearly to be understood.

376. **Might we not say that the perfect love of God justifies the soul only in case of necessity, as, for instance, when at the point of death, it is not possible to have a confessor?**
He who should say this would in effect say that perfect charity may subsist in the soul together with mortal sin, and would assert a proposition

precisely condemned in Baius.[102] If charity is perfect, that is to say, if God is loved above all things because he is an infinite good, mortal sin is immediately taken away from the soul.

377. **Suppose a man to have been justified by some act of perfect love of God, including the intention of confession at a convenient time; if such a one should change his intention, and resolve never to go to confession again, would the mortal sins, which were canceled by his act of the love of God, return once more to stain his soul?**

It is a most certain truth that sins which have been once canceled cannot again return to stain the soul: other similar sins may be committed, but the same sins cannot return again. Take the following comparison: you drop a pocket-handkerchief in the mud, so that it is dirty and stained; you rinse it out in a stream, and the stains and dirt are washed out by the water; that dirt, those particular stains are removed, they are gone with the stream, and it is impossible that the handkerchief can be stained by them anymore, although it might be stained anew, should you again let it fall in the mud. Observe, however, that a person who should have the evil intention of going no more to confession would commit a fresh mortal sin, and would immediately lose the love of God and his grace.

378. **If the perfect love of God has so great an efficacy as to restore the soul to a state of grace, even beyond the case of necessity, a person in mortal sin need not think it of great consequence to confess his sin at once, but may rest satisfied with making acts of the love of God and acts of contrition.**

Beware of drawing such a conclusion, for it is false. Not all who make acts of the love of God and acts of contrition make them with that perfection which is requisite in order that they may take away sin from the soul; and therefore, many persons might believe themselves to be justified, whilst they were really in mortal sin. Moreover, although the acts of the love of God and the acts of contrition might be perfect, they would not confer

[102] This is the proposition of Baius: "By contrition, even with perfect charity, and with a desire of receiving the sacrament, sin is not remitted, save in case of necessity, or of martyrdom, without actual reception of the sacrament."

sacramental grace, which is given solely in the sacrament of penance when the penitent receives absolution. Hence, the soul would remain without the great help of this grace, of which we shall speak in answer to Question 400, below. Therefore, when one falls into mortal sin, let him immediately make acts of contrition, in order that by making one perfectly, he may speedily recover the grace of God; but then, without waiting for the obligation of annual confession, or even for his own convenience, let him go as soon as he can to confession, in order to provide for his soul in the best way possible in a matter of so great importance.

The doctrine of the efficacy and value of contrition must be taught, because it is the doctrine of the Church, and because everyone ought to know the value of the virtue of charity and of acts of charity; but no one must take occasion from this doctrine to defer going to confession after having committed mortal sin. However great may be the contrition which he feels in his heart, let the sinner go to confession as soon as he can, even if it be to his own inconvenience.

379. **How ought we to love our neighbor?**
We ought to love him as we love ourselves, and for the love of God. Thus, the love of our neighbor is founded in the love of God, inasmuch as we love our neighbor in regard of God, and for the love we bear to God.

380. **If a man love his neighbor because he is of a good disposition, because he is learned, rich, his benefactor, his friend, or his relation, does he love him with the love of charity?**
If he love him for these titles and reasons only, he loves him with a natural love, which is found even in infidels, and therefore does not love him with supernatural love, such as the love of charity is; besides all these motives, then, he must love him also for the love of God, and because God wills that he should love him.

381. **Must we love all our neighbors, absolutely and without distinction?**
We must love all our neighbors absolutely, whether friends or enemies, good or bad, faithful or unfaithful to us; nevertheless, there may be

distinctions in our love, seeing we ought to prefer our friends and relations, our benefactors, those who are faithful, etc., to those who are not so. Thus, for example, if we had to clothe two poor persons, one of whom was a relation, and the other not, and we had but one coat to give away, we ought to give it to our relation.

382. **In order to love our neighbor, does it not suffice to do him good, without, however, loving him in our heart?**
It does not suffice; and Pope Innocent XI condemned two propositions which said that we are not bound to love our neighbor with internal and formal acts, but that we can satisfy the precept by mere external acts. Therefore, it is necessary to love our neighbor with affection of the heart, and hence to do to him what we would reasonably wish done to us, and not to do to him what we would not reasonably have done to us.

383. **Are we obliged to make acts of charity equally with acts of faith and hope?**
We are; and theologians agree that we are even obliged to make them more frequently.

384. **Does the precept of charity oblige us to refer all our actions to the service and glory of God?**
Certainly; it obliges us to refer to the glory of God and to his service all our actions, even such indifferent actions as eating, sleeping, suitable amusements, recreations, etc.

385. **Is it necessary in every action that we perform to say expressly: "I intend to do this for the glory of God"?**
This is not necessary; it suffices that, from time to time, we renew our intention of doing all our actions for the glory of God.

The Sacraments

The Sacraments in General

386. **How do you define the word *sacrament*?**
A sacrament is a sacred sign, visible and permanent, instituted by Christ, which effects, *ex opere operato*, our sanctification. This definition belongs to all the sacraments of the new law, that is to say, to all the sacraments of the Church.

387. **Are there then other sacraments besides those of the new law?**
Before Christ instituted the sacraments which are administered in the Church, that is to say, before his coming, there were sacraments, but they were very inferior to ours, and such as it is not necessary to speak of in this compendium. It is sufficient to observe that he who should say that the sacraments of the old law were of equal value with the sacraments of the new law, that is to say, with the sacraments of holy Church, would be a heretic.[103]

388. **For what reason is the word *sacrament* defined as a sign?**
Because it makes known to us the thing which it signifies. Thus, in baptism, the washing makes known to us the purity which the soul acquires in receiving this sacrament.

389. **Why is it called a sacred sign?**
Because the use of such a sign is a religious act pertaining to the worship of God.

[103] Cf. Council of Trent, Session 7, "On the Sacraments in General," Can. 2

390. **Why is it called visible?**

It is called visible, because it is necessary that it fall under the cognizance of the senses, that is to say, that in some way it should be material; therefore, here the term *visible* is used in the signification of "sensible." Anything purely spiritual could not be a sacrament.

391. **Why is it called permanent?**

Because the sacraments are the foundations of religion, and, like religion, must endure perpetually; hence, the sacraments are rites which will continue even to the end of the world.

392. **Why is a sacrament said to be instituted by Jesus Christ?**

Because he is the author of all the sacraments which are administered in the Church, as is defined by the holy Council of Trent.[104]

393. **Why is it said, to effect our sanctification, *ex opere operato*?**

Because the sacraments have the intrinsic virtue of conferring grace on the soul, so that it is not the good dispositions which confer grace when we receive the sacraments, but the sacraments themselves which confer it. That they confer it *ex opere operato* is an article of the faith, defined by the holy Council of Trent.[105]

394. **It is of no importance then to approach the sacraments with good dispositions?**

It is of the utmost importance, and moreover, necessary, in order that the sacraments may produce their effect, in the same way that it is of importance and necessary that wood should be dry, in order that it may burn quickly. If you take dry wood and put it on the fire, it soon burns; if you take wood full of spring sap, you will find it impossible to kindle it into a flame. The property of burning, however, is neither in the dry nor in the green wood, the property of burning is in the fire. In like manner when

[104] Cf. Council of Trent, Session 7, "On the Sacraments in General," Can. 1
[105] Cf. Council of Trent, Session 7, "On the Sacraments in General," Can. 8

the sacraments are given to one who is well-disposed for their reception, he acquires either grace or an augmentation of grace, because there exists no impediment to hinder their effect; if, on the contrary, they are given to one who is not well-disposed for their reception, he does not acquire grace, because there exists the impediment of his bad dispositions, which impediment does not suffer them to produce their effect, just as the quantity of moisture does not suffer the fire to burn the green wood. Therefore, I repeat, that as the property of burning is in the fire, and not in the dispositions of the wood, so the property of conferring grace is in the sacraments, and not in the dispositions of him who receives them.

395. **Will not the effect of the sacrament be greater or less, according to the greater or less disposition of him who receives it?**
Certainly it is so; just as we see that the effect of fire is greater or less, according as the wood which is set on fire is more or less dry.

396. **Why do you say that the sacraments either confer or increase grace?**
Because some of the sacraments are instituted in order to confer sanctifying grace on those who lack it; and others to increase grace in those who already possess it. Baptism and penance confer grace on those who do not possess it; all the other sacraments, on the contrary, increase grace in those who have already received it and preserved it. The first two are called sacraments of the dead, and all the others, sacraments of the living; because the first two are given to those who are dead to the grace of God, and the others to those who are alive by the same grace.

397. **May there not be cases in which the sacraments of the dead increase grace in those who already possess it, and in which the sacraments of the living confer grace on those who are deprived of it?**
Such cases may certainly occur. Suppose that a catechumen, by a perfect act of contrition, puts himself into a state of grace before he receives baptism; when he afterward receives baptism, the sacrament cannot confer grace on him, but can only increase it. The same may be said of the sacrament of penance: when the penitent, by his perfect contrition, is already in

a state of grace before he receives absolution; or, if he have only venial sins to confess. In such cases, the sacraments of the dead increase sanctifying grace in those who already possess it. All this is certain; and there is no room for doubt in regard to it. On the other hand, the sacraments of the living sometimes confer sanctifying grace on those who are deprived of it, as theologians, with St. Thomas,[106] commonly teach. Suppose a person with simple attrition makes his confession to a priest who has not the necessary jurisdiction, or to a layman who pretends to be a priest. Such a person, in spite of his confession, remains in a state of mortal sin; but if, afterward, believing himself to be validly absolved, he approaches to the holy table, then Holy Communion puts him in a state of grace—the most Holy Eucharist, which is a sacrament of the living, conferring on him that grace which, as yet, he does not possess. What I say of the most Holy Eucharist holds good in regard to all the other sacraments of the living, whenever, without fault on his own part, they are received by a person in a state of mortal sin, but who has repented of his mortal sin with the sorrow of attrition. The reason is that attrition removes from the soul the evil will which would be an impediment to the acquisition of grace.

398. **If this be so, we can always approach the sacraments of the living with simple attrition, without the necessity of confession. By attrition we shall remove the impediment of an evil will, and thus the sacraments of the living will confer on us sanctifying grace.**

By no means; the sacraments of the living were not instituted by Jesus Christ in order that of their institution they should confer sanctifying grace on those who are deprived of it; but in order that they should give augmentation of grace to those who already possess it; and therefore, there is an express divine command that men are not to approach those sacraments, except in a state of grace. So that he who knows himself to be still in mortal sin, and yet chooses to approach them, transgresses this divine command, and, by so doing, commits a fresh mortal sin: hence, in him the attrition would be false, because it would be united to the will to transgress a divine

[106] Cf. *Summa Theologiae*, III, q. 79, a. 3, c.; q. 80, a. 4, rep. 5

command, and could not remove the impediment to obtaining sanctifying grace. Only, *per accidens*, as theologians say, that is to say, when a man is in good faith, and has done all that he knows he ought to do in order to place himself in the grace of God, when he believes himself to be justified and rightly disposed, so that if he were conscious of having still the stain of sin upon his soul, he would abstain from receiving this or that sacrament of the living—in this case only, and having, moreover, attrition for his mortal sins, by receiving one of these sacraments, he obtains sanctifying grace.

399. **You mean to say, then, that in order worthily to receive the sacraments of the living, we must first either confess our sins with attrition, or excite ourselves to perfect contrition; and that one or other of these, it matters not which, will suffice, since both one and the other places us in a state of grace?**

If you mean that one or other of these indifferently suffices for all the sacraments of the living, you greatly err; for in order to receive the most Holy Eucharist, it is not sufficient that those who are in mortal sin should make an act of contrition; they are under obligation, except in case of indispensable necessity, of going to confession; the sacred Council of Trent[107] having thus understood the precept of St. Paul: *Probet autem seipsum homo*; "Let a man prove himself."[108] In like manner, those who are in mortal sin and find themselves at the point of death should confess their sins, because presently they will be unable to satisfy the precept of confession; and so they could not receive extreme unction without confession, and with merely making an act of contrition. In regard, however, to confirmation, holy orders, and matrimony, there is no express command that confession should precede them; it would suffice therefore, that those who are about to receive any one of these sacraments should repent of their sins with true contrition, having, however, the intention of confessing in due time. Observe, nevertheless, that this doctrine is not to be preached to simple people; it is well that they should be ignorant of it, lest they should abuse it to their own injury, and with a mere imperfect act of contrition on the tip

[107] Cf. Council of Trent, Session 13, "Decree Concerning the Most Holy Sacrament of the Eucharist," Ch. 7; Can. 11

[108] 1 Cor 11:28

of their tongue; approach the sacraments of confirmation and matrimony. You should know this doctrine, as a rule for yourselves, in order that you may not preach that there is equal necessity that confession should precede confirmation and matrimony, as Communion, which would be false; inasmuch as in regard to Communion, there is the precept of St. Paul, which is not found in regard to the three foresaid sacraments. Preach, however, nonetheless, that the means left us by Jesus Christ to cleanse the soul from mortal sin is sacramental confession; and that, therefore, everyone who finds himself guilty of grievous sin, must go to confession before approaching to receive any sacrament whatsoever.

400. **Do the sacraments confer other graces, besides sanctifying grace?**
They each confer a grace proper to the sacrament, to wit, a right founded on the sanctifying grace conferred by the sacrament, to receive at opportune times certain aids, or actual graces, in order that a man may obtain the end of the sacrament. Hence the sacramental grace of baptism entitles one to seasonable aids to lead a life worthy of a Christian; the sacramental grace of confirmation gives one special aids to confess the faith courageously; that of the Eucharist, to nourish, that is, to preserve and increase charity; that of penance, to avoid sin for the future; that of extreme unction, to make a good and tranquil passage to the other life; that of holy orders, to comport oneself worthily and with zeal in the sacred ministry; that of matrimony, that the wedded may lead a peaceable life, and train up their children in the holy fear of God.

401. **Who has given so great an efficacy to the sacraments?**
Jesus Christ, who is the author of them, and who has merited it for them by the merits of his incarnation, passion, and death.

402. **Do the sacraments produce any other effect, besides conferring sanctifying and sacramental grace?**
Three of the sacraments, namely, baptism, confirmation, and order, confer character, that is, a spiritual, indelible mark imprinted on the soul, by means of which those who shall have received all three, or any one of these

sacraments, will be distinguished to all eternity from those who have not received them. This character will be for a special glory to the blessed; and for a special confusion to the damned. Observe also that it is an article of the faith that those three sacraments can be received but once.

403. **Is it of faith that this character will be indelible to all eternity?**
It is certainly an article of the faith, defined by the Council of Trent, that this character can never be canceled during this life;[109] but it is not a matter expressly defined as of faith that it shall be indelible also for all eternity. Such is, however, the teaching of St. Thomas,[110] and the general sentiment of the faithful.

404. **Would one, who should receive these three sacraments with bad dispositions, remain forever deprived of the effects of those sacraments?**
When any one of these sacraments has been received validly, but bad dispositions have hindered the effect of the sacrament—for instance, if one have received baptism, with an affection to mortal sin, or confirmation, or order, in a state of mortal sin—theologians say that if the bad dispositions be removed by a good confession, or, at least, by an act of contrition including the desire of confession, as has been already shown,[111] then the effect of these sacraments, however badly received, revives, so that the sacramental aids of which the man was deprived when he received these sacraments will be obtained. They teach the same in regard to matrimony and extreme unction, because they suppose that the divine compassion will not suffer penitent sinners to be deprived of the special aids which the wedded need for the whole or nearly the whole of their lives, and which the dying need in order to make a good passage into eternity. The sacraments however of penance and the Eucharist, which may be received as often as we will, do not revive in their effects; and those who have received them badly must repair the loss by receiving them well another time. If,

[109] Cf. Council of Trent, Session 23, "The True and Catholic Doctrine, Touching the Sacrament of Order," Ch. 4; Can. 4

[110] Cf. *Summa Theologiae*, III, q. 63, a. 5, rep. 3

[111] See the section, "The Virtue of Charity," on p. 115-120, above.

however, a sacrament has been received, not only with bad dispositions, but invalidly, it is certain that it must be received anew; and this even in the case of baptism.

405. **What things are required to the validity of the sacraments?**
Matter, form, a proper minister, and intention.

406. **What is the matter in the sacraments?**
The matter is the thing used in conferring the sacrament; for example, in baptism, the matter is water.

407. **What is the form?**
The words which are uttered in conferring the sacrament; for instance, in baptism, the form is: "I baptize thee, in the name of the Father, and of the Son, and of the Holy Ghost."

408. **Can the Church change the matter or form of the sacraments?**
The Church, as the sacred Council of Trent teaches, has no authority to change the matter or form of the sacraments;[112] hence, if the matter or form were changed, the sacraments would be valueless.

409. **Still, in different places there is some difference in the form of the sacraments.**
There are accidental differences in words, which do not substantially change the meaning. If in any place a form were used which changed the sense of the form instituted by Christ, the sacrament would be without effect, and the Church would not permit it.

410. **Who is the minister of the sacraments?**
The sacraments have a primary minister and a secondary minister. The primary minister is Jesus Christ, who is the author of the sacraments; the

[112] Cf. Council of Trent, Session 21, "Decree on Communion under Both Species, and the Communion of Infants," Ch. 2

secondary minister is he who has received from Jesus Christ authority to confer them. Who are the different ministers of the different sacraments we shall see when we come to speak of each sacrament in particular. I merely remark here that the Council of Trent has defined, against heretics, that not all Christians are ministers of all the sacraments; to affirm the contrary, therefore, would be heresy.[113]

411. **Are faith and sanctifying grace requisite in the minister of the sacraments?**
In order that he may confer them worthily and with merit, it is undoubtedly requisite that he have faith, and that he be in a state of grace; but in respect of the validity of the sacrament, it is an article of the faith that neither the one nor the other is requisite; and so baptism, conferred by an impious heretic, has the same validity as if conferred by a pious Catholic.

412. **Is intention necessary in the minister?**
It is of faith that in conferring the sacraments, it is necessary to have the intention of doing what the Church does; without such intention the minister would confer the sacrament invalidly.

413. **Suppose heretics, who do not believe in the holy Catholic Church, or idolaters, Turks, etc., who attach no value to the sacraments, were to administer baptism, would they not administer it invalidly, because they could have no intention of doing what the Church does: for in regard to heretics, they do not believe in her, and in regard to idolaters, Turks, and Jews, they believe neither in her nor in her sacraments?**
It is not necessary for the validity of the sacrament that the minister intend to do a holy action, to confer a sacrament, nor that he believe in the virtue of the sacraments, nor that he have the intention of doing what the true Catholic and Roman Church does; it is sufficient that he have the intention of doing what the Church in general does. So a Lutheran, who supposes that the true Church exists in his sect, when he baptizes with the intention of doing what the Church does, baptizes validly. In like manner,

[113] Cf. Council of Trent, Session 7, "On the Sacraments in General," Can. 10

if a Turk, to annoy and spite another Turk, should seriously baptize a child, intending to give him the baptism of the Christians, that child would be validly baptized.

414. **Would baptism, absolution, or any other sacrament be valid if given in sport and jest?**
They would be invalid, as was declared by holy Church against Luther. Hence, if anyone should take an unbaptized child, pour water on his head, and utter the form, saying: "This is what the parish priest will do when he baptizes him," that child would not be baptized. Observe that such jesting in regard to the sacraments is mortal sin.

415. **What sort of intention is required in him who is the minister of the sacraments?**
The intention may be actual, as, for example, when he who baptizes says to himself, whilst he baptizes: "I intend to baptize." Or it may be virtual, as, for example, when one sets out with the intention of baptizing, and afterward in the act of baptizing, from some distraction, does not reflect on what he is doing. Or, finally, the intention may be habitual, as, for example, when one who is accustomed to baptize administers this sacrament at a time that from some disease he is deprived of the use of reason. The first is not necessary; the second suffices; but not so the third, because with it the minister of the sacrament does not perform a human act.

416. **What intention is required in those who receive the sacraments?**
It is most certain that no intention whatever is required to receive the sacrament of baptism in children before the use of reason, and in adults who have never had free use of reason. Moreover, it is an express article of the faith that baptism, conferred on children before the use of reason, is valid, as we gather from the sacred Council of Trent, and from the practice of the universal Church of baptizing children as soon as they are born.[114] But, on

[114] Cf. Council of Trent, Session 5, "Decree Concerning Original Sin," Can. 3, 4; Session 7, "On Baptism," Can. 13

the other hand, in adults who have perfect use of reason, or, at least, who have once had it, it is necessary either that they have actually the will to receive baptism, or that, having had that will, they have not retracted it. Such will is still more requisite in the sacraments of penance, matrimony, and perhaps even of order.[115] To receive the sacraments of confirmation, the Eucharist, and extreme unction, however, interpretative intention suffices, which consists in this: that he who wishes to be a Christian wishes also to enjoy all the privileges and graces of a Christian, and therefore also the graces of these sacraments.

417. **You think then that a sick person, deprived of his senses, would receive confirmation, the Eucharist, and extreme unction with profit, although he might not, while in his senses, have asked for these sacraments?**
If he were in the grace of God, he would receive them with profit, or, at all events, if, before the loss of his senses, he had had a sincere sorrow of attrition, as we pointed out in the answer to Question 397. It is evident from the practice of the Church, which in early times gave the Eucharist to infants, that these sacraments may be received with profit, without that positive intention which the other sacraments require. It is even now permitted to give confirmation to infants, in cases where there is good reason to fear that they will not be able to receive it when they shall have attained the use of reason, as we shall show in the section, "Confirmation," below.

Extreme unction is given to sick persons deprived of their senses, not only when they have previously asked for it, but even when from unforeseen attacks, they have not had time to ask for it, and are in immediate danger of death. This the Church would not have permitted were it necessary to have a positive intention in order to receive these sacraments with profit.

Observe, however, that the Eucharist must not be given to sick persons wholly deprived of their senses, by reason of the irreverence which might occur in such cases.

[115] It has been a matter of controversy among theologians whether the sacrament of order can be validly administered to children.

418. **Is it an article of the faith that there are seven sacraments?**
It is an article of the faith, expressly defined by the sacred Council of Trent; and so, he would be a heretic who should assert that there are more than seven sacraments, or less than seven sacraments. They are: baptism, confirmation, the Eucharist, penance, extreme unction, order, and matrimony.[116]

419. **What is required in a sacred rite in order that it may be called a sacrament of the new law?**
There must be an external sign, divine institution, and power of conferring grace. These three things united are only found in the foresaid seven sacraments, recognized in the Catholic Church.

Baptism

420. **How do you define the sacrament of baptism?**
It is a sacrament of the new law, instituted by Christ, for the spiritual regeneration of man.

421. **What do these words, "for the spiritual regeneration of man," signify?**
Man, by sin, is born dead to the grace of God, and by means of baptism, he is born again to this grace, which is the supernatural life of the soul. In this spiritual regeneration, he is admitted to make part of Christ's faithful, that is to say, he becomes a member of his Church, and he acquires the right to receive the other sacraments.

422. **What is the matter of this sacrament?**
Natural water, whether from a well, a spring, or from the sea. In solemn baptism, however, that is, in baptism conferred with the accustomed ceremonies, the holy water, blessed in the font on Holy Saturday, should be used.

[116] Cf. Council of Trent, Session 7, "On the Sacraments in General," Can. 1

423. **Would not any other liquid, such as wine, oil, etc., suffice in case of necessity for the administration of baptism?**
It is of faith that true, natural water is necessary for the valid administration of baptism. Hence, if any other liquid whatsoever were made use of, the baptism would be invalid.

424. **Suppose that true, natural water were used, but that some other liquid or matter were mixed with it, in that case would the baptism be likewise invalid?**
If a small quantity of other matter were mixed with the water, the baptism would not be invalid: we see, in fact, that a little oil and chrism is mixed with the water which is blessed in the font on Holy Saturday, and this is the water which, except in case of necessity, ought to be used for baptizing. If, however, the liquid or other matter mixed with the water were in such quantity that it could no longer be called water—if, for example, so much earth were mixed with the water that it became mud—in that case the baptism would be invalid, that is to say, it would have no effect.

425. **What is the form of the sacrament of baptism?**
I baptize thee in the name of the Father, and of the Son, and of the Holy Ghost.

426. **Would the baptism be invalid if any one of these words were changed, or omitted to be expressed?**
If the change or omission were not essential, the baptism would be valid, but if essential, then it would be invalid. For instance, if the word *Ego* were omitted, the baptism would retain its effect; but if the word *baptizo* were omitted, it would have no virtue whatever.

427. **To what must attention be paid in the act of baptizing?**
To pouring water over the head of the child, in such quantity that it flow over the head, pronouncing meanwhile, with great precision, the words of the form.

428. **Why must attention be paid to pouring water over the head?**
Because, although the baptism might probably be valid if the water were poured over any other part of the body, especially if it were any principal part, such as the breast or shoulders, still its validity would not be so certain as if it were poured over the head. And therefore, it is prescribed by the *Roman Ritual* that, if a child shall have been baptized on any other part of the body, he is to be rebaptized under condition.

Moreover, in pouring water upon the head, care must be taken that it does not merely flow upon the hair, if the person baptized have thick hair, because some doubt whether, unless the water touch the skin, the baptism be valid. There is small foundation for this doubt, but as to a sacrament of so great necessity, we should adopt every precaution, and so take care that the water flow over the forehead or temples.

429. **Why is it requisite that water should be poured in such quantity as to flow?**
Because baptism is a washing, and it could not be called so unless the water flowed; we certainly could not say a thing was washed if only a few drops of water were let fall upon it, and remained where they fell.

430. **Is it necessary that the water be poured three times over the head of the baptized?**
The Church so prescribes, and therefore, this rite ought to be observed: the baptism, however, would certainly be valid, even if the water were only poured once.

431. **Why is it requisite that the form should be pronounced at the same moment that the water is poured upon the head of the baptized?**
Because, in all the sacraments the form should always be applied to the matter, and if there were any considerable interval between pronouncing the form and applying the matter, the sacrament would be invalid.

432. **Who is the minister of the sacrament of baptism?**

The ordinary minister of the sacrament of baptism is a priest, the extraordinary minister of this sacrament is a deacon, who, when there is just cause, may be delegated to administer it with the accustomed ceremonies. Should it happen, however, that neither priest nor deacon can be had, then any person, even a child, provided he have the use of reason, nay, even an infidel, may administer baptism. This is defined by the Fourth Lateran Council.[117]

433. **If a cleric not yet ordained deacon, or a layman should baptize a child when it was not a case of necessity, would such baptism be valid?**

It would be valid, certainly: but it would be a grave sin for any ordinary person to presume to baptize, when it was not a case of necessity.

434. **Is baptism necessary for everyone?**

Baptism is necessary for all, in order that they may attain eternal salvation; and this is an article of the faith defined by the sacred Council of Trent.[118] Theologians, however, distinguish three sorts of baptism: the baptism of blood, the baptism of desire, and the baptism of water. This latter alone is properly a sacrament; the other two may stand in place of the sacrament, but they are not sacraments.

435. **What is the baptism of blood?**

The baptism of blood is martyrdom. If a child were killed out of hatred to the faith, before he had been baptized, he would be saved. When, during the persecutions, adult Christians and even their infants were killed, such infants, although not baptized, were saved.

436. **What is the baptism of desire?**

The desire to receive baptism. If a Turk, finding himself at the point of death, desired baptism, but had no one at hand to baptize him, he would be saved.

[117] Cf. Fourth Lateran Council, Const. 1

[118] Cf. Council of Trent, Session 5, "Decree Concerning Original Sin," Can. 5; Session 6, "Decree on Justification." Ch. 7; Session 7, "On Baptism," Can. 5

437. **What is requisite to constitute martyrdom?**

In the case of children, it is required that they be killed out of hatred to Christ and his faith; nothing more is requisite. In this way the Holy Innocents, whom Herod caused to be put to death, were truly martyrs. In the case of adults, however, it is required: 1) that they accept death from a right and supernatural motive, hence should anyone accept martyrdom out of vainglory in order to be honored as a martyr, his death would not have the merit of martyrdom; nor, should anyone accept it in order to free himself from a life made grievous to him by indigence, would he be a martyr; 2) that they have no will to defend themselves; because to die in battle for the faith is not properly martyrdom; 3) in the case of one guilty of mortal sin, repentance of his sin, at least by attrition, is requisite.

Observe also, that martyrdom, being an act of the virtue of fortitude, should be voluntary. It is not, however, necessary to have the actual will, nor even the virtual will of meeting death in order to bear witness to the faith; the habitual will suffices. For example, in time of persecution, a Christian, resolved to die rather than to renounce his faith, were he surprised by the persecutors whilst asleep, and killed, would be a true martyr because of such habitual disposition. Observe, further, that martyrdom does not free a man from all his other obligations at the point of death, if he has time to fulfill them. If he has not been baptized, he is obliged, if possible, to receive baptism; and in the case of a baptized person, if he have any mortal sin on his soul still unconfessed, he would be obliged to confess it, were there a priest at hand to absolve him.

438. **Would one be a martyr who should suffer death in order not to offend against some other virtue, as, for example, against chastity?**

Certainly; and the virgins who suffered death, rather than yield to the seductions of those who attempted their chastity, are venerated as martyrs.

439. **Can those be called true martyrs who suffer death through their charity in serving the sick in time of pestilence?**

They could not be called martyrs in the strict sense of the term, because martyrdom is an act of the virtue of fortitude in defense of the faith, or of some other Christian virtue; and in exposing themselves to danger of death by serving the plague-stricken, they make an act of fortitude, not in defense of the virtue of charity, but in the practice of it. Still, in God's sight, this may have a merit equal to that of real martyrdom; and the Church, in her Martyrology of the 28th of February, venerates as martyrs those who died in the service of the sick in time of pestilence.[119]

440. **Does martyrdom supply all the effects of baptism?**
Martyrdom supplies by infusion of grace and remission of sins, but it cannot supply the other effects of baptism, of which we shall speak presently; and for which the baptism of water, that is, the sacrament, is requisite. With regard to the remission of sins, you must observe that in martyrdom they are all remitted with the same fullness with which they are remitted in baptism, so that the martyr has no remains of temporal punishment to suffer in the other life, but no sooner is his martyrdom consummated, than he is admitted to the estate of eternal beatitude.

441. **In case of necessity, is the simple desire of baptism sufficient for the attainment of eternal salvation?**
The simple desire of baptism is not sufficient if it be not accompanied by an act of contrition, or of charity; because, apart from the sacrament, save in the case of martyrdom, sins are not remitted without contrition, that is to say, unless the sinner detests them from the motive of the pure love of God.

442. **Is it, however, certain that children can be validly baptized?**
It is an article of the faith, defined by the sacred Council of Trent, and he who should say that children so baptized are not really Christians, or that, on attaining the use of reason, they ought to be re-baptized, or that it is

[119] *Quos velut martyres religiosa fides venerare consuevit.* "Them a religious faith is wont to venerate as martyrs."

better to defer baptism till they have attained the use of reason, would be a heretic, and excommunicated by the said council.[120]

443. **Supposing children, on attaining the use of reason, are dissatisfied at having been baptized, are they in such case bound to live as Christians?**
Baptism constitutes them subjects of holy Church; hence they would be bound to live as Christians; nor must any attention be paid to their dissatisfaction, it being most unreasonable and unjust.

444. **But would not this be to do violence to conscience?**
To oblige a person to do what is his positive duty cannot be called doing violence to conscience. If men, who are constituted subjects of the Church through baptism, could, when they attain the use of reason, refuse to remain subjects to the Church; much more could they, when they attain the use of reason, refuse to submit to the authority of the lawful government of the state in which they are born. I say "much more," because the authority which the Church has over baptized persons is more sacred and inviolable than the authority which any sovereign has over his people. In fact, we are not made subjects by any sacrament, nor do we receive any indelible character constituting us such in perpetuity in regard to the lawful sovereign in whose states we are born. If we change our country, we are no longer his subjects. But we can go to no part of the world where we can withdraw ourselves from subjection to the Church, after having been once baptized.[121]

445. **What are the effects of baptism?**
There are six effects of the sacrament of baptism. 1) It remits original sin and every actual sin, as well in respect of the guilt, as in respect of even

[120] Cf. Council of Trent, Session 5, "Decree Concerning Original Sin," Can. 3, 4; Session 7, "On Baptism," Can. 13

[121] By this we do not mean to say that the authority which the sovereign has over his subjects is not sacred and inviolable. It is sacred because princes derive their authority from God; and inviolable because, except in case of a prince commanding what would be a crime, and which case would be not a use of authority but an abuse of power, it cannot happen that subjects should have the right to disobey their sovereign.

the temporal punishment due to actual sin; so that, should an adult pass out of this life immediately after having received baptism, he would have no debt of temporal punishment to pay in purgatory; and therefore, if an adult were baptized when dying, no indulgence could be given him. 2) It confers sanctifying grace, infused virtues, and the other supernatural gifts whereby a man is sanctified and interiorly renewed. 3) It gives a certain right of receiving the actual graces necessary to attainment of his end, that is to say, the graces necessary to enable a man to live a Christian and holy life. This last constitutes the sacramental grace of which we have spoken in the preceding section, in answer to Question 400.

4) It imprints an indelible character on the soul; and for this reason, baptism can be received but once. 5) It constitutes us members of the Church; and subjects us to her jurisdiction. 6) It gives us the capability and the right to receive the other sacraments; and it makes us participators in the common treasures of the Church, such as indulgences, the fruits of the Sacrifice of the Mass, etc.

446. **When adults receive baptism, ought they to have sorrow for their sins?**
They need not have sorrow for original sin, because we can only repent of sins which we have committed from our own proper, individual, personal malice. It is certain, however, that they ought to repent of actual mortal sins, at least with the sorrow of attrition, because those sins are forgiven to no one who has not sorrow for them.

Confirmation

447. **How do you define the sacrament of confirmation?**
Confirmation is a sacrament of the new law, by which the strength of the Holy Spirit is given to baptized persons, in order that they may remain firm in the faith and profess it intrepidly.

448. **Who is the minister of this sacrament?**

It is an article of the faith, declared by the sacred Council of Trent, that bishops alone are the ordinary ministers of this sacrament.[122] The supreme pontiff can, however, delegate even a simple priest to confer confirmation. In such case, that priest is the extraordinary minister of this sacrament.

449. **What is the matter in confirmation?**

The imposition of hands, and the unction of the sacred chrism.

450. **What is the form in confirmation?**

These words: "I sign thee with the sign of the cross. I confirm thee with the chrism of salvation."

451. **Who are the subjects of this sacrament?**

All baptized persons; hence it was in ancient times given to infants immediately after baptism; although now, according to the present discipline of the Church, it ought not to be conferred on children under seven years of age, except in cases of necessity.

452. **What dispositions are requisite in those who receive this sacrament?**

When the bishop believes there is sufficient cause to confer this sacrament on children before the use of reason, all that is required is that they should have been baptized. But when this sacrament is conferred on adults, or on children who have attained the use of reason, it is required that they be in a state of grace, and that they be properly instructed in matters of faith, and in regard to the nature and effects of this sacrament.

453. **Is this sacrament necessary in order to the attainment of eternal salvation?**

It is not necessary absolutely speaking; for otherwise simple priests would have been the ministers of this sacrament, in order that it might be an easy matter for all to receive it. Still, everyone who has it in his power is

[122] Cf. Council of Trent, Session 23, "The True and Catholic Doctrine, Touching the Sacrament of Order," Ch. 4; Can. 7

obliged to receive this sacrament under pain of mortal sin; as Benedict XIV commanded the bishops to teach those who had not yet received it.

454. **What are the effects of this sacrament?**
There are two: 1) the indelible character; as we have shown in answer to Question 402, above; 2) the fullness of the Holy Spirit, which gives a special strength to the soul, enabling it easily to overcome temptations against the faith, and to endure with invincible constancy persecutions for its sake. This fullness of the Holy Spirit includes also increase of sanctifying grace.

The Holy Eucharist

455. **Is the Holy Eucharist a sacrament of the new law?**
It is a true sacrament of the new law, and that it is so is an express article of the faith.

456. **Is it also a true sacrifice?**
It is likewise an express article of the faith that the Holy Eucharist is a true sacrifice.

457. **How do you define the Holy Eucharist—as it is a sacrament?**
The Holy Eucharist is a sacrament of the new law, which really contains the body and blood of Jesus Christ under the species of bread and wine, and was instituted for the spiritual refection of the faithful.

458. **What is the matter of this sacrament?**
Bread made of wheat, and wine made of grapes.

459. **What is the form of this sacrament?**
The words of consecration which the priest pronounces over the bread and wine in the Holy Mass.

460. **What change is wrought in the bread and wine when the words of consecration are pronounced?**
It is an article of the faith that the whole substance of the bread is changed into the body of Jesus Christ, and that the whole substance of the wine is changed into his blood.

461. **Why do you say "the whole substance"?**
Because it is an article of the faith, declared by the Church against certain heretics, that, after the words of consecration, there remains nothing of the substance of the bread and of the wine, but that it is all changed into the body and blood of Christ; and to denote that the species, that is, the color, smell, taste, and quantity, as well of the bread as of the wine, remain; and so, these substances being changed into the body and blood of Christ, there remain the appearances of bread and wine.

462. **Then, in the consecrated host there is only the body, and in the consecrated chalice there is only the blood of Christ?**
This would be a heresy, for it is of faith that the whole Christ, and therefore his soul and his divinity, is as well in the host under the species of bread, as in the chalice under the species of wine. We say that the bread is changed into the body of Christ, and the wine into his blood, because by virtue of the words of consecration the bread is changed into his body, which, as a living body, contains his blood; and because, by virtue of the words of consecration of the chalice, the wine is changed into the blood of Christ, which, as living blood, is united to his body, and so by concomitance his blood is along with his body, and his body along with his blood.

463. **Then we receive the living and whole Christ as much under the species of bread, as under the species of wine?**
Certainly; and this is an article of the faith.

464. **What kind of bread ought to be consecrated?**
Any kind of bread, provided it be made of wheaten flour, can be validly consecrated; and so, whether the bread be made with leaven or without

leaven, by the words of consecration it is changed into the body of the Lord. You must observe, however, that the Church commands us to use bread made without leaven, and prohibits the consecration of leavened bread. At the same time, many of the Greeks having an ancient custom of consecrating leavened bread, the Church permits this use to them; nay, not only permits it, but desires that it be maintained.

465. **Would it not be well that lay persons also, when they communicate, should receive the Blessed Sacrament under the species of wine, as well as under the species of bread?**
For many wise reasons the Church has prohibited the administration of the Blessed Sacrament to lay persons under the species of wine; nor can even priests communicate under the species of wine, except when they celebrate the Holy Mass. Moreover, it would be a heresy, condemned by the sacred Council of Trent, to say that Christians are obliged to communicate also under the species of wine.[123] Observe further, that, receiving the living and whole Christ, as well under the species of bread as under the species of wine, he who receives him only under the species of bread is not defrauded of any part of the fruit of the sacrament.

466. **When a consecrated host is divided, what happens to the body of Christ?**
No change nor alteration takes place in the body of Christ; but it is of faith that when the host is broken into small particles, the living and whole Christ is under each particle; and the same happens if the species of wine in the chalice is divided into small drops.

467. **For how long a time does the body and the blood of Christ remain really present in the Blessed Sacrament?**
It is an article of the faith that the body and blood of Christ remain present therein so long as the species are not consumed or have become corrupted. Therefore, if the species of wine were left in the chalice until

[123] Cf. Council of Trent, Session 21, "Decree on Communion under Both Species, and the Communion of Infants," Ch. 1-3; Can. 1-3

it evaporated, or became vinegar, there would no longer be the blood of Christ in that chalice.

468. **When we communicate, for how long time does the real presence of Christ remain in us?**
It remains in us so long as the heat of the stomach does not change the sacramental species; therefore, according to the greater or less activity of the stomach, Christ remains a greater or less time really present in us.

469. **Who is the minister of the sacrament of the Eucharist?**
Priests alone can consecrate the bread and wine; therefore, not even in case of necessity can one who is not a priest consecrate validly. Hence, for example, should a deacon say Mass, he would not consecrate, and the bread would still remain bread, and the wine would still remain wine. This is of the faith.

Moreover, the administration of this sacrament belongs also to priests alone, so that no other, ordinarily speaking, can give Communion. I say "ordinarily speaking," because, in case of necessity, a deacon also can give Communion, and so deacons are the extraordinary ministers of this sacrament, not in respect of consecration, but of administration.

470. **Who are the subjects of this sacrament?**
All baptized persons are the subjects of this sacrament, that is to say, they are capable of receiving it; but in adults, to receive it with profit, the necessary dispositions are requisite.

471. **May children then also receive Communion?**
For many centuries it was the custom of the Church to give Communion to children before the use of reason, but this custom has now ceased; so that according to the present discipline of the Church, it is not lawful to give them Communion. Observe, moreover, that the sacred Council of Trent

excommunicates those who should assert that Communion is necessary for children before they attain the use of reason.[124]

472. **What dispositions are requisite in adults?**
Sanctifying grace; knowledge of the sacrament, that is to say, that they know what they are receiving; and, except in the case of danger of death, fasting from every kind of food and drink, even though it were medicinal. These are the most essential dispositions; there are others which cause us to receive this sacrament with greater fruits, but the masters of the spiritual life will instruct you in regard to these.

473. **Suppose a person in mortal sin were about to communicate, would it suffice that he put himself in a state of grace by an act of perfect contrition?**
In the answer to Question 399, above, we have said that it would not suffice, there being the precept of St. Paul, which obliges all those who would communicate to go first to confession every time they have been guilty of any mortal sin. This is meant speaking generally, for if there were urgent necessity to communicate, and no confessor could be had, a person might receive Holy Communion with an act of perfect contrition alone. But it is for moralists to discuss such cases of necessity, as well as the obligation which remains of confessing the sin.

474. **What are the effects of this sacrament?**
The first effect is spiritual nourishment of the soul, through the increase of sanctifying grace; the second effect is deliverance from venial sins; the third, preservation from mortal sins. The sacred Council of Trent assigns these effects to this sacrament. The Councils of Florence and Vienne add a fourth effect, which is spiritual delectation;[125] this, however, as St. Bernard observes, is only conferred on those who are thoroughly detached from

[124] Cf. Council of Trent, Session 21, "Decree on Communion under Both Species, and the Communion of Infants," Ch. 4; Can. 4

[125] Cf. Council of Trent, Session 13; Council of Florence, Session 8, "Bull of Union with the Armenians"

earthly affections and very fervent in spirit. Such as these, when they communicate, experience in a sensible manner how sweet is the Lord.

475. **What necessity is there to receive Holy Communion?**
All adults, by divine and ecclesiastical precept, are bound to communicate, and the Church has fixed this obligation at once a year, so that he who should not fulfill this obligation would not be saved. There is also obligation to communicate when death is approaching; but moral theologians will tell you of these obligations. Observe, however, that this necessity is only of precept, so that should an adult find it impossible to receive Holy Communion, he might notwithstanding be saved.

476. **Is the practice of daily Communion to be approved in the case of lay persons?**
It is doubtless to be approved, 1) because such was the common practice of the early Church; 2) because it is in conformity with the desire of the Council of Trent;[126] 3) because the *Roman Catechism* directs parish priests frequently to exhort the faithful to practice it;[127] 4) because a decree of the Sacred Congregation, approved by Innocent XI, forbids that even married persons, or those engaged in business, should be debarred from daily Communion, and orders it to be left to the judgment of confessors as to who shall be admitted or not admitted to it. Much more is daily Communion to be approved for persons living in religious communities.

477. **You said that the Blessed Eucharist is not only a sacrament, but that it is also a true sacrifice. I should like, in the first place, to know what a sacrifice is.**
A sacrifice may be defined as: an oblation or offering of a sensible thing, made to God by his legitimate minister, in recognition of his supreme dominion over all creatures—and this offering must import some destruction

[126] Cf. Council of Trent, Session 13, "Decree Concerning the Most Holy Sacrament of the Eucharist," Ch. 8

[127] Cf. *Roman Catechism*, "The Obligation of Communion." Editor's note: See p. 274–277 of Volume VII of this series, which includes the *Catechism of the Council of Trent*, also called the *Roman Catechism*.

of the thing or victim which is offered; otherwise, should this destruction be wanting, it is no longer a sacrifice, but a simple oblation. This definition belongs also to the sacrifices of the old law, in which animals were offered to God by lawful priests, in recognition of his supreme authority, and they offered them by putting them to death.

478. **How can this definition be applied to the Holy Eucharist?**
In the Holy Mass there is the oblation of a sensible thing, that is, of the body and blood of Jesus Christ, under the species of bread and wine. There is a legitimate minister, that is, the priest, and there is the immolation or destruction of a victim, which immolation was made really in the sacrifice of the cross, when Jesus Christ really shed his blood and really died; but in the Holy Mass this immolation is made mystically, for Jesus Christ does not shed his blood anymore, nor die anymore really, but mystically, inasmuch as by virtue of the words of consecration the body alone of Christ is made present under the species of bread, and the blood alone of Christ under the species of wine; and although along with his body there is also his blood, and along with his blood there is also his body, this happens not by virtue of the words of consecration, but by way of concomitance, inasmuch as the blood of Christ cannot now be again really separated from his body. Therefore, in the Mass, the body and blood of the Lord are offered as if separated under the diverse species of bread and wine; and this suffices for mystical destruction or immolation of the victim.

479. **What kind of sacrifice must we say is the Sacrifice of the Mass?**
The sacred Council of Trent has defined that the Holy Mass is the same sacrifice as that of the cross, differing from it only as to the manner in which it is offered; for the same victim who was offered then, is offered now upon our altars, that is to say, Jesus Christ, who was made a victim for our sins, and it is the same priest who offers that victim, inasmuch as Jesus Christ is the principal offerer, offering himself as he did upon Calvary, but through the ministry of his priests. Therefore, when Holy Mass is celebrated, the sacrifice of the cross is renewed; which then was a bloody

sacrifice, that is, with a real blood-shedding; and now is an unbloody sacrifice, that is, with a not real but mystical blood-shedding.[128]

480. **What are the qualities of the Sacrifice of the Holy Mass?**
It is *latreutic*, that is to say, it is a sacrifice of praise, rendering infinite praise to God. It is *eucharistic*, that is to say, it is a sacrifice of thanksgiving, which avails to thank him for all possible benefits. It is *propitiatory*, that is to say, it is such as to appease him for all sins. It is *impetratory*, that is to say, it can impetrate for us every grace.

481. **Had not the sacrifice of the cross all these characteristics, and was it not all-sufficient? Why, then, must we acknowledge the Holy Mass to be a true sacrifice?**
In the first place, you must observe, as St. Thomas shows,[129] that the true religion must have a sacrifice to offer to God. Now we have no other sacrifice, for the ancient sacrifices were abrogated; and therefore, if it were not for the Holy Mass, the Christian religion could offer no sacrifice to God.

In the second place, observe that, although the sacrifice of the cross was all-sufficient, and more than all-sufficient, yet by the Holy Mass the honor which God received from the sacrifice of the cross is renewed; and it is a most powerful means by which the merits of that same sacrifice, which our Savior offered upon the cross, are applied to us.

482. **Does the Sacrifice of the Holy Mass aid only the living?**
It is an article of the faith, defined by the sacred Council of Trent, that the Sacrifice of the Holy Mass aids not only the living, but also the dead who are in purgatory.[130]

[128] Cf. Council of Trent, Session 22

[129] Cf. *Summa Theologiae*, II-II, q. 85

[130] Cf. Council of Trent, Session 22, "Doctrine on the Sacrifice of the Mass," Ch. 2; Can. 3; Session 25, "Decree Concerning Purgatory"

483. **Can Masses be celebrated in honor of the saints?**

It is likewise an article of the faith, defined in the said council,[131] that it is well to celebrate Masses in honor of the saints. Observe, however, that the holy sacrifice can only be offered to God in thanksgiving for the great graces which he has bestowed upon the saints, and to obtain their patronage. Hence the Holy Mass can be offered to no saint, but only to God, in thanksgiving for the graces which he has bestowed upon them, and in order that he may deign to make us partakers of their intercession. Nevertheless, since all this redounds to the honor of the saints, we say rightly that Masses are celebrated in honor of the saints.

484. **Who can offer the Sacrifice of the Holy Mass?**

Jesus Christ, who instituted it at the last supper, and who then thus offered a true sacrifice of his body and blood under the species of bread and wine, is truly and properly the principal offerer of the Holy Mass. In the second place, priests alone can, immediately and properly, as ministers, offer this sacrifice, as we have already said; nor could it be validly celebrated by any person whatever who was not a priest. In the third place, all the faithful, as members of the Church, when they hear Holy Mass, offer the holy sacrifice together with the priest, as appears from the prayers of the Canon.

485. **If all the faithful offer the sacrifice together with the priest, ought they not all to communicate when they hear Mass?**

It is well that all who are disposed should communicate. The Council of Trent desires that all who are present should dispose themselves to receive Holy Communion from the priest who celebrates, as we have already shown; nevertheless, this is not a matter of necessity. Moreover, the same council excommunicates anyone who should assert that Holy Mass cannot be celebrated unless the assistants communicate.[132]

[131] Cf. Council of Trent, Session 22, "Doctrine on the Sacrifice of the Mass," Ch. 3; Can. 5

[132] Cf. Council of Trent, Session 22, "Doctrine on the Sacrifice of the Mass," Ch. 6; Can. 8

486. **Is it necessary to put a little water in the wine which is consecrated in Holy Mass?**

It is not necessary for validity, because, by the words of consecration, the wine would be changed into the blood of Christ, although no water were put into the chalice; but it is necessary to add the water, because, as the holy fathers declare, Christ did so at the last supper, it has always been the custom of the Church, and the Church has most rigorously commanded it. Moreover, the Council of Trent excommunicates anyone who should assert that this small quantity of water is not to be put in the wine.[133] You must be careful, however, not to put too great a quantity of water into the chalice, because if the wine were mixed with much water, it would no longer be fit matter for the consecration.

487. **Would it not be better if the Holy Mass were celebrated in the vulgar tongue, and in a loud voice, so that the people might understand all the prayers?**

He who should say that the Mass ought to be celebrated only in the vulgar tongue, and the whole of it, including the Canon and the words of consecration, in a loud voice, would incur the excommunication fulminated by the Council of Trent. In like manner, he who should despise the ceremonies, rites, or vestments which are used in celebrating the Holy Mass, would incur the excommunication fulminated by the same council.[134]

Penance

488. **Is penance a sacrament of the new law?**

Penance is a supernatural moral virtue, which inclines the sinner to detest and grieve for his sins, inasmuch as they are offenses against God, and to have a purpose of amendment and satisfaction. This virtue was always necessary for sinners, even under the old law, in order that they might

[133] Cf. Council of Trent, Session 22, "Doctrine on the Sacrifice of the Mass," Ch. 7; Can. 9

[134] Cf. Council of Trent, Session 22, "Doctrine on the Sacrifice of the Mass," Ch. 5, 8; Can. 7, 9

obtain the pardon of their sins, and Jesus Christ raised it to the rank of a sacrament, so that, when penance has the due requisites, according to the institution of Christ, it is a true sacrament.

489. **Is not penance then always a sacrament?**
When there is not only sorrow for sin committed, not only purpose of amendment, and of making satisfaction to the divine justice, but also confession of sins made to a priest approved for confession, and absolution received from him, then it is of faith that penance is a true sacrament; but when these two last are wanting, it is a simple virtue.

490. **How do you define the sacrament of penance?**
Penance is a sacrament, instituted by Jesus Christ, in which, by the acts of the penitent and the absolution of an approved priest, sins committed after baptism are remitted.

491. **What is the matter of this sacrament?**
Sins committed after baptism are the remote matter of this sacrament; contrition, confession of the same sins, and satisfaction are the proximate matter.

492. **Are all sins committed after baptism equally the matter of this sacrament?**
Mortal sins never previously confessed are the necessary matter, so that, except in case of real inability, they must be confessed in order to obtain pardon; venial sins, however, and all mortal sins already confessed are sufficient matter; so that there is no obligation to confess them, but they may be confessed, and, there being no other sins to confess, absolution may be received for them.

493. **In case of real inability, how are mortal sins forgiven without confession?**
They are pardoned by means of perfect contrition, which includes the desire or purpose of confession, as we pointed out in the section, "The Virtue of Charity," above.

494. **Is it a good thing to frequent confession when we have no mortal sins to confess?**

It is certainly a good thing, and conformable to the desire of the Church, and the practice of fervent Christians.

495. **What is contrition?**

The Council of Trent defines contrition as "a hearty sorrow and detestation of sins committed, accompanied by a purpose not to sin anymore."[135] Contrition is perfect when this sorrow springs from perfect love of God. It is imperfect when it springs from a supernatural motive, indeed, but not from the perfect love of God. If a person repents of having offended God because he has offended the supreme good who merits to be loved above everything, he has perfect contrition. If, on the other hand, he repents for having forfeited heaven and merited hell, he has imperfect contrition.

496. **Is perfect or imperfect contrition necessary for confession?**

Perfect contrition is undoubtedly desirable, but it is not necessary; since otherwise, everyone who went to confession would go already in a state of grace, there being no doubt, as we have said in the section, "The Virtue of Charity," above, in that perfect charity and perfect contrition place the soul in the grace of God, before receiving sacramental absolution, and that, too, apart from case of necessity. Imperfect contrition therefore suffices for confession.

497. **What conditions ought contrition, that is, sorrow for sin, to have?**

It must be internal, that is to say, it must come from the heart. It must be supreme, that is to say, it must cause us to detest sin above every other evil. It must be universal, making us abhor all mortal sins whatsoever. It must be supernatural, that is to say, it must spring from a motive revealed by the holy faith.

[135] Council of Trent, "Doctrine on the Sacrament of Penance," Ch. 4

498. **Is a sorrow which has these conditions necessary in confession, when we have only to accuse ourselves of venial sins?**
There is no doubt of it, except in regard to the third condition; for it is not necessary that the penitent should have a universal sorrow for all his venial sins; it is sufficient that, when confessing only venial sins, he should repent of some one of them. He must, however, have an internal, supreme, supernatural sorrow on account of that of which he repents, so that he may be disposed to suffer anything whatever, rather than commit it anymore.

499. **Could a person who had only venial sins to confess, and who did not feel this sorrow, go to confession?**
Such a one could not receive absolution, otherwise the sacrament would be void, as wanting an essential part. On this account theologians advise persons who frequent holy confession and who accuse themselves only of habitual venial sins, to add to their confession some graver sin of their past life for which they have a more certain sorrow, in order that the matter of the sacrament may not be wanting. For want of such caution it is possible that not a few persons who frequent holy confession receive absolution in vain. But we leave this to be discussed by moral theologians.

500. **Of what sort ought our purpose of amendment to be?**
Our purpose of amendment must be firm, that is to say, the will must be resolute never more to return to the sin which we detest. It must be universal, so that it be resolute to guard against committing any mortal sin whatsoever. It must be efficacious, so that it be disposed to adopt all the necessary means to avoid sin.

501. **What is confession?**
Confession is accusation of one's own sins, committed after baptism, made by the penitent, in the presence of the priest, in order to obtain absolution.

502. **Can we not obtain pardon of mortal sins without confessing them?**
This is an article of the faith, defined by the sacred Council of Trent,[136] because there is an express divine command to confess all and each of our mortal sins; and if the pardon of such mortal sins is obtained by means of perfect contrition, it is obtained, because in that perfect contrition there is included the purpose or desire of confession.

503. **How often are we under obligation to fulfill this precept?**
Generally speaking, there is obligation to fulfill it once a year, and at the point of death. There may, however, be other circumstances which also oblige us to fulfill this precept, as may be seen in the moral theology.

504. **What is satisfaction?**
Satisfaction, which is a part of the sacrament of penance, is the acceptance and voluntary fulfillment of the penance enjoined by the confessor, in order to compensate for the injury we have done to God by the sin.

505. **The guilt of sin being pardoned, do we remain debtors to any punishment?**
Contrition is sometimes so powerful and vehement that it takes away not only the guilt, but also all the punishment; but for the most part, as the Council of Trent teaches, there remains a debt of temporal punishment due for sin, after the guilt is pardoned, and we must satisfy this either by works of penance in this life, or in purgatory in the next.[137]

506. **It seems to me that the penance should be performed before receiving absolution.**
The practice of the Church is contrary to this, which enjoins a penance and, if he who confesses his sins be rightly disposed, gives absolution immediately, leaving him to perform the penance enjoined afterward. Moreover, the Church has condemned certain modern rigorists, who pretended that

[136] Cf. Council of Trent, "Doctrine on the Sacrament of Penance," Ch. 5; Can. 7

[137] Cf. Council of Trent, "Doctrine on the Sacrament of Penance," Ch. 8-9; Can. 12, 13, 15

the penance enjoined by the confessor ought to be performed before receiving absolution.

507. **Is the penance enjoined by the confessor an essential part of the sacrament?**
It is not an essential part of the sacrament, for, in cases where it cannot be imposed or cannot be fulfilled, the sacrament still produces its effect, that is, the justification of the sinner. On the other hand, it is a necessary part of the sacrament, for it is of divine precept that this penance should be imposed and performed, except in cases where there is an impossibility of fulfilling it. Therefore, should anyone go to confession with the intention of not performing his penance, he would have a bad intention, which would render him ill-disposed, and he would receive the absolution unworthily, and his sins would not be forgiven him.

508. **Is this penance entirely in the power of the confessor?**
It is not in such manner in the power of the confessor that he can impose penances according to his own caprice; but it is so far in the power of the confessor, that, after prudently considering the number and quality of the sins and the dispositions of the penitent, it rests with him to assign such penance as he shall prudently judge to be most fitting and salutary; such penance being directed, as the sacred Council of Trent teaches, not only as a punishment for past sins, but also as a remedy to preserve from future sins.[138]

509. **What is the form of the sacrament of penance?**
"I absolve thee from thy sins, in the name of the Father, and of the Son, and of the Holy Ghost." These last words, however, are not essential, for though he who should omit them would sin by so doing, the absolution would be valid. The essential words are: "I absolve thee."

[138] Cf. Council of Trent, "Doctrine on the Sacrament of Penance," Ch. 8

510. **What is the meaning of these words?**

The meaning of these words is: "I administer to thee the sacrament of absolution." This is the explanation of St. Thomas.[139] Or: "I give thee, insofar as I can, the grace which reconciles, or which remits sins." In this sense the form is true, even for those who approach the sacrament already freed from sin, by perfect contrition, and who in reality could not have their sins taken away, because they have been taken away already. In such sense the form is true; because the sinner receives grace which, of its nature, is directed to the taking away of sin; because he reconciles himself more perfectly to God, and advances in his friendship; and because in the sacrament a part of the temporal pain due to sin is condoned.

511. **Who is the minister of the sacrament of penance?**

Only priests who have been approved for the hearing of confessions. All priests who have cure of souls are so approved, and also all others on whom jurisdiction to hear confessions has been conferred.

512. **Who can give priests jurisdiction to hear confessions?**

The pope for the whole Church, as universal pastor; a bishop in his own diocese; and a regular prelate to the religious subject to him. Observe, however, that regulars cannot hear the confessions of nuns, even of those who are exempt from the jurisdiction of the bishop and subject to the regular prelate, without the approbation of the bishop of the place.

513. **Cannot priests, not approved for the hearing of confessions, absolve from venial sins?**

It is certain that they cannot absolve even from venial sins, as was declared by the congregation of cardinals under Innocent XI, in 1679.

[139] Cf. *Summa Theologiae*, III, q. 84, a. 3, rep. 5

514. **Can some sins be reserved, so that priests otherwise approved for the hearing of confessions shall not have jurisdiction in regard of such sins?**
It is an article of the faith, declared in the sacred Council of Trent, that bishops can reserve to themselves certain sins, for which ordinary confessors cannot give absolution; and what each bishop can do for his own diocese, the pope can do for the whole Church.[140]

515. **The Church orders that all the faithful shall confess once a year to their own priest; what is meant by "their own priest"?**
By "their own priest" is meant the parish priest; at the present day, however, it is sufficient to confess to any priest approved by the bishop; such is the present practice recognized by the supreme pontiff, and by all the bishops.

516. **What are the effects of the sacrament of penance?**
Five principal effects may be enumerated: 1) the remission of sin, and of the eternal punishment which sin merits, if it be mortal; 2) the diminution of the temporal punishment due to sin, a diminution greater or less, according to the more or less perfect disposition of the penitent; 3) renewal of friendship with God, which has been violated; 4) the restitution or revival of virtues and merits which have been lost by sin; 5) the aids of actual grace, that is to say, a certain right to have such aids in time of need, by means of which the penitent is strengthened against falling anew into sin, and strengthened to persevere in good.

517. **What is meant by the virtues or merits being restored which have been lost by sin?**
Sin causes us to lose the habits of virtue; the sin of infidelity, for example, causes us to lose faith; the sin of despair causes us to lose hope, etc.; and by means of a good confession, these virtues are restored to the soul. Similarly,

[140] Cf. Council of Trent, Session 14, "Doctrine on the Sacrament of Penance," Ch. 7; Can. 11

sin strips the soul of all the merits it had acquired for eternal life, and by means of confession, those merits are restored to the soul.

On Indulgences

518. **What is an indulgence?**
An indulgence is a remission of the temporal punishment which remains due to us on account of our sins, after their guilt has been pardoned; which remission is given us outside the sacrament by those who have the faculty to dispense the spiritual treasures of the Church.

519. **Explain this to me more distinctly.**
An indulgence is said to be a remission of punishment, because it is not the sin which is remitted by the indulgence, but the punishment due for the sin. It is said to be a remission of temporal punishment, because the eternal punishment due to mortal sin is not remitted by the indulgence: that is remitted only in the sacrament of penance. This temporal punishment remains due after the guilt is pardoned, because, as we have already shown, after absolution has been received, there remains, for the most part, some debt of temporal punishment which we must satisfy, either by works of penance in this life, or by purgatory in the next. Observe further: this remission is given outside the sacrament, which means that we must not confound an indulgence with the remission of that part of the temporal punishment which is obtained by virtue of the sacrament of penance, in proportion to the more or less perfect dispositions of the penitent.

In conclusion, the indulgence is given by those who have the faculty to dispense, etc., because no one can grant indulgences who has not legitimate authority to distribute the common treasures of the Church. The pope has this power, without limit, for the whole Church; the bishops have it, limited, for their own dioceses, and restricted by the Fourth Lateran Council, so that they can only grant indulgences of forty days, and of one year in the dedication of a basilica.[141]

[141] Cf. Fourth Lateran Council, Const. 62

520. **Of what does the spiritual treasury of the Church consist?**

The spiritual treasury of the Church is formed of the infinite merits of Jesus Christ and of the Blessed Virgin Mary and of all the saints; also, of the merits of the just still living upon earth, as Clement VI teaches in his bull *Unigenitus* of the year 1350. The Church has authority to dispense these treasures, in remission of the temporal punishment due to God on account of sin.

521. **Is it certain that in the Church there is this power to grant indulgences?**

It is an article of the faith, as declared by the sacred Council of Trent.[142]

522. **Are there different kinds of indulgences?**

Some indulgences are plenary, and some partial. Plenary indulgences remit the whole of the temporal punishment due to the divine justice. Hence, to obtain the full effect of a plenary indulgence, it is necessary not only to be in a state of grace, but also to be detached from all affection to venial sin. Partial indulgences remit a part of the temporal punishment corresponding to forty days, seven years, or the like, of the penances formerly imposed.

523. **What was this penance formerly imposed?**

In early times, for many sins the canons appointed penances either of days or years, which penances were to be performed by sinners when they were converted to God; these penances were called "the pains" imposed. They are now no longer prescribed; but when an indulgence of forty days, seven years, or the like is granted, so much temporal punishment is remitted as would have been remitted to the penitent had he fulfilled a penance of forty days, seven years, etc.

524. **Can indulgences be given also for the dead?**

They can, and such is the practice of the Church. You must observe, however, that to the living, over whom the Church has jurisdiction, they are given by way of absolution; to the dead, over whom the Church has no longer jurisdiction, they are given by way of suffrage.

[142] Cf. Council of Trent, Session 25, "Decree Concerning Indulgences"

Extreme Unction

525. **Is extreme unction a sacrament?**

That it is a true sacrament is an article of the faith, as defined by the Council of Trent.[143]

526. **What is the matter of this sacrament?**

The matter of this sacrament is the oil blessed by the bishop on Maundy Thursday.

527. **What is the form?**

The prayer which is offered by the priest while he is anointing the senses of the sick person.

528. **Who is the minister of it?**

Priests alone are ministers of this sacrament.

529. **Who are the subjects of it?**

Sick persons alone, in peril of death, who have arrived at the use of reason; because, for children who have not yet sinned, such a form could not be used as: "By this holy anointing, and by his most piteous mercy, the Lord pardon thee, whereinsoever thou hast sinned by seeing, hearing," etc.

530. **What are the effects of this sacrament?**

The first is sanctifying grace, with a right to actual graces given to comfort and strengthen the soul of the sick person amidst the pains and troubles of his sickness, and against the temptations of the devil. The second is to free him from the relics of sin, which are the weakness, languor, tepidity in good, anxiety, and timidity which sin leaves behind it in the soul; besides this, the temporal punishments still due to sin[144] are taken away or

[143] Cf. Council of Trent, Session 7, "On the Sacraments in General," Can. 1; Session 14, "On the Sacrament of Extreme Unction," Ch. 1; Can. 1

[144] See the section, "Penance," on p. XX-XX, above.

pardoned, according to the more or less perfect disposition of him who receives this sacrament. The third effect is to free him from venial sins, and even from mortal sins, if there be no possibility of confessing them, or if they have been forgotten, provided there be the repentance of attrition, as we have already shown in the section, "The Sacraments in General," above. The fourth is bodily healing, if it be expedient for the salvation of the soul.

531. **Is there any necessity to receive this sacrament?**
You may see clearly, from the importance of the foresaid effects, that everyone ought to be careful to fortify himself with this sacrament at the terrible approach of death.

Order

532. **Is order a true sacrament of the new law?**
This is an article of the faith, expressly declared by the sacred Council of Trent.[145] Order is defined to be: a sacrament of the new law, whereby the spiritual power is given to baptized men, of consecrating bread and wine in the most august Sacrament of the Altar, of administering the sacraments, and of exercising other ecclesiastical ministries.

533. **What powers must we recognize as derived from this sacrament?**
Two powers: the first is called the power of order, which regards the holy sacrifice, or the real body of Christ; the second is called the power of jurisdiction, which regards the governing of the mystical body of Christ, that is to say, of the Christian people.

534. **Have these two powers distinct grades?**
It is certain that they have distinct grades, of which the ecclesiastical hierarchy is formed. It is defined by the sacred Council of Trent that there

[145] Cf. Council of Trent, Session 7, "On the Sacraments in General," Can. 1; Session 23, "The True and Catholic Doctrine, Touching the Sacrament of Order," Ch. 3; Can. 3

is such a hierarchy.[146] This hierarchy is composed of bishops, priests, and the inferior ministers.

535. **Are several orders to be recognized in sacred ordination?**
It is of faith that several orders are to be recognized, the greater orders and the minor orders, as the sacred Council of Trent has defined.[147]

536. **Which are the greater orders?**
The greater orders are three in number: priest, deacon, and subdeacon.

537. **Which are the minor orders?**
There are four minor orders: ostiarius, lector, exorcist, and acolyte.

538. **Who are the ministers of the sacrament of order?**
Bishops alone, as defined by the sacred Council of Trent.[148]

539. **What is the matter of this sacrament, and what is its form?**
The matter is the imposition of the hands of the bishop upon the person to be ordained; the form consists of the words with which the bishop accompanies this action.[149]

540. **What dispositions are required in those who aspire to the priesthood?**
The principal dispositions are: 1) vocation from God, for without a positive vocation—which, moreover, must be well examined—no one should dare to aspire to so eminent an estate in the Church; 2) sanctity

[146] Cf. Council of Trent, Session 23, "The True and Catholic Doctrine, Touching the Sacrament of Order," Ch. 4; Can. 6

[147] Cf. Council of Trent, Session 23, "The True and Catholic Doctrine, Touching the Sacrament of Order," Ch. 2; Can. 2

[148] Cf. Council of Trent, Session 23, "The True and Catholic Doctrine, Touching the Sacrament of Order," Ch. 4; Can. 7

[149] It is to be observed, that in regard to the different greater and lesser orders, to the episcopate, and to the matter and form of this sacrament, much more might be said, but we omit it here, as not necessary for the scope of this work. Moreover, such subjects, being somewhat difficult, would require to be treated at length, in order to be made intelligible to uninstructed persons.

of life; for he who does not live habitually in the grace of God, cannot pretend to occupy himself with the most sacred mysteries; 3) the gift of perpetual continence; and he who does not feel himself disposed to preserve this continence should on no account aspire to the sacerdotal state; 4) competent knowledge; for an ignorant man can never be a useful minister of Holy Church; 5) immunity from all censures and irregularities.

541. **Cannot the ecclesiastical state be entered on, like any other, when family convenience requires it, provided there be the intention of living in a manner conformable to that state?**
No family convenience, nor any other temporal motive, should determine one to embrace that estate, but the divine vocation alone. He who should receive holy orders without such vocation could not expect to live in a manner conformable to the ecclesiastical state, because he could not expect that God would give him the grace which he bestows on those whom he calls to serve him in the priesthood.

542. **Then he who should have received sacred orders without this divine vocation could not hope for salvation?**
Such a one would be in great peril; still, if, considering this peril, and detesting his rashness, he have recourse to the mercy of God, he will obtain the graces necessary for him to save his soul in the state he has entered on, and from which he can never withdraw, because it is a state which is immutable.

543. **What are the effects of this sacrament?**
1) The indelible character which it imprints on the soul, and 2) grace, as we observed in the section, "The Sacraments in General," above.

Matrimony

544. **Did Jesus Christ raise the marriage contract to the dignity of a sacrament?**
This is an article of the faith, as affirmed by the sacred Council of Trent.[150]

545. **Is it lawful for a man to have more than one wife?**
Under the old law, a man was permitted to have more than one wife at the same time; but it is forbidden by the new law. If, however, the first wife dies, it is lawful to take another; nay, it is an article of the faith that to marry successively a second, a third, or a fourth wife is lawful.

546. **Is marriage, after it is consummated, indissoluble?**
It is an article of the faith that, in the case of Christians, it is indissoluble. Marriage, in the case of infidels, may be dissolved if the party who is converted to the faith have good reason for ceasing to cohabit with the party who remains in infidelity.

547. **Is marriage indissoluble when only ratified, that is to say, after the marriage has been contracted, but before the wedded persons have yet cohabited?**
It is an article of the faith that it may be dissolved by means of religious profession. If the man enters an approved religious order, and makes his profession, the woman is free; and vice versa.

548. **Has the Church authority to declare impediments to marriage, which in certain cases may render the marriage unlawful and even invalid?**
This is an article of the faith, as declared by the sacred Council of Trent.[151]

549. **Is marriage commanded for all?**
Marriage is commanded to no one in particular; on the contrary, as of greater perfection, it is better to preserve oneself in perfect chastity. This is also an article of the faith, recognized as such in all ages of the Church, and

[150] Cf. Council of Trent, Session 7, "On the Sacraments in General," Can. 1; Session 24, "Doctrine on the Sacrament of Matrimony"; Can. 1

[151] Cf. Council of Trent, Session 24, Can. 4

so declared by the Council of Trent, where it is defined: "If anyone shall say that the married state is to be preferred to the estate of virginity or celibacy, and that it is not a better and a happier condition to remain in virginity or celibacy than to be joined in matrimony, let him be excommunicated."[152]

Appendix I

ON THE MODE OF TEACHING CHRISTIAN DOCTRINE TO CHILDREN

The Importance of This Teaching

1. Man's first and highest need is to know God and the truths which he has revealed. Without this knowledge, life must pass unhappily in this world, and will end in eternal misery in the next. This first and highest need of man becomes of urgent necessity, as soon as the light of reason dawns upon the understanding. Hence, while all other kinds of instruction may be deferred till the child has advanced in years, instruction in the truths of religion must not be delayed. On this account the teaching of Christian doctrine to children is of the highest importance, nay! of absolute necessity.

2. Moreover we must consider that the tenderest age is the best suited for such instruction; for if the first ideas which are communicated to children, when they attain the use of reason, are Christian ideas, these will become, as it were, natural to them, and will remain profoundly impressed on their minds: they will seem to have been born Christians rather than to have been made Christians; nor in later years will they easily suffer those ideas to be altered or effaced. Christian instruction, begun with the first development of the understanding, and carried on afterward, as it ought to

[152] Council of Trent, Session 24, Can. 10. Many other things might be mentioned concerning this sacrament, but as they are not suited to the primary scope of this little work, it is thought better to omit them.

be, with patient and diligent perseverance, is the surest guarantee we can have that the child will become a good youth and a good man.

3. For this reason, general councils, the supreme pontiffs, and the bishops have ever prescribed, by most earnest and vigorous precepts, that children should not be left without this instruction; and hence, also, men the most distinguished for learning and sanctity have always promoted it with indefatigable zeal, and have taken delight in making it their own personal care.

On the Method to Be Observed in This Instruction

1. This instruction should be uniform. Hence children should be taught only the catechism of the diocese, and, if possible, made to learn it word for word. Great confusion would be caused by the use of different catechisms. Moreover, a particular form of words is more easily retained, and keeps longer alive in the memory the substance or understanding of the things taught.

2. It is not meant, however, that the mere letter of the catechism is alone to be taught. Persons who are not instructed in theology should confine themselves to this, and content themselves with teaching the catechism as it stands, without expatiating on it or explaining it, because, as they are wanting in the necessary theological knowledge, they might very possibly teach grave error; but let those who are sufficiently instructed endeavor to dilate upon and explain it according to the children's capacity, in order that they may the better understand it, and that the truths which it contains may make a deeper impression on their minds.

3. But be careful not to think it always easy or desirable to explain too minutely to children the truths of Christian doctrine. This is not an easy matter, because in the mysteries of the faith we cannot know all that we should like to know, but only what God has chosen to manifest to us. St. Athanasius said, in regard to the mystery of the most Blessed Trinity, that we must be content to know just so much as the Church teaches us concerning it, and that the rest is covered by the wings of the cherubim. In like manner, as to the mystery of the incarnation, in regard to grace, and

to all other mysteries, you must not attempt to give a reason for every difficulty that you meet with, or expect to understand and be able to explain everything. Neither is it desirable; for, even supposing that he who is teaching Christian doctrine be very learned and capable of treating Catholic truths with profound depth and subtlety, still this would not be suitable for children, who are scarcely able to understand the subjects of primary importance, and that in a general way. Explain, therefore, Christian doctrine, but not too minutely, so that children may learn what is necessary, without having their minds confused rather than enlightened.

4. Another important caution is not to touch on those objections which cannot be answered so as fully to satisfy the unformed intellects of children, nor on those difficulties which cannot be cleared away by evident, or, so to speak, palpable reasons, of which alone the minds of children are capable. Such knowledge as is important for all, should be given to children, and that with the greatest possible clearness and simplicity; they have not to confute heretics, nor to sit in the chair of the teacher. This caution is very necessary for clerical students, who are sometimes apt to set to work to teach children what they themselves are learning in the schools.

5. Children must be taught gradually, beginning with such things as are most necessary to be known, and proceeding from these to the rest; hence they ought not to be taught a multitude of things at once. For example, you should begin by teaching them the existence of God, his attributes, the mysteries of the Trinity, the incarnation, etc., and so lead them on from one subject to another without confusion. You must, however, it is true, often recur to the previous subjects, in order that they may not be forgotten. And here I would insist on the importance of so explaining the divine attributes that children may conceive a grand idea of God, and the grandest idea possible; for this grand idea will be of the utmost service in causing the maxims of the holy love and fear of God to make a great impression on their hearts. We know that the reason why God is so little loved and so little feared by many Christians is because they have too little knowledge of his goodness and of his greatness.

6. Remember that in teaching children you cannot expect the same success with all. Therefore, let those who are quick and bright, and have

good memories, learn more; while you must be content that those who are slow and dull, and of feeble memory, should learn only those things that are really necessary. You will only lose time if you try to make dull children learn as many things as children of better capacity, and you will only puzzle them. Hence the prudent catechist will seek to instruct children of dull understanding only in such truths as are most important, and indispensably necessary for them to know.

The Maxims to Be Instilled into Children

1. Teaching children Christian doctrine should not be a bare, dry teaching of the truths of the faith, such as to tell them: there is a God; there is a hell; there is a heaven; there are seven sacraments, etc.; but it should be a teaching full of life and vigor, which inflames the heart at the same time that it enlightens the mind. This will be effected by teaching and explaining good Christian maxims; and I will here put down a few principal ones, by way of example. The first maxim is this: that God has placed us in this world, not that we may eat and drink and amuse ourselves, etc., but that we may know him, love him, and serve him now, and afterward enjoy him in heaven; you must thoroughly explain this fundamental maxim, and make children understand that whoever does not live in this world for the end of knowing, loving, and serving God and gaining heaven, lives ill, and deserves to be removed from the world, just as a vine which does not bear grapes, or a fig tree which bears no figs would deserve to be cut down and consumed.

2. That the grace of God is the greatest treasure, nay, the only real treasure that there is in the world; that, to preserve the grace of God in our hearts, we should throw overboard the whole world, if it were ours, and if it were necessary so to do in order to preserve the grace of God.

3. That the greatest evil is sin, which deprives us of the grace of God, and that it would be better to keep a live serpent in our bosoms than a mortal sin in our souls; and that, as he who should carry a live serpent in his bosom would be unable to eat, or sleep, or amuse himself, from the fear that at any moment this serpent might sting him to death, so it should

seem impossible that a person, who has ever so little faith, could eat, or sleep, or amuse himself, while he has on his soul a mortal sin, which at any moment might cast him into hell; and so, if a child have the misfortune—the greatest of all misfortunes—to commit a mortal sin, he should immediately make a lively act of contrition, and then, as soon as possible, go and confess it.

4. That he who has wicked companions has no need of the devil to tempt him, that he may go to hell; for it often happens that a wicked companion does more hurt to the soul than the devil himself. Moreover, unrestricted intercourse between boys and girls, if not evil, is always dangerous, and is displeasing to their guardian angels.

5. That it is far better not to go to confession at all, than to make a bad confession by concealing sins. With this object, it would be well for you to bring forward some terrible example of badly-made confessions.

6. That they must exercise themselves in acts of the love of God, which, according to St. Teresa, are like the wood which maintains and increases in the heart the holy fire of God's love. And here it will be well to suggest to children the practice of making them often in the course of the day, such, for instance, as, "My God, I love thee above all things"; "I love thee, O Lord, with my whole heart." Theologians are of opinion, that as soon as children attain the use of reason, they are bound to make acts of the love of God; yet, generally speaking, they are not instructed or incited to fulfill this duty, and, from the natural thoughtlessness of childhood, they themselves think but little of it. In order, therefore, that they may acquire the habit of making frequent acts of the love of God, it will be well for you to examine them from time to time as to this.

7. That a person, truly devout to our Blessed Lady, was never lost. And here I would exhort you carefully to instill into the hearts of children this tender and fervent devotion, teaching them ever to regard Mary as a most loving Mother, and to have recourse to her in all their needs. Among other practice, you might suggest to them the following easy and most fruitful devotion: that every morning and evening they should say three *Aves*, adding this short prayer: "Dear Mother, keep me from mortal sin. Dear Mother, let me rather die than offend God."

8. If such and similar maxims are instilled into the hearts of children and young persons, at the same time that you teach them Christian doctrine, they will be easily trained to goodness and piety: and these maxims, being thoroughly impressed on their hearts in early years, will never be effaced in later life.

The Qualifications Which Persons Who Teach Children Christian Doctrine Should Strive to Acquire

1. He who has to teach children must be patient, grave, and kind. He must, in the first place, be patient, because children, either from a heaviness of disposition, or from a rude upbringing, or from thoughtlessness and levity, are often tiresome and difficult to manage. You must compassionate them: all the evil which is in them is not pure malice, and sometimes certain defects exist which you must put up with. Hence that saint said well when he said to children: "Be wise, if you can." You must affect not to see many faults and acts of thoughtlessness, which after all are of no great consequence. When the faults are really considerable, you must take the opportunity of scolding them, or punishing them; but, if a child finds himself scolded and punished for every trifle, while he knows not how to avoid all these scoldings and punishments, he will begin to care for neither the one nor the other, and so will gradually become insensible, and therefore incorrigible.

2. You must preserve a befitting gravity, in order that the children may always have the necessary respect for their master, without which there will be neither attention nor profit. The catechist, therefore, must always preserve a certain decorum of countenance and manner, in order that the children may respect him. This caution is especially necessary, even on other accounts, for all who teach children.

3. But gravity must not be separated from kindness, in order that children may take pleasure in being with those who teach them Christian doctrine. If your manners are harsh and repulsive, you will alienate the minds of the children from your teaching, and the few who are present will soon grow weary, be distracted, and learn nothing.

4. Those, however, who teach Christian doctrine with true zeal, will never find themselves deficient in the requisite qualifications, for the love of God will teach them how to profit by all means and opportunities. Cultivate, therefore, a great love of God, reflect how important a thing it is to instruct the mind and form the heart of youth, and then you may hope for abundant fruit from your labors. In the eyes of some, those labors may appear of small esteem and little honor, because they are expended on children of tender age, and often of rude natures and low birth, but in the eyes of God, who does not regard things with the prejudices of human vanity, they are of priceless value.

Appendix II

IMPORTANT INSTRUCTIONS REGARDING THE ADMINISTRATION OF THE HOLY SACRAMENTS TO THE SICK

Instruction I: In Regard to Confession

All Christians, whether men or women, who are prevented by sickness from repairing to the Church, even although not in danger of death, may be confessed at home; and this for many reasons. First, because they may be in a state of mortal sin, and so have need of confession that they may regain the grace of God. Secondly, because it often happens that illnesses, which at the beginning do not appear dangerous, unexpectedly become serious, so as even to deprive the patient of the use of his senses. Moreover, this doctrine goes back to the decrees of the Lateran Council under Pope Innocent III and St. Pius V. These decrees are common both to men and women, as the reasons which induced the Church to issue them are common to both. Observe that there is no need to ask the doctor's permission to receive this sacrament, nay, that it would be ridiculous to ask the doctor's permission to do that which the Church not only permits but commands.

Instruction II: In Regard to the Holy Viaticum

The holy viaticum, according to the teaching of all theologians, may be administered whenever the illness is serious, and there is danger of death, although there may yet be good hope of recovery. I say "a serious illness with danger of death," because a serious illness necessarily implies peril of life; nay, in all grave maladies, fatal and sudden danger is to be feared. Except in clear cases, the doctor will judge of the gravity and danger of the illness. But observe that if the patient have reason to believe his illness serious and dangerous, (provided the doctor do not absolutely affirm the contrary) he may insist on the administration of the holy viaticum, even though he may be told, in all sincerity, that his illness is not desperate, nay that there is every probable appearance of his recovery.

Instruction III: In Regard to Extreme Unction

Observe, in the first place, that this sacrament is so called, not because it is to be administered at the last moment of life, but because it is the extreme, or last of the sacred unctions which the Church gives.

Observe, secondly, that extreme unction, like the holy viaticum, may be administered every time there is serious illness with danger of death, as already stated. And, as this is a point on which great ignorance commonly prevails, it is well you should hear how St. Alphonsus Liguori speaks of it. Here is a faithful translation of his words: "The doctors of the Church, such as Suarez, Layman, Castropalao, Bonacina, Conninch, the Salmanticenses and others, are commonly agreed, that it suffices that the sickness be perilous to life, at least remotely." It suffices, therefore, that there be remote danger. He goes on to prove this doctrine from the authority of the Councils of Aquisgrana, Magonza, Florence, and Trent. And he then proceeds thus: "This was confirmed still more clearly by Benedict XIV in the bull already quoted, in which it is said that the sacrament of extreme unction is not to be administered to those who are in health, but only to those who are seriously ill; on which account, Castropalao says correctly that whenever the Holy Communion can be given to a sick person as the viaticum and, therefore, without fasting, extreme unction may be given, and it is expedient to give it." Therefore, when a sick person has received the holy viaticum, he may ask for extreme unction, and he has a right to receive it.[153]

These instructions may be useful as rules, not only for the sick themselves, but also for their relations and for doctors.

Profession of the Catholic Faith

I, N. N., with a firm faith believe and profess all and every one of those things which are contained in that Creed which the holy Roman Church maketh use of. To wit:

I believe in one God, the Father Almighty, Maker of heaven and earth, and of all things visible and invisible; and in one Lord Jesus Christ, the only begotten Son of God, born of the Father before all ages; God of God; light of light; true God of true God; begotten, not made, consubstantial with the Father, by whom all things were made. Who for us men, and for our salvation, came down from heaven, and was incarnate by the Holy Ghost of the Virgin Mary, and was made man. Crucified also for us under Pontius Pilate, he suffered, and was buried. And the third day he rose again according to the scriptures; he ascended into heaven, sitteth at the right hand of the Father, and shall come again with glory to judge the living and the dead; of whose kingdom there shall be no end. I believe in the Holy Ghost, the Lord and lifegiver, who proceedeth from the Father and the Son: who together with the Father and the Son is adored and glorified; who spake by the prophets. And in one, holy, Catholic, and apostolic

[153] At Paris it is customary to give extreme unction immediately after the viaticum, as we read in the life of Victorine de Gallard, who died in 1836 (*Life*, Pt. 4).

Church. I confess one baptism for the remission of sins, and I look for the resurrection of the dead, and the life of the world to come. Amen.

I most steadfastly admit and embrace the apostolical and ecclesiastical traditions, and all other observances and constitutions of the same Church. I also admit the holy scriptures, according to that sense which our holy mother the Church hath held and doth hold, to whom it belongeth to judge of the true sense and interpretation of the scriptures: neither will I ever take and interpret them otherwise than according to the unanimous consent of the fathers.

I also profess that there are truly and properly seven sacraments of the new law, instituted by Jesus Christ our Lord, and necessary for the salvation of mankind, though not all for everyone; to wit: baptism, confirmation, the Eucharist, penance, extreme unction, order, and matrimony; and that they confer grace; and that of these, baptism, confirmation, and order cannot be repeated without sacrilege. I also receive and admit the received and approved ceremonies of the Catholic Church, used in the solemn administration of the aforesaid sacraments.

I embrace and receive all and every one of the things which have been defined and declared in the holy Council of Trent, concerning original sin and justification.

I profess, likewise, that in the Mass there is offered to God a true, proper, and propitiatory sacrifice for the living and the dead. And that in the most Holy Sacrament of the Eucharist there is truly, really, and substantially the body and blood, together with the soul and divinity of our Lord Jesus Christ; and that there is made a conversion of the whole substance of the bread into the body; and of the whole substance of the wine into the blood; which conversion the Catholic Church calls transubstantiation. I also confess that under either kind alone, Christ is received whole and entire, and a true sacrament.

I constantly hold that there is a purgatory, and that the souls, therein detained, are helped by the suffrages of the faithful.

Likewise, that the saints, reigning together with Christ, are to be honored and invocated, and that they offer prayers to God for us, and that their relics are to be had in veneration.

I most firmly assert that the images of Christ, of the Mother of God, ever Virgin, and also of other saints, ought to be had and retained, and that due honor and veneration are to be given them.

I also affirm that the power of indulgences was left by Christ in the Church, and that the use of them is most wholesome to Christian people.

I acknowledge the holy, Catholic, apostolic, and Roman Church for the mother and mistress of all churches; and I promise true obedience to the bishop of Rome, successor of St. Peter, prince of the apostles, and vicar of Jesus Christ.

I likewise undoubtedly receive and profess all other things delivered, defined, and declared by the sacred canons and general councils, and particularly by the holy Council of Trent. And I condemn, reject, and anathematize all things contrary thereto, and all heresies which the Church has condemned, rejected, and anathematized.

I, N. N., do at this present freely profess and sincerely hold this true Catholic faith, without which no one can be saved; and I promise most constantly to retain and confess the same, entire and inviolate, by God's assistance, to the end of my life, and to procure, as far as in me lies, that it shall be preached, taught, and observed by all those who depend on me, and all those who shall be committed to my charge.

So help me God.

The Catholic Christian has in this Profession an excellent act of faith, and a certain rule by which to recognize all protestants.

COMPENDIO

DELLA

DOTTRINA CRISTIANA

PRESCRITTO DA S. S. PAPA PIO X

ILLUSTRATO CON SIMILITUDINI ED ESEMPI

CATECHISMO MAGGIORE

PRIMO VOLUME

Del Credo e dell' Orazione

MILANO

Premiata Tipografia Pontif. ed Arciv. di S. Giuseppe

Via S. Calocero N. 9

1906

Cover of the first "illustrated" edition of the Compendium: *Milan, 1906.*

COMPENDIO

DELLA

DOTTRINA CRISTIANA

PRESCRITTO DA S. S. PAPA PIO X

ILLUSTRATO CON SIMILITUDINI ED ESEMPI

CATECHISMO MAGGIORE

PRIMO VOLUME

Del Credo e dell' Orazione

MILANO

Premiata Tipografia Pontif. ed Areiv. di S. Giuseppe

Via S. Calocero N. 9

1906

Translator's Introduction (Excerpt)

The catechism, as we now know it, is of comparatively recent origin. Previous to the invention of printing, and the consequent possibility of the spread of books and education among the masses of the people, the widespread use of a catechism was plainly out of the question. Its place was supplied by brief formulae, not infrequently set to rhyme, which were committed to memory and handed down from generation to generation, conveying a brief statement of the truths more necessary to salvation. The nearest approaches to the modern catechism would be St. Cyril's *Catechesis*, St. Augustine's *Instruction of the Ignorant*, and, later on, certain works of Alcuin, Rabanus Maurus, and Gerson.

The publication and widespread diffusion of an infinity of catechisms compiled by Luther and his followers for the purpose of disseminating their new doctrines, stimulated the energies of Catholic writers in a similar direction; and accordingly several Catholic catechisms were issued within the next few years giving a clear and simple statement of Catholic doctrine, particularly on those points that were being attacked by the reformers. Of these, several of which were prescribed for diocesan use, the principal were those of Erasmus, Witzel, Dietenberg, Fabri, Titelmann, Hosius, and Blessed Peter Canisius, in Germany; of Parvi, de Bourbon, du Bellay, de Thou, in France; of Sonnius, Hessel, and Hunnaeus, in the Low Countries; of Dominic Soto, John of St. Thomas, and Florez, in Spain; of Bartholomew of the Martyrs and Louis of Granada, in Portugal; and of Cardinal Contarini, Marini, and Crispoldi, in Italy.

But, as already pointed out, the fathers of the Council of Trent showed at a very early date that they were satisfied with none of the existing works, and that they were fully alive to the need and necessity of preparing an authoritative catechism. The realization of their desire, however, was retarded for several years by events over which they had little control; and when the work was finally taken in hand another idea prevailed, resulting in the publication of a manual for the use of the clergy, and not, as originally suggested, a catechism for children and uninstructed adults.

Of the countless catechisms that continued to appear, two—those of Bellarmine and Canisius[1]—have steadily held their ground ever since, and to a large extent have served as the models of nearly all subsequent compilations of the kind. The influence of Canisius, however, has on the whole been limited to Germany; whereas Bellarmine's catechism, which was written by command of Pope Clement VIII in 1597, has been copied in almost every other country in the world. At an early date it was translated into Arabic, Latin, Modern Greek, French, Spanish, German, English, and Polish. It had the warm approbation of Clement VIII, who prescribed it for use in the Papal States; of Urban VIII, who directed it to be adopted in all the Eastern missions; of Innocent XIII and Benedict XIV; particularly of the very important council of all Italy, held at Rome, in 1725, which made it obligatory in all the dioceses of the peninsula; and finally of the Vatican Council which indicated it as the model for a proposed universal catechism.

Though Bellarmine's catechism was largely followed as a model all over the world, yet, owing to the modifications introduced in diocesan editions, it came to pass in the course of time that almost every diocese had its own catechism, differing in many respects from the catechisms of other dioceses.

The obvious inconvenience of this bewildering multiplicity of catechisms occupied the attention of the fathers of the Vatican Council, the great majority of whom were agreed as to the desirability of having a uniform small catechism for the faithful all over the world. Early during the sittings of the council, forty-one of the assembled fathers devoted six sessions (February 10 to February 22) to an examination of the question; and the report which they drew up occupied the attention of the whole council during the sittings of April 29 and 30. The question being put to a vote on May 4, an immense majority was found to be in favor of the compilation of a small uniform catechism, to be compiled in Latin, translated into every

[1] Editor's note: St. Robert Bellarmine's *A Shorte Catechisme* is included in Volume II of this series. The catechism of St. Peter Canisius is included in Volume IX of this series.

language, and made obligatory in every diocese.[2] But the approach of the Italian troops toward the walls of Rome brought the council to an untimely end and there was no time to promulgate the constitution on the proposed uniform catechism, so that it has not the force of law.

The idea, however, has never been lost sight of. During the sitting of the first Catechetical Congress in 1880, the then bishop of Mantua (now Pius X) proposed that the holy father be petitioned to arrange for the compilation of a simple, plain, brief, and popular catechism for uniform use all over the world. Shortly after his elevation to the chair of Peter, Pius X at once set about realizing, within certain limits, his own proposal of 1880, by prescribing a uniform catechism—the *Compendium of Christian Doctrine*—for use in the dioceses of the ecclesiastical province of Rome, at the same time indicating that it was his earnest desire to have the same manual adopted all over Italy. The text selected was, with slight modifications, that which had been adopted for some years by the united hierarchy of Piedmont, Liguria, Lombardy, Emilia, and Tuscany. It contains three catechisms. The first, which is intended for infant schools and for the home, and which covers about thirteen pages, sets forth briefly the more elementary truths of faith, chiefly by way of formulae to be committed to memory. The second part, called the *Short Catechism*, is intended chiefly for primary schools and for children preparing for the sacraments. It contains about sixty pages devoted to a brief exposition of the doctrine of the Creed, sacraments, commandments, and prayer. The *Larger Catechism*, which forms the third part, explains these at greater length in about two hundred pages. It is succeeded by an explanation of the principal feasts of the year, covering sixty pages, followed by forty pages of a brief history of religion, and concludes with a certain number of daily prayers, and prayers for special occasions.

[2] Cf. *Coll. Lac.*, vol. 7, 666-667

Preliminary Lesson

On Christian Doctrine and Its Principal Parts

1. **Are you a Christian?**
Yes, I am a Christian, by the grace of God.

2. **Why do you say, "by the grace of God"?**
I say, "by the grace of God," because to be a Christian is a perfectly gratuitous gift of God, which we ourselves could not have merited.

3. **Who is a true Christian?**
A true Christian is he who is baptized, who believes and professes the Christian doctrine, and obeys the lawful pastors of the Church.

4. **What is Christian doctrine?**
Christian doctrine is the doctrine which Jesus Christ our Lord taught us to show us the way of salvation.

5. **Is it necessary to learn the doctrine taught by Jesus Christ?**
It certainly is necessary to learn the doctrine taught by Jesus Christ, and those who fail to do so are guilty of a grave breach of duty.

6. **Are parents and guardians bound to send their children and those dependent on them to catechism?**
Parents and guardians are bound to see that their children and dependents learn Christian doctrine, and they are guilty before God if they neglect this duty.

7. **From whom are we to receive and learn Christian doctrine?**
We are to receive and learn Christian doctrine from the holy Catholic Church.

8. **How are we certain that the Christian doctrine which we receive from the holy Catholic Church is really true?**
We are certain that the doctrine which we receive from the holy Catholic Church is true, because Jesus Christ, the divine author of this doctrine, committed it through his apostles to the Church, which he founded and made the infallible teacher of all men, promising her his divine assistance until the end of time.

9. **Are there other proofs of the truth of Christian doctrine?**
The truth of Christian doctrine is also shown by the eminent sanctity of numbers who have professed it and who still profess it, by the heroic fortitude of the martyrs, by its marvelous and rapid propagation in the world, and by its perfect preservation throughout so many centuries of ceaseless and varied struggles.

10. **What and how many are the principal and most necessary parts of Christian doctrine?**
The principal and most necessary parts of Christian doctrine are four: the Creed, the Our Father, the commandments, and the sacraments.

11. **What does the Creed teach us?**
The Creed teaches us the principal articles of our holy faith.

12. **What does the Our Father teach us?**
The Our Father teaches us all that we are to hope from God, and all we are to ask of him.

13. **What do the commandments teach us?**
The commandments teach us all that we are to do to please God—all of which is summed up in loving God above all things and our neighbor as ourselves for the love of God.

14. **What does the doctrine of the sacraments teach us?**

The doctrine of the sacraments shows us the nature and right use of those means which Jesus Christ has instituted to remit our sins, give us his grace, infuse into and increase in us the virtues of faith, hope, and charity.

SECTION I

The Symbol of the Apostles, Commonly Called the Creed

The Creed in General

15. **What is the first part of Christian doctrine?**
The first part of Christian doctrine is the Symbol of the apostles, commonly called the Creed.

16. **Why do you call the Creed the Symbol of the apostles?**
The Creed is called the Symbol of the apostles because it is a summary of the truths of faith taught by the apostles.

17. **How many articles are there in the Creed?**
There are twelve articles in the Creed.

18. **Recite them.**
1) I believe in God, the Father Almighty, Creator of heaven and earth; 2) and in Jesus Christ, his only Son, our Lord; 3) who was conceived by the Holy Ghost; born of the Virgin Mary; 4) suffered under Pontius Pilate, was crucified, dead, and buried; 5) he descended into hell; the third day he rose again from the dead; 6) he ascended into heaven, sitteth at the right hand of God the Father Almighty; 7) from thence he shall come to judge the living and the dead. 8) I believe in the Holy Ghost; 9) the holy Catholic Church; the communion of saints; 10) the forgiveness of sins; 11) the resurrection of the body; 12) life everlasting. Amen.

19. **What is meant by the word, *I believe,* which you say at the beginning of the Symbol?**
The word, *I believe*, means I hold everything that is contained in these twelve articles to be perfectly true; and I believe these truths more firmly than if I saw them with my eyes, because God, who can neither deceive nor be deceived, has revealed them to the holy Catholic Church and through this Church to us.

20. **What do the articles of the Creed contain?**
The articles of the Creed contain the principal truths to be believed concerning God, Jesus Christ, and the Church, his spouse.

21. **Is it useful to recite the Creed frequently?**
It is most useful to recite the Creed frequently, so as to impress the truths of faith more and more deeply on our hearts.

The First Article of the Creed

God the Father Almighty

22. **What does the first article of the Creed: "I believe in God, the Father Almighty, Creator of heaven and earth," teach us?**
The first article of the Creed teaches us that there is one God, and only one; that he is omnipotent and has created heaven and earth and all things contained in them, that is to say, the whole universe.

23. **How do we know that there is a God?**
We know that there is a God because reason proves it and faith confirms it.

24. **Why do we call God the Father?**
We call God the Father because by nature he is the Father of the second Person of the Blessed Trinity, that is to say, of the Son begotten of him; because God is the Father of all men, whom he has created and whom he preserves and governs; finally, because by grace he is the Father of all good Christians, who are hence called the adopted sons of God.

25. **Why is the Father the first Person of the Blessed Trinity?**
The Father is the first Person of the Blessed Trinity, because he does not proceed from any other Person, but is the principle of the other two Persons, that is, of the Son and of the Holy Ghost.

26. **What is meant by the word *omnipotent*?**
The word *omnipotent* means that God can do all that he wills.

27. **God can neither sin nor die, how then do we say he can do all things?**
Though he can neither sin nor die, we say God can do all things, because to be able to sin or die is not an effect of power, but of weakness which cannot exist in God who is most perfect.

On the Creation

28. **What is meant by the words: "Creator of heaven and earth"?**
To create means to make out of nothing; hence, God is called the "Creator of heaven and of earth," because he made heaven and earth and all things contained therein, that is, the whole universe, out of nothing.

29. **Was the world created by the Father alone?**
The world was created by all the three divine Persons, because whatever one Person does with regard to creatures is done by the other two Persons in one and the selfsame act.

30. **Why then is creation specially attributed to the Father?**
Creation is specially attributed to the Father because creation is a work of divine omnipotence, which is specially attributed to the Father, just as wisdom is attributed to the Son, and goodness to the Holy Ghost, though all three Persons possess the same omnipotence, wisdom, and goodness.

31. **Does God take any interest in the world and in the things created by him?**
Yes, God takes an interest in the world and in all things created by him; he preserves them, and governs them by his infinite goodness and wisdom; and nothing happens here below that he does not either will or permit.

32. **Why do you say that nothing happens here below that he does not either will or permit?**
We say that nothing happens here below that he does not either will or permit, because there are some things which God wills and commands, while there are others which he simply does not prevent, such as sin.

33. **Why does not God prevent sin?**
God does not prevent sin, because even from the very abuse man makes of the liberty with which he is endowed, God knows how to bring forth good and to make his mercy or his justice become more and more resplendent.

The Angels

34. **Which are the noblest of God's creatures?**
The noblest creatures created by God are the angels.

35. **Who are the angels?**
The angels are intelligent and purely spiritual creatures.

36. **Why did God create the angels?**
God created the angels so as to be honored and served by them, and to give them eternal happiness.

37. **What form and figure have the angels?**
The angels have neither form nor material figure of any kind, because they are pure spirits created by God in such a way as to exist without having to be united to a body.

38. **Why then are the angels represented under sensible forms?**
The angels are represented under sensible forms: 1) as a help to our imagination; and 2) because they have thus appeared many times to men, as we read in sacred scripture.

39. **Were all the angels faithful to God?**
No, the angels were not all faithful to God, many of them through pride claimed to be his equals and independent of him—for which sin they were banished forever from paradise and condemned to hell.

40. **How are the angels called who were banished forever from paradise and condemned to hell?**
The angels banished forever from paradise and condemned to hell are called demons, and their chief is called Lucifer or Satan.

41. **Can the demons do us any harm?**
Yes, the demons can do us great harm both in soul and body, especially by tempting us to sin, provided God permits them to do so.

42. **Why do they tempt us?**
The demons tempt us because of the envy they bear us, which makes them desire our eternal damnation; and because of their hatred of God, whose image is reflected in us. God on the other hand permits these temptations in order that we may overcome them by his grace, and thus practice virtue and acquire merit for heaven.

43. **How are temptations conquered?**
Temptations are conquered by watchfulness, prayer, and Christian mortification.

44. **How are the angels called who remained faithful to God?**

The angels who remained faithful to God are called the good angels, heavenly spirits, or simply angels.

45. **What became of the angels who remained faithful to God?**

The angels who remained faithful to God were confirmed in grace, forever enjoy the vision of God, love him, bless him, and praise him eternally.

46. **Does God use the angels as his ministers?**

Yes, God uses the angels as his ministers, and especially does he entrust to many of them the office of acting as our guardians and protectors.

47. **Should we have a particular devotion to our guardian angel?**

Yes, we should have a particular devotion to our guardian angel; we should honor him, invoke his aid, follow his inspirations, and be grateful to him for the continual assistance he affords us.

Man

48. **Which is the noblest creature God has placed on earth?**

The noblest creature God has placed on earth is man.

49. **What is man?**

Man is a rational creature composed of soul and body.

50. **What is the soul?**

The soul is the noblest part of man, because it is a spiritual substance, endowed with intelligence and will, capable of knowing God and of possessing him for all eternity.

51. **Can the human soul be seen and touched?**

Our soul can neither be seen nor touched, because it is a spirit.

52. **Does the human soul die with the body?**
The human soul never dies: faith and our very reason prove that it is immortal.

53. **Is man free in his actions?**
Yes, man is free in his actions and each one feels within himself that he can do a thing or leave it undone, or do one thing rather than another.

54. **Explain human liberty by an example.**
If I voluntarily tell a lie, I know that I could have left it unsaid or that I could have remained silent, and that, on the other hand, I could also speak differently and tell the truth.

55. **Why do we say that man was created to the image and likeness of God?**
We say that man was created to the image and likeness of God because the human soul is spiritual and rational, free in its operations, capable of knowing and loving God and of enjoying him forever—perfections which reflect a ray of the infinite greatness of the Lord in us.

56. **In what state did God place our first parents, Adam and Eve?**
God placed our first parents, Adam and Eve, in the state of innocence and grace; but they soon fell away by sin.

57. **Besides innocence and sanctifying grace did God confer any other gifts on our first parents?**
Besides innocence and sanctifying grace, God conferred on our first parents other gifts, which, along with sanctifying grace, they were to transmit to their descendants; these were: integrity, that is, the perfect subjection of sense reason; immortality; immunity from all pain and sorrow; and a knowledge in keeping with their state.

58. **What was the nature of Adam's sin?**
Adam's sin was a sin of pride and of grave disobedience.

59. **What chastisement was meted out to the sin of Adam and Eve?**
Adam and Eve lost the grace of God and the right they had to heaven; they were driven out of the earthly paradise, subjected to many miseries of soul and body, and condemned to death.

60. **If Adam and Eve had not sinned, would they have been exempt from death?**
If Adam and Eve had not sinned and if they had remained faithful to God, they would, after a happy and tranquil sojourn here on earth, and without dying, have been transferred by God into heaven, to enjoy a life of unending glory.

61. **Were these gifts due to man?**
These gifts were in no way due to man, but were absolutely gratuitous and supernatural; and hence, when Adam disobeyed the divine command, God could without any injustice deprive both Adam and his posterity of them.

62. **Is this sin proper to Adam alone?**
This sin is not Adam's sin alone, but it is also our sin, though in a different sense. It is Adam's sin because he committed it by an act of his will, and hence in him it was a personal sin. It is our sin also because Adam, having committed it in his capacity as the head and source of the human race, it was transmitted by natural generation to all his descendants: and hence in us it is original sin.

63. **How is it possible for original sin to be transmitted to all men?**
Original sin is transmitted to all men because God, having conferred sanctifying grace and other supernatural gifts on the human race in Adam, on the condition that Adam should not disobey him; and Adam having disobeyed, as head and father of the human race, rendered human nature rebellious against God. And hence, human nature is transmitted to all the descendants of Adam in a state of rebellion against God, and deprived of divine grace and other gifts.

64. **Do all men contract original sin?**

Yes, all men contract original sin, with the exception of the Blessed Virgin, who was preserved from it by a singular privilege of God, in view of the merits of Jesus Christ our Savior.

65. **Could not men be saved after Adam's sin?**

After Adam's sin men could not be saved, if God had not shown mercy toward them.

66. **What was the mercy shown by God to the human race?**

The mercy shown by God to the human race was that of immediately promising Adam a divine Redeemer or Messiah, and of sending this Messiah in his own good time to free men from the slavery of sin and of the devil.

67. **Who is the promised Messiah?**

The promised Messiah is Jesus Christ, as the second article of the Creed teaches.

The Second Article of the Creed

68. **What are we taught in the second article: "And in Jesus Christ his only Son our Lord"?**

The second article of the Creed teaches us that the Son of God is the second Person of the Blessed Trinity; that, like the Father, he is God eternal, omnipotent, Creator, and Lord; that he became man to save us; and that the Son of God, made man, is called Jesus Christ.

69. **Why is the second Person called the Son?**
The second Person is called the Son, because he is begotten by the Father from all eternity by way of intelligence; and for this reason he is also called the eternal Word of the Father.

70. **Since we also are sons of God, why is Jesus Christ called the only Son of God the Father?**
Jesus Christ is called the only Son of God the Father, because he alone is his Son by nature, whereas we are his sons by creation and adoption.

71. **Why is Jesus Christ called our Lord?**
Jesus Christ is called our Lord, because, not only did he, together with the Father and the Holy Ghost, create us as God; but he has also redeemed us as God and man.

72. **Why is the Son of God made man called Jesus?**
The Son of God made man is called Jesus, that is to say, "Savior," because he has saved us from the eternal death merited by our sins.

73. **Who gave the name of Jesus to the Son of God made man?**
The eternal Father himself, through the archangel Gabriel, gave the name of Jesus to the Son of God made man, at the moment when the archangel announced to the Blessed Virgin the mystery of the incarnation.

74. **Why is the Son of God made man also called Christ?**
The Son of God made man is also called Christ, that is to say, "anointed" or "consecrated," because kings, priests, and prophets were anointed of old; and Jesus is the King of kings, high priest, and supreme prophet.

75. **Was Jesus Christ really anointed and consecrated with a material anointing?**
The anointing of Jesus Christ was not material, like that of the kings, priests, and prophets of old, but wholly spiritual and divine, because the fullness of the divinity dwells in him substantially.

76. **Had men any idea of Jesus Christ previous to his coming?**
Yes, previous to his coming men had some idea of Jesus Christ in the promise of the Messiah, which God made to our first parents, Adam and Eve, and which he renewed to the holy patriarchs; and also in the prophecies and the many figures which foreshadowed him.

77. **How do we know that Jesus Christ is truly the Messiah and promised Redeemer?**
We know that Jesus Christ is truly the Messiah and promised Redeemer from the fact that in him are verified: 1) all that the prophecies foretold, and 2) all that the figures of the old testament foreshadowed.

78. **What did the prophecies foretell of the Redeemer?**
Regarding the Redeemer, the prophecies foretold the tribe and the family from which he was to come; the place and time of his birth; his miracles and the most minute circumstances of his passion and death; his resurrection and ascension into heaven; and his spiritual, perpetual, and universal kingdom, that is, the holy Catholic Church.

79. **Which are the principal figures of the Redeemer in the old testament?**
The principal figures of the Redeemer in the old testament are: the innocent Abel; the high priest Melchizedech; the sacrifice of Isaac; Joseph sold by his brethren; the prophet Jonah; the paschal lamb; and the brazen serpent set up by Moses in the desert.

80. **How do you know that Jesus Christ is true God?**
We know that Jesus Christ is true God: 1) from the testimony of the Father saying: "This is my beloved Son in whom I am well pleased, hear ye him";[3] 2) from the attestation of Jesus Christ himself, confirmed by the most stupendous miracles; 3) from the teaching of the apostles; 4) from the unvarying tradition of the Catholic Church.

[3] Mt 17:5; 3:17; Mk 9:6; Lk 9:35; 2 Pt 1:17

81. **Mention the chief miracles wrought by Jesus Christ.**
Besides his resurrection, the chief miracles wrought by Jesus Christ are: the restoring of health to the sick, of sight to the blind, of hearing to the deaf, and of life to the dead.

The Third Article of the Creed

82. **What is taught in the third article: "Who was conceived by the Holy Ghost, born of the Virgin Mary"?**
The third article of the Creed teaches that by the operation of the Holy Ghost the Son of God took a body and soul like ours, in the chaste womb of the Virgin Mary, and that he was born of that Virgin.

83. **Did the Father and the Son also take part in forming the body and creating the soul of Jesus Christ?**
Yes, the whole three divine Persons cooperated in forming the body and in creating the soul of Jesus Christ.

84. **Why then is it simply said, "He was conceived by the Holy Ghost"?**
It is simply said, "He was conceived by the Holy Ghost," because the incarnation of the Son of God is a work of goodness and love, and the works of goodness and love are attributed to the Holy Ghost.

85. **In becoming man did the Son of God cease to be God?**
No, the Son of God became man without ceasing to be God.

86. **Jesus Christ, then, is God and man at the same time?**
Yes, the incarnate Son of God, that is, Jesus Christ, is both God and man, perfect God and perfect man.

87. **Are there, then, two natures in Jesus Christ?**
Yes, in Jesus Christ, who is both God and man, there are two natures, the divine and the human.

88. **In Jesus Christ are there also two Persons, the divine and the human?**
No, in the Son of God made man there is only one Person, namely, the divine.

89. **How many wills are there in Jesus Christ?**
In Jesus Christ there are two wills, the one divine, the other human.

90. **Did Jesus Christ possess free will?**
Yes, Jesus Christ possessed free will, but he could not do evil, since to be able to do evil is a defect, and not a perfection, of liberty.

91. **Are the Son of God and the Son of Mary one and the same Person?**
Yes, the Son of God and the Son of Mary are one and the same Person, that is, Jesus Christ, true God and true man.

92. **Is the Blessed Virgin the Mother of God?**
Yes, the Blessed Virgin is the Mother of God, because she is the Mother of Jesus Christ, who is true God.

93. **How did Mary become the Mother of Jesus Christ?**
Mary became the Mother of Jesus Christ solely through the operation and power of the Holy Ghost.

94. **Is it of faith that Mary was always a Virgin?**
Yes, it is of faith that the most holy Mary was always a Virgin, and she is called the Virgin of virgins.

The Fourth Article of the Creed

95. **What are we taught in the fourth article: "Suffered under Pontius Pilate, was crucified, dead, and buried"?**
The fourth article of the Creed teaches us that to redeem the world by his precious blood Jesus Christ suffered under Pontius Pilate, the governor of Judea, died on the tree of the cross, and, on being taken down therefrom, was buried.

96. **What does the word *suffered* denote?**
The word *suffered* denotes all the pains endured by Jesus Christ during his passion.

97. **Did Jesus Christ suffer as God or as man?**
Jesus Christ suffered as man alone; as God he could neither suffer nor die.

98. **What class of punishment was that of the cross?**
The punishment of the cross in those days was the cruelest and the most ignominious of all punishments.

99. **Who was it that condemned Jesus Christ to be crucified?**
He who condemned Jesus Christ to be crucified was Pontius Pilate, the governor of Judea who, through recognizing his innocence, cravenly yielded to the threats of the people of Jerusalem.

100. **Could not Jesus Christ have freed himself from the hands of Pilate and the Jews?**
Yes, Jesus Christ could have freed himself from the hands of Pilate and the Jews, but knowing it was his eternal Father's will that he should suffer and die for our salvation, he voluntarily submitted; nay, he himself went forth to meet his enemies and freely permitted himself to be taken and led to death.

101. **Where was Jesus Christ crucified?**
Jesus Christ was crucified on Mount Calvary.

102. **What did Jesus Christ do while on the cross?**
On the cross Jesus Christ prayed for his enemies; gave his own most Blessed Mother as a Mother to St. John, and, in his person, to all of us; offered up his death in sacrifice; and satisfied the justice of God for the sins of men.

103. **Would it not have been enough for an angel to come and make satisfaction for us?**
No, it would not have been enough for an angel to come and make satisfaction for us, because the offense given to God by sin was, in a certain sense, infinite, and to satisfy for it a person possessing infinite merit was required.

104. **To satisfy divine justice, was it necessary that Jesus Christ should be both God and man?**
Yes; to be able to suffer and die it was necessary that Jesus Christ should be man; while for his sufferings to be of infinite value it was necessary that he should be God.

105. **Why was it necessary that the merits of Jesus Christ should be of infinite value?**
It was necessary that the merits of Jesus Christ should be of infinite value, because God's majesty, which had been offended by sin, is infinite.

106. **Was it necessary for Jesus Christ to suffer as much as he actually did?**
No, it was not absolutely necessary for Jesus Christ to suffer as much as he did, because each of his acts being of infinite value, the least of his sufferings would have sufficed for our redemption.

107. **Why, then, did Jesus suffer so much?**
Jesus Christ suffered so much in order to satisfy divine justice all the more abundantly; to display his love for us still more; and to inspire us with the deepest horror of sin.

108. **Did anything remarkable happen at the death of Jesus Christ?**
Yes, at the death of Jesus Christ, the sun was darkened, the earth trembled, graves opened, and many of the dead arose.

109. **Where was the body of Jesus Christ buried?**
The body of Jesus Christ was buried in a new grave, hewn out of a rock, on the mount not far from where he had been crucified.

110. **Was the divinity separated from the body and soul of Jesus Christ by his death?**
The divinity was separated from neither the body nor the soul of Christ in death; only the soul was separated from the body.

111. **For whom did Jesus Christ die?**
Jesus Christ died for the salvation of all men, and made satisfaction for all.

112. **If Jesus Christ died for the salvation of all men, why are not all men saved?**
Jesus Christ died for all, but not all are saved, because not all will acknowledge him; all do not observe his law; all do not avail themselves of the means of salvation he has left us.

113. **To be saved is it enough that Jesus Christ has died for us?**
No, it is not enough for our salvation that Jesus Christ has died for us; it is also necessary that the fruits of his passion and death be applied to each one of us, which is accomplished especially by means of the sacraments instituted for this end by Jesus Christ himself; and as many either do not receive the sacraments at all, or do not receive them well, they thus render the death of Jesus Christ useless in their regard.

The Fifth Article of the Creed

114. **What are we taught in the fifth article: "He descended into hell; the third day he rose again from the dead"?**
The fifth article of the Creed teaches us that the soul of Jesus Christ, on being separated from his body, descended to the limbo of the holy fathers, and that on the third day it became united once more to his body, never to be parted from it again.

115. **What is here meant by hell?**
Hell here means the limbo of the holy fathers, that is, the place where the souls of the just were detained, in expectation of redemption through Jesus Christ.

116. **Why were not the souls of the holy fathers admitted into heaven before the death of Jesus Christ?**
The souls of the holy fathers were not admitted into heaven before the death of Jesus Christ, because heaven was closed by the sin of Adam, and it was but fitting that Jesus Christ, who reopened it by his death, should be the first to enter it.

117. **Why did Jesus Christ defer his own resurrection until the third day?**
Jesus Christ deferred his own resurrection until the third day to show clearly that he was really dead.

118. **Was the resurrection of Jesus Christ like the resurrection of other men who had been raised from the dead?**
No, the resurrection of Jesus Christ was not like the resurrection of other men who had been raised from the dead, because he rose by his own power, while the others were raised by the power of God.

The Sixth Article of the Creed

119. **What are we taught in the sixth article: "He ascended into heaven, sitteth at the right hand of God, the Father Almighty"?**
The sixth article of the Creed teaches us that Jesus Christ, forty days after his resurrection, ascended of himself into heaven in the sight of his apostles; and that while as God he was equal to his Father in glory, as man he has been raised above all the angels and saints, and constituted Lord of all things.

120. **Why did Jesus Christ remain forty days on earth after his resurrection before ascending into heaven?**
After his resurrection Jesus Christ remained forty days on earth before ascending into heaven: to prove by several apparitions that he was truly risen, to instruct the apostles still further, and to confirm them in the truths of faith.

121. **Why did Jesus Christ ascend into heaven?**
Jesus Christ ascended into heaven: 1) to take possession of the kingdom he had merited by his death; 2) to prepare the place of our glory, and to be our mediator and advocate with the Father; and 3) to send the Holy Ghost upon his apostles.

122. **Why is it said of Jesus Christ that he ascended, and of his most holy Mother that she was assumed, into heaven?**
It is said of Jesus Christ that he ascended into heaven, and of his most holy Mother that she was assumed, because, Jesus Christ, being man-God, ascended into heaven by his own power; but his Mother, being a creature, even though the greatest of all creatures, was taken up into heaven by the power of God.

123. **Explain the words: "Sitteth at the right hand of God, the Father Almighty."**
The word *sitteth* signifies the peaceful possession which Jesus Christ has of his glory; and the words "at the right hand of God, the Father Almighty," denote that he has a place of honor above all creatures.

The Seventh Article of the Creed

124. **What are we taught in the seventh article: "From thence he shall come to judge the living and the dead"?**
The seventh article of the Creed teaches us that at the end of the world Jesus Christ, in all his glory and majesty, will come from heaven to judge all men, both good and bad, and to give to each of them the reward or the punishment he shall have merited.

125. **If everyone has to be judged by Jesus Christ in the particular judgment immediately after death, why must all be judged in the general judgment?**
We must all be judged in the general judgment for several reasons: 1) that God may be glorified; 2) that Jesus Christ may be glorified; 3) that the saints may be glorified; 4) that the wicked may be confounded; and 5) that along with the soul the body may receive its sentence of reward or punishment.

126. **How will God's glory be manifested in the general judgment?**
God's glory will be manifested in the general judgment in this way: that all shall then know how justly God governs the world, even though the good are often afflicted and the wicked in prosperity here on earth.

127. **How will the glory of Jesus Christ be manifested in the general judgment?**
The glory of Jesus Christ will be manifested in the general judgment in this way: that he who was unjustly condemned by men shall then come before the whole world as the supreme judge of all.

128. **How will the glory of the saints be manifested in the general judgment?**
The glory of the saints will be manifested in the general judgment in this way: that many of them who died despised by the wicked shall be glorified before the whole world.

129. **How great will be the confusion of the wicked in the general judgment?**
In the general judgment great indeed shall be the confusion of the wicked, especially of those who have oppressed the just and who have tried in this life to be esteemed as men of virtue and goodness; for they shall then see even their most hidden sins laid bare before the whole world.

The Eighth Article of the Creed

130. **What are we taught in the eighth article: "I believe in the Holy Ghost"?**
The eighth article of the Creed teaches us that there is a Holy Ghost, the third Person of the Blessed Trinity; and that, like the Father and the Son, he is God eternal, infinite, omnipotent, Creator, and Lord of all things.

131. **From whom does the Holy Ghost proceed?**
The Holy Ghost proceeds from the Father and the Son, as from one principle, by way of will and love.

132. **If the Son proceeds from the Father, and the Holy Ghost proceeds from the Father and the Son, it would seem as if the Father and the Son are prior to the Holy Ghost; how then can it be said that all the three Persons are eternal?**
It is said that all the three Persons are eternal, because the Father has begotten the Son from all eternity, and the Holy Ghost proceeds from the Father and from the Son from all eternity.

133. **Why is the third Person of the Blessed Trinity specially designated by the name of the Holy Spirit?**
The third Person of the Blessed Trinity is specially designated by the name of the Holy Spirit, because he proceeds from the Father and from the Son by way of spiration and of love.

134. **What work is especially attributed to the Holy Ghost?**
To the Holy Ghost is specially attributed the sanctification of souls.

135. **Do the Father and the Son sanctify us equally with the Holy Ghost?**
Yes, all the three divine Persons equally sanctify us.

136. **If this is so, why is the sanctification of souls specially attributed to the Holy Ghost?**
The sanctification of souls is specially attributed to the Holy Ghost, because it is a work of love, and the works of love are attributed to the Holy Ghost.

137. **When did the Holy Ghost descend on the apostles?**
The Holy Ghost descended on the apostles on the day of Pentecost, that is, fifty days after the resurrection of Jesus Christ, and ten days after his ascension.

138. **Where were the apostles during the ten days preceding Pentecost?**
The apostles were gathered together in the supper room with the Virgin Mary and the other disciples, and were persevering in prayer in expectation of the Holy Ghost, whom Jesus Christ had promised them to send.

139. **What effects did the Holy Ghost produce in the apostles?**
The Holy Ghost confirmed the apostles in the faith, filled them with light, strength, charity, and an abundance of all his gifts.

140. **Was the Holy Ghost sent for the apostles alone?**
The Holy Ghost was sent for the whole Church and for every faithful soul.

141. **What does the Holy Ghost do in the Church?**
The Holy Ghost gives life to the Church by his grace and by his gifts, as the soul gives life to the body; he establishes in her the kingdom of truth and of love; and he helps her to lead her children in safety along the way to heaven.

The Ninith Article of the Creed

The Church in General

142. **What does the ninth article, "the holy Catholic Church, the communion of saints," teach us?**
The ninth article of the Creed teaches us that Jesus Christ founded a visible society on earth called the Catholic Church, and that all those who belong to this Church are in communion with one another.

143. **Why immediately after the article that treats of the Holy Ghost is mention made of the Catholic Church?**
Immediately after the article that treats of the Holy Ghost mention is made of the Catholic Church to indicate that the Church's holiness comes from the Holy Ghost, who is the author of all holiness.

144. **What does the word *church* mean?**
The word *church* means a "calling forth" or "assembly of many."

145. **Who has convoked or called us into the Church of Jesus Christ?**
We have been called into the Church of Jesus Christ by a special grace of God, to the end, that by the light of faith and the observance of the divine law, we may render him the worship due to him, and attain eternal life.

146. **Where are the members of the Church to be found?**
The members of the Church are found partly in heaven, forming the Church triumphant; partly in purgatory, forming the Church suffering; partly on earth, forming the Church militant.

147. **Do these various parts of the Church constitute one sole Church?**
Yes, these various parts of the Church constitute one sole Church and one sole body for they have the same head, Jesus Christ, the same Spirit animating and uniting them, and the same end, eternal happiness, which some already enjoy and the rest hope for.

148. **To which part of the Church does this ninth article principally refer?**
This ninth article of the Creed principally refers to the Church militant, which is the Church we actually belong to.

The Church in Particular

149. **What is the Catholic Church?**
The Catholic Church is the union or congregation of all the baptized who, still living on earth, profess the same faith and the same law of Jesus Christ, participate in the same sacraments, and obey their lawful pastors, particularly the Roman pontiff.

150. **State distinctly what is necessary to be a member of the Church?**
To be a member of the Church it is necessary to be baptized, to believe and profess the teaching of Jesus Christ, to participate in the same sacraments, and to acknowledge the pope and the other lawful pastors of the Church.

151. **Who are the lawful pastors of the Church?**
The lawful pastors of the Church are the Roman pontiff, that is, the pope, who is supreme pastor, and the bishops. Other priests, also, and especially parish priests, have a share in the pastoral office, subject to the bishop and the pope.

152. **Why do you say that the Roman pontiff is supreme pastor of the Church?**
Because Jesus Christ said to St. Peter, the first pope: "Thou art Peter, and upon this rock I will build my church…And I will give to thee the keys of the kingdom of heaven, and whatsoever thou shalt bind on earth shall be bound also in heaven, and whatsoever thou shalt loose on earth shall be loosed also in heaven."[4] And again: "Feed my lambs, feed my sheep."[5]

153. **The many societies of persons who are baptized but who do not acknowledge the Roman pontiff as their head do not, then, belong to the Church of Jesus Christ?**
No, those who do not acknowledge the Roman pontiff as their head do not belong to the Church of Jesus Christ.

154. **How can the Church of Jesus Christ be distinguished from the numerous societies or sects founded by men, and calling themselves Christian?**
From the numerous societies or sects founded by men and calling themselves Christian, the Church of Jesus Christ is easily distinguished by four notes: she is one, holy, Catholic, and apostolic.

155. **Why is the Church called one?**
The true Church is called one, because her children of all ages and places are united together in the same faith, in the same worship, in the same law; and in participation of the same sacraments, under the same visible head, the Roman pontiff.

156. **Can there not be several churches?**
No, there cannot be more churches than one; for as there is but one God, one faith, and one baptism, there is and can be but one true Church.

[4] Mt 16:18-19
[5] Cf. Jn 21:15-17

157. **But are not the faithful of a whole nation or diocese also called a church?**
The faithful of a whole nation or diocese are also called a church, but they ever remain mere parts of the universal Church and form but one Church with her.

158. **Why is the true Church called holy?**
The true church is called holy because holy is her invisible head, Jesus Christ; holy are many of her members; holy are her faith, her laws, her sacraments; and outside of her there is not and cannot be true holiness.

159. **Why is the Church called Catholic?**
The true Church is called Catholic, or universal, because she embraces the faithful of all times, of all places, of all ages and conditions; and all peoples are called to belong to her.

160. **Why is the Church also called apostolic?**
The true Church is also called apostolic because she goes back without break to the apostles; because she believes and teaches all that the apostles believed and taught; and because she is guided and governed by their lawful successors.

161. **And why is the true Church called Roman?**
The true Church is called Roman, because the four marks of unity, sanctity, Catholicity, and apostolicity are found in that Church alone which acknowledges as head the bishop of Rome, the successor of St. Peter.

162. **What is the constitution of the Church of Jesus Christ?**
The Church of Jesus Christ has been constituted as a true and perfect society; and in her we can distinguish a soul and a body.

163. **In what does the soul of the Church consist?**
The soul of the Church consists in her internal and spiritual endowments, that is, faith, hope, charity, the gifts of grace and of the Holy Ghost,

together with all the heavenly treasures which are hers through the merits of our Redeemer, Jesus Christ, and of the saints.

164. **In what does the body of the Church consist?**
The body of the Church consists in her external and visible aspect, that is, in the association of her members, in her worship, in her teaching-power, and in her external rule and government.

165. **To be saved, is it enough to be any sort of member at all of the Catholic Church?**
No, to be saved it is not enough to be any sort of member of the Catholic Church; it is necessary to be a living member.

166. **Who are the living members of the Church?**
The living members of the Church are the just, and the just alone, that is, those who are actually in the grace of God.

167. **And who are the dead members?**
The dead members of the Church are the faithful in mortal sin.

168. **Can one be saved outside the Catholic, apostolic, and Roman Church?**
No, no one can be saved outside the Catholic, apostolic, and Roman Church, just as no one could be saved from the flood outside the ark of Noah, which was a figure of the Church.

169. **How, then, were the patriarchs of old, the prophets, and the other just men of the old testament, saved?**
The just of the old testament were saved in virtue of the faith they had in Christ to come, by means of which they spiritually belonged to the Church.

170. **But if a man through no fault of his own is outside the Church, can he be saved?**
If he is outside the Church through no fault of his, that is, if he is in good faith, and if he has received baptism, or at least has the implicit desire of

baptism; and if, moreover, he sincerely seeks the truth and does God's will as best he can; such a man is indeed separated from the body of the Church, but is united to the soul of the Church and consequently is on the way of salvation.

171. **Suppose that a man is a member of the Catholic Church, but does not put her teaching in practice, will he be saved?**
He who is a member of the Catholic Church and does not put her teaching in practice is a dead member, and hence will not be saved; for toward the salvation of an adult not only baptism and faith are required, but, furthermore, works in keeping with faith.

172. **Are we obliged to believe all the truths the Church teaches us?**
Yes, we are obliged to believe all the truths the Church teaches us, and Jesus Christ declares that he who does not believe is already condemned.

173. **Are we also obliged to do all that the Church commands?**
Yes, we are obliged to do all that the Church commands, for Jesus Christ has said to the pastors of the Church: "He who hears you, hears me, and he who despises you, despises me."[6]

174. **Can the Church err in what she proposes for our belief?**
No, the Church cannot err in what she proposes for our belief, since according to the promise of Jesus Christ she is unfailingly assisted by the Holy Ghost.

175. **Is the Catholic Church infallible, then?**
Yes, the Catholic Church is infallible, and hence those who reject her definitions lose the faith and become heretics.

[6] Lk 10:16

176. **Can the Catholic Church be destroyed or perish?**
No; the Catholic Church may be persecuted, but she can never be destroyed or perish. She will last till the end of the world, because Jesus Christ, as he promised, will be with her to the end of time.

177. **Why is the Catholic Church so persecuted?**
The Catholic Church is so persecuted because even her divine founder, Jesus Christ, was thus persecuted, and because she reproves vice, combats the passions, and condemns all acts of injustice and all error.

178. **Has a Catholic any other duties toward the Church?**
Every Catholic ought to have a boundless love for the Church, ought to consider himself infinitely honored and happy in belonging to her, and ought to labor for her glory and advancement by every means in his power.

The Church Teaching and the Church Taught

179. **Is there any distinction between the members of the Church?**
There is a very notable distinction between the members of the Church; for there are some who rule and some who obey; some who teach and some who are taught.

180. **How do you call that part of the Church which teaches?**
That part of the Church which teaches is called the teaching Church.

181. **How do you call that part of the Church which is taught?**
That part of the Church which is taught is called the learning Church, or the Church taught.

182. **Who has set up this distinction in the Church?**
Jesus Christ himself has established this distinction in the Church.

183. **Are the Church teaching and the Church taught, then, two churches?**
The Church teaching and the Church taught are two distinct parts of one and the same Church, just as in the human body the head is distinct from the other members, and yet forms but one body with them.

184. **Of whom is the teaching Church composed?**
The teaching Church is composed of all the bishops, with the Roman pontiff at their head, be they dispersed throughout the world or assembled together in council.

185. **And the Church taught, of whom is it composed?**
The Church taught is composed of all the faithful.

186. **Who, then, are they who possess the teaching power in the Church?**
The teaching power in the Church is possessed by the pope and the bishops, and, dependent on them, by the other sacred ministers.

187. **Are we obliged to hear the teaching Church?**
Yes, without doubt we are obliged under pain of eternal damnation to hear the teaching Church; for Jesus Christ has said to the pastors of his Church, in the persons of the apostles: "He who hears you, hears me, and he who despises you, despises me."[7]

188. **Besides her teaching power has the Church any other power?**
Yes, besides her teaching power the Church has in particular the power of administering sacred things, of making laws, and of exacting the observance of them.

189. **Does the power possessed by the members of the hierarchy come from the people?**
The power possessed by the hierarchy does not come from the people, and it would be heresy to say it did: it comes solely from God.

[7] Ibid.

190. **To whom does the exercise of this power belong?**
The exercise of this power belongs solely to the hierarchy, that is, to the pope and to the bishops subordinate to him.

The Pope and the Bishops

191. **Who is the pope?**
The pope, who is also called the sovereign pontiff, or the Roman pontiff, is the successor of St. Peter in the see of Rome, the vicar of Jesus Christ on earth, and the visible head of the Church.

192. **Why is the Roman pontiff the successor of St. Peter?**
The Roman pontiff is the successor of St. Peter because St. Peter united in his own person the dignity of bishop of Rome and that of head of the Church; by divine disposition he established his seat at Rome, and there died; hence, whosoever is elected bishop of Rome is also heir to all his authority.

193. **Why is the Roman pontiff the vicar of Jesus Christ?**
The Roman pontiff is the vicar of Jesus Christ because he represents him on earth and acts in his stead in the government of the Church.

194. **Why is the Roman pontiff the visible head of the Church?**
The Roman pontiff is the visible head of the Church because he visibly governs her with the authority of Jesus Christ himself, who is her invisible head.

195. **What, then, is the dignity of the pope?**
The dignity of the pope is the greatest of all dignities on earth, and gives him supreme and immediate power over all and each of the pastors and of the faithful.

196. **Can the pope err when teaching the Church?**
The pope cannot err, that is, he is infallible, in definitions regarding faith and morals.

197. **How is it that the pope is infallible?**
The pope is infallible because of the promise of Jesus Christ, and of the unfailing assistance of the Holy Ghost.

198. **When is the pope infallible?**
The pope is infallible when, as pastor and teacher of all Christians and in virtue of his supreme apostolic authority, he defines a doctrine regarding faith or morals to be held by all the Church.

199. **What sin would a man commit who should refuse to accept the solemn definitions of the pope?**
He who refuses to accept the solemn definitions of the pope, or who even doubts them, sins against faith; and should he remain obstinate in this unbelief, he would no longer be a Catholic, but a heretic.

200. **Why has God granted to the pope the gift of infallibility?**
God has granted the pope the gift of infallibility in order that we all may be sure and certain of the truths which the Church teaches.

201. **When was it defined that the pope is infallible?**
That the pope is infallible was defined by the Church in the Vatican Council;[8] and should anyone presume to contradict this definition he would be a heretic and excommunicated.

202. **In defining that the pope is infallible, has the Church put forward a new truth of faith?**
No, in defining that the pope is infallible the Church has not put forward a new truth of faith; but to oppose new errors she has simply defined that

[8] Editor's note: See First Vatican Council, *Pastor Aeternus*, Ch. 4

the infallibility of the pope, already contained in sacred scripture and in tradition, is a truth revealed by God, and therefore to be believed as a dogma or article of faith.

203. **How should every Catholic act toward the pope?**
Every Catholic must acknowledge the pope as father, pastor, and universal teacher, and be united with him in mind and heart.

204. **After the pope, who are they who by divine appointment are to be most venerated in the Church?**
After the pope, those who by divine appointment are to be most venerated in the Church are the bishops.

205. **Who are the bishops?**
The bishops are the pastors of the faithful; placed by the Holy Ghost to rule the Church of God in the sees entrusted to them, in dependence on the Roman pontiff.

206. **What is a bishop in his own diocese?**
A bishop in his own diocese is the lawful pastor, the father, the teacher, the superior of all the faithful, ecclesiastic and lay belonging to his diocese.

207. **Why is the bishop called the lawful pastor?**
The bishop is called the lawful pastor because the jurisdiction, or the power which he has to govern the faithful of his diocese, is conferred upon him according to the laws and regulations of the Church.

208. **To whom do the pope and the bishops succeed?**
The pope is the successor of St. Peter, the prince of the apostles; and the bishops are the successors of the apostles, in all that regards the ordinary government of the Church.

209. **Must the faithful be in union with their bishop?**
Yes, all the faithful, ecclesiastic and lay, should be united heart and soul with their bishop, who is in favor and communion with the apostolic see.

210. **How should the faithful act toward their own bishop?**
Each one of the faithful, both ecclesiastic and lay, should revere, love, and honor his own bishop, and render him obedience in all that regards the care of souls and the spiritual government of the diocese.

211. **By whom is the bishop assisted in the care of souls?**
The bishop is assisted in the care of souls by priests, and especially by parish priests.

212. **Who is the parish priest?**
The parish priest is a priest deputed to preside over and direct with due dependence on his bishop a portion of the diocese called a parish.

213. **What are the duties of the faithful toward their parish priest?**
The faithful should be united with their parish priest, listen to him with docility, and show him respect and submission in all that regards the care of the parish.

The Communion of Saints

214. **What are we taught by these words of the ninth article: "The communion of saints"?**
In the words "the communion of saints," the ninth article of the Creed teaches us that the Church's spiritual goods, both internal and external, are common to all her members because of the intimate union that exists between them.

215. **Which are the internal goods that are common in the Church?**
The internal goods that are common in the Church are: the graces received through the sacraments; faith, hope, and charity; the infinite merits of Jesus

Christ; the superabundant merits of the Blessed Virgin and of the saints; and the fruit of all the good works done in the same Church.

216. **Which are the external goods that are common in the Church?**
The external goods that are common in the Church are: the sacraments, the Sacrifice of the Mass, public prayers, religious functions, and all the other outward practices that unite the faithful.

217. **Do all the children of the Church share in this communion of goods?**
All Christians who are in the grace of God share in the communion of internal goods, while those who are in mortal sin do not participate in these goods.

218. **Why do not those who are in mortal sin participate in these goods?**
Because that which unites the faithful with God, and with Jesus Christ as his living members, rendering them capable of performing meritorious works for life eternal, is the grace of God which is the supernatural life of the soul; and hence as those who are in mortal sin are without the grace of God, they are excluded from perfect communion in spiritual goods, nor can they accomplish works meritorious toward life eternal.

219. **Do Christians then, who are in mortal sin derive no advantage from the internal and spiritual goods of the Church?**
Christians who are in mortal sin still continue to derive some advantage from the internal and spiritual goods of the Church, inasmuch as they still preserve the Christian character which is indelible, and the virtue of faith which is the basis of justification. They are aided, too, by the prayers and good works of the faithful toward obtaining the grace of conversion to God.

220. **Can those in mortal sin participate in the external goods of the Church?**
Those in mortal sin can participate in the external goods of the Church, unless indeed they are cut off from the Church by excommunication.

221. **Why are the members of this communion, taken together, called saints?**
The members of this communion are called saints because all are called to sanctity and have been sanctified by baptism, and because many of them have really attained perfect sanctity.

222. **Does the communion of saints extend also to heaven and purgatory?**
Yes, the communion of saints also extends to heaven and purgatory, because charity unites the three Churches—the triumphant, the suffering, and the militant; the saints pray God both for us and for the souls in purgatory; while we on our part give honor and glory to the saints, and are able to relieve the suffering souls in purgatory by applying in their behalf Masses, alms, indulgences, and other good works.

Those outside the Communion of Saints

223. **Who are they who do not belong to the communion of saints?**
Those who are damned do not belong to the communion of saints in the other life; and in this life those who belong neither to the body nor to the soul of the Church, that is, those who are in mortal sin, and who are outside the true Church.

224. **Who are they who are outside the true Church?**
Outside the true Church are: infidels, Jews, heretics, apostates, schismatics, and the excommunicated.

225. **Who are infidels?**
Infidels are those who have not been baptized and do not believe in Jesus Christ, because they either believe in and worship false gods as idolaters do, or though admitting one true God, they do not believe in the Messiah, neither as already come in the Person of Jesus Christ, nor as to come; for instance, Mohammedans and the like.

226. **Who are the Jews?**

The Jews are those who profess the law of Moses; have not received baptism; and do not believe in Jesus Christ.

227. **Who are heretics?**

Heretics are those of the baptized who obstinately refuse to believe some truth revealed by God and taught as an article of faith by the Catholic Church; for example, the Arians, the Nestorians, and the various sects of protestants.

228. **Who are apostates?**

Apostates are those who abjure, or by some external act, deny the Catholic faith which they previously professed.

229. **Who are schismatics?**

Schismatics are those Christians who, while not explicitly denying any dogma, yet voluntarily separate themselves from the Church of Jesus Christ, that is, from their lawful pastors.

230. **Who are the excommunicated?**

The excommunicated are those who, because of grievous transgressions, are struck with excommunication by the pope or their bishop, and consequently are cut off as unworthy from the body of the Church, which, however, hopes for and desires their conversion.

231. **Should excommunication be dreaded?**

Excommunication should be greatly dreaded, because it is the severest and most terrible punishment the Church can inflict upon her rebellious and obstinate children.

232. **Of what goods are the excommunicated deprived?**

The excommunicated are deprived of public prayers, of the sacraments, of indulgences, and of Christian burial.

233. **Can we in any way help the excommunicated?**
We can in some way help the excommunicated and all others who are outside the true Church by salutary advice, by prayers and good works, begging God in his mercy to grant them the grace of being converted to the faith and of entering into the communion of saints.

The Tenth Article of the Creed

234. **What are we taught by the tenth article: "The forgiveness of sins"?**
The tenth article of the Creed teaches us that Jesus Christ has left to his Church the power of forgiving sins.

235. **Can the Church forgive every sort of sin?**
Yes, the Church can forgive all sins, no matter how many or how grave they may be, because Jesus Christ has given her full power to bind and to loose.

236. **Who exercises this power of forgiving sins in the Church?**
Those who exercise the power of forgiving sins in the Church are, first of all, the pope, who alone possesses this power in all its plenitude; then the bishops, and, dependent upon the bishops, the priests.

237. **How does the Church forgive sins?**
The Church forgives sins through the merits of Jesus Christ by conferring the sacraments instituted by him for this purpose; especially the sacraments of baptism and penance.

The Eleventh Article of the Creed

238. **What are we taught by the eleventh article: "The resurrection of the body"?**
The eleventh article of the Creed teaches us that all men will rise again, every soul resuming the body it had in this life.

239. **How will the resurrection of the dead be accomplished?**
The resurrection of the dead will be accomplished by the virtue of the omnipotent God, to whom nothing is impossible.

240. **When will the resurrection of the dead take place?**
The resurrection of the dead shall take place at the end of the world, and shall be followed by the general judgment.

241. **Why does God will the resurrection of the body?**
God wills the resurrection of the body, in order that the soul, having done good or evil while united with the body, may also be rewarded or punished along with it.

242. **Will all rise in the same way?**
No, there will be a vast difference between the bodies of the elect and the bodies of the damned; because only the bodies of the elect shall have, like the risen Christ, the endowments of glorified bodies.

243. **What are the endowments that are to adorn the bodies of the elect?**
The endowments that shall adorn the bodies of the elect are: 1) impassibility, by which they can never again be subject to evil, nor to any kind of pain, nor to need of food, of rest, or the like; 2) brightness, by which they shall shine as the sun and as so many stars; 3) agility, by which they shall be able to pass in a moment and without fatigue from one place to another and from earth to heaven; 4) subtlety, by which without hindrance they

shall be able to penetrate any body, as did Jesus Christ when risen from the dead.

244. **And the bodies of the damned, what of them?**
The bodies of the damned shall be destitute of all the endowments of the glorified bodies of the blessed, and shall bear upon them the appalling mark of eternal reprobation.

The Twelfth Article of the Creed

245. **What are we taught by the last article: "life everlasting"?**
The last article of the Creed teaches us that, after the present life there is another life, eternally happy for the elect in heaven, or eternally miserable for the damned in hell.

246. **Can we comprehend the bliss of heaven?**
No, we cannot comprehend the bliss of heaven, because it is beyond the scope of our limited minds, and because the goods of heaven cannot be compared with the goods of this world.

247. **In what does the happiness of the elect consist?**
The happiness of the elect consists in forever seeing, loving, and possessing God, the source of all good.

248. **In what does the misery of the damned consist?**
The misery of the damned consists in being forever deprived of the vision of God and punished with eternal torments in hell.

249. **Are the happiness of heaven and the miseries of hell for the soul alone?**
The happiness of heaven and the miseries of hell at present affect the soul alone, because at present the soul alone is in heaven or in hell; but after

the resurrection of the flesh, man in the fullness of his nature, that is, in body and in soul, will be forever happy or forever tormented.

250. **Shall the bliss of paradise and the miseries of hell be the same for all men?**
The bliss of heaven in the case of the blessed, and the miseries of hell in the case of the damned, will be the same in substance and in eternal duration; but in measure, or degree, they will be greater or less according to the extent of each one's merits or demerits.

251. **What does the word *Amen* signify at the end of the Creed?**
The word *Amen* at the end of a prayer signifies "so be it"; at the end of the Creed it signifies "so it is," that is to say, "I believe that all things contained in these twelve articles are most true, and I am more certain of them than if I had seen them with my eyes."

SECTION II

On Prayer

Prayer in General

252. **What does this part of Christian doctrine treat of?**
This part of Christian doctrine treats of prayer in general, and of the Our Father in particular.

253. **What is prayer?**
Prayer is an elevation of the mind to God to adore him, to thank him, and to ask him for what we need.

254. **How is prayer divided?**
Prayer is divided into mental and vocal prayer. Mental prayer is that made with the mind alone; and vocal prayer is that expressed in words accompanied by attention of mind and devotion of heart.

255. **Can prayer be divided in any other way?**
Prayer may also be divided into private and public prayer.

256. **What is private prayer?**
Private prayer is that which each one says individually for himself or for others.

257. **What is public prayer?**
Public prayer is that said by the sacred ministers in the name of the Church and for the salvation of the faithful. That prayer also which is said in common and publicly by the faithful, in processions, pilgrimages, and in God's house, may also be called public prayer.

258. **Have we a well-founded hope of obtaining by means of prayer the helps and graces of which we stand in need?**
The hope of obtaining from God the graces of which we stand in need is founded on the promises of the omnipotent, merciful, and all-faithful God, and on the merits of Jesus Christ.

259. **In whose name should we ask of God the graces we stand in need of?**
We should ask of God the graces we stand in need of in the name of Jesus Christ, as he himself has taught us and as is done by the Church, which always ends her prayers with these words: "Through our Lord Jesus Christ."

260. **Why should we beg graces of God in the name of Jesus Christ?**
We should beg graces of God in the name of Jesus Christ because he is our mediator, and it is through him alone that we can approach the throne of God.

261. **If prayer is so powerful how is it that many times our prayers are not heard?**
Many times our prayers are not heard, either because we ask things not conducive to our eternal salvation, or because we do not ask properly.

262. **Which are the chief things you should ask of God?**
The chief things we should ask of God are his own glory, our eternal salvation, and the means of obtaining it.

263. **Is it not also lawful to ask for temporal goods?**
Yes, it is lawful also to ask God for temporal goods, but always with the condition that these be in conformity with his holy will and not a hindrance to our salvation.

264. **If God knows all that is necessary for us, why should we pray?**
Although God knows all that is necessary for us, he nevertheless wills that we should pray to him so as to acknowledge him as the giver of every good gift, to attest our humble submission to him, and to merit his favors for ourselves.

265. **What is the first and best disposition to render our prayers efficacious?**
The first and best disposition to render our prayers efficacious is to be in the state of grace; or if we are not in that state, to desire to put ourselves in it.

266. **What other dispositions are required in order to pray well?**
To pray well we specially require recollection, humility, confidence, perseverance, and resignation.

267. **What is meant by praying with recollection?**
It means remembering that we are speaking to God; and hence we should pray with all respect and devotion, as far as possible avoiding distractions, that is, every thought foreign to our prayers.

268. **Do distractions lessen the merit of prayer?**
Yes, when we ourselves bring them about, or when we do not promptly drive them away; but if we do all we can to be recollected in God, then our distractions do not lessen the merit of our prayer, and may even increase it.

269. **What is required to pray with recollection?**
Before prayer we should banish all occasions of distraction, and during prayer we should reflect that we are in the presence of God who sees and hears us.

270. **What is meant by praying with humility?**
It means sincerely acknowledging our own unworthiness, powerlessness, and misery; and as well as this, observing a respectful posture.

271. **What is meant by praying with confidence?**
It means that we should have a firm hope of being heard, if it is to God's glory and our own true welfare.

272. **What is meant by praying with perseverance?**
It means that we should not grow tired of praying, if God does not at once hear us, but that we should ever continue to pray with increased fervor.

273. **What is meant by praying with resignation?**
It means that we should conform our will to the will of God, even when our prayers are not heard, because he knows better than we do what is necessary for our eternal salvation.

274. **Does God always hear prayers when well said?**
Yes, God always hears prayers when well said; but in the way he knows to be most conducive to our eternal salvation, and not always in the way we wish.

275. **What effects does prayer produce in us?**
Prayer makes us recognize our dependence on God, the supreme Lord, in all things; it makes us think on heavenly things; it makes us advance in virtue; it obtains for us God's mercy; it strengthens us against temptations; it comforts us in tribulation; it aids us in our needs; and it obtains for us the grace of final perseverance.

276. **When should we especially pray?**
We should especially pray when in danger, in temptation, and at the hour of death; moreover, we should pray often, and it is advisable we should do so morning and night, and when beginning the more important actions of the day.

277. **For whom should we pray?**
We should pray for all; first, for ourselves, then for our relatives, superiors, benefactors, friends, and enemies; for the conversion of poor sinners, and of those outside the true Church, and for the holy souls in purgatory.

The Lord's Prayer

The Lord's Prayer in General

278. **Which is the most excellent of all vocal prayers?**
The most excellent of all vocal prayers is that which Jesus Christ taught us, that is to say, the Our Father.

279. **Why is the Our Father the most excellent of all prayers?**
The Our Father is the most excellent of all prayers because Jesus Christ himself composed it and taught it to us; because it contains clearly and in a few words all we can hope for from God; and because it is the standard and model of all other prayers.

280. **Is the Our Father also the most efficacious of prayers?**
Yes, it is also the most efficacious of prayers, because it is the most acceptable to God, since in it we pray in the very words his divine Son has taught us.

281. **Why is the Our Father called the Lord's prayer?**
The Our Father is called the Lord's Prayer, precisely because Jesus Christ our Lord has taught it to us with his own lips.

282. **How many petitions are there in the Our Father?**
In the Our Father there are seven petitions preceded by an introduction.

283. **Say the Our Father.**
Our Father who art in heaven, 1) hallowed be thy name; 2) thy kingdom come; 3) thy will be done on earth as it is in heaven. 4) Give us this day our daily bread; 5) and forgive us our trespasses, as we forgive those who trespass against us. 6) And lead us not into temptation; 7) but deliver us from evil. Amen.

284. **When invoking God in the beginning of the Lord's Prayer, why do we call him "Our Father"?**
In the beginning of the Lord's Prayer we call God "Our Father," to foster confidence in his infinite goodness by the remembrance that we are his children.

285. **How can we say that we are the children of God?**
We are the children of God: first, because he has created us to his own image, and preserves and governs us by his providence; and secondly, because by an act of special benevolence he has adopted us in baptism as brothers of Jesus Christ and co-heirs with him to eternal glory.

286. **Why do we call God "Our Father" and not "My Father"?**
We call God "Our Father" and not "My Father," because we are all his children, and hence we should look on and love one another as brothers and pray for one another.

287. **God being in every place, why do we say: "who art in heaven"?**
God is in every place; but we say, "Our Father who art in heaven," to raise our hearts to heaven, where God manifests his glory to his children.

The First Petition

288. **What do we ask in the first petition when we say: "hallowed be thy name"?**
In the first petition, "hallowed be thy name," we ask that God may be known, loved, honored, and served by the whole world and by ourselves in particular.

289. **What do we intend when we ask that God may be known, loved, honored, and served by the whole world?**
We intend to beg that infidels may come to the knowledge of the Lord God, that heretics may recognize their errors, that schismatics may return to the unity of the Church, that sinners may repent, and that the just may persevere in well-doing.

290. **Why do we first of all ask that the name of God may be sanctified?**
We first of all ask that the name of God may be sanctified, because the glory of God should be nearer our hearts than all other goods and interests.

291. **How can we promote the glory of God?**
We can promote the glory of God by prayer, by good example, and by directing to him all our thoughts, affections, and actions.

The Second Petition

292. **What do we mean by the "kingdom of God"?**
By the "kingdom of God" we mean a threefold spiritual kingdom; that is, the reign of God in us, or the reign of grace; the reign of God on earth, or the holy Catholic Church; and the reign of God in heaven, or paradise.

293. **In the words "thy kingdom come," what do we ask with regard to grace?**
With regard to grace we beg that God may reign in us by his sanctifying grace, by which he deigns to dwell within us as a king in his palace; and that he may keep us ever united to himself by the virtues of faith, hope, and charity, through which he reigns over our intellect, our heart, and our will.

294. **In the words "thy kingdom come," what do we ask regarding the Church?**
Regarding the Church we beg that she may be spread and propagated ever more and more throughout the world for the salvation of mankind.

295. **In the words "thy kingdom come," what do we ask regarding heaven?**
Regarding heaven we beg to be one day admitted into that paradise for which we were created and where we shall be perfectly happy.

The Third Petition

296. **What do we ask in the third petition: "thy will be done on earth as it is in heaven"?**
In the third petition, "thy will be done on earth as it is in heaven," we beg the grace to do the will of God in all things by obeying his commandments as promptly as the angels and saints obey him in heaven; and we also beg the grace to correspond to divine inspirations and to live resigned to the will of God should he send us tribulations.

297. **Is it necessary to do the will of God?**
It is as necessary to do the will of God as it is to work out our salvation, because Jesus Christ has said that they alone who have done the will of his Father shall enter into the kingdom of heaven.

298. **In what way can we know the will of God?**
We can know the will of God especially by means of the Church and of the spiritual superiors appointed by God to guide us along the way of salvation; we may also learn his most holy will from the divine inspirations that come to us and from the very surroundings in which the Lord has placed us.

299. **Should we always recognize the will of God in adversity as well as in prosperity?**
Both in prosperity and adversity we should always recognize the will of God, who directs or permits all things for our good.

The Fourth Petition

300. **What do we ask in the fourth petition: "Give us this day our daily bread"?**
In the fourth petition we beg of God all that is daily necessary for soul and body.

301. **What do we ask of God for our soul?**
For our soul we ask of God the sustentation of our spiritual life, that is, we pray the Lord to give us his grace of which we stand in continual need.

302. **How is the life of the soul nourished?**
The life of the soul is nourished principally by the food of the word of God and by the most Holy Sacrament of the Altar.

303. **What do we ask of God for the body?**
For the body we ask all that is necessary for the sustentation of our temporal life.

304. **Why do we say, "Give us this day our daily bread," rather than, "Give us bread this day"?**
We say, "Give us this day our daily bread," rather than, "Give us bread this day," to exclude all desire of what is another's; and hence we beg the Lord to help us in acquiring just and lawful gains, so that we may procure our maintenance by our own toil and without theft or fraud.

305. **Why do we say, "Give us bread," and not, "Give me bread"?**
We say, "Give us," rather than, "Give me," to remind us that as everything comes from God, so if he gives us his gifts in abundance, he does it in order that we may share what we do not need with the poor.

306. **Why do we add *daily*?**
We add *daily*, because we should desire that which is necessary to life, and not an abundance of food and other goods of the earth.

307. **What more does *daily* signify in the fourth petition?**
The word *daily* signifies that we should not be too solicitous regarding the future, but that we should simply ask what we need at present.

The Fifth Petition

308. **What do we ask in the fifth petition: "and forgive us our trespasses, as we forgive them that trespass against us"?**
In the fifth petition, "and forgive us our trespasses as we forgive them that trespass against us," we ask God to pardon us our sins as we pardon those who offend us.

309. **Why are our sins called debts?**
Our sins are called debts, because we must satisfy God's justice for them either in this life or in the next.

310. **Can those who do not forgive their neighbor hope that God will pardon them?**
Those who do not forgive their neighbor have no reason to hope that God will pardon them; especially since they condemn themselves when they ask God to forgive them as they forgive their neighbor.

The Sixth Petition

311. **What do we ask in the sixth petition: "And lead us not into temptation"?**
In the sixth petition, "And lead us not into temptation," we ask God to deliver us from temptation either by not allowing us to be tempted, or by giving us grace not to be conquered.

312. **What are temptations?**
Temptations are an incitement to sin that comes from the devil, or from the wicked, or from our own evil passions.

313. **Is it a sin to have temptations?**
No, it is no sin to have temptations; but it is a sin to consent to them, or voluntarily to expose oneself to the danger of consenting to them.

314. **Why does God allow us to be tempted?**
God allows us to be tempted so as to test our fidelity, increase our virtue, and augment our merits.

315. **What should we do to avoid temptations?**
To avoid temptation we should fly dangerous occasions, guard our senses, receive the sacraments frequently, and have recourse to the practice of prayer.

The Seventh Petition

316. **What do we ask in the seventh petition: "but deliver us from evil"?**
In the seventh petition, "but deliver us from evil," we ask God to free us from evils, past, present, and future, and particularly from the greatest of all evils which is sin, and from eternal damnation, which is its penalty.

317. **Why do we say, "deliver us from evil" and not, "from evils"?**
We say, "deliver us from evil," and not, "from evils," because we should not desire to be exempt from all the evils of this life, but only from those which are not good for our souls; and hence we beg liberation from evil in general, that is, from whatever God sees would be bad for us.

318. **Is it not lawful to beg liberation from some evil in particular, for example, from sickness?**
Yes, it is lawful to beg liberation from some evil in particular but always in bowing to the will of God, who may even ordain that particular affliction for the good of our soul.

319. **How do the tribulations, which God sends us, help us?**
Tribulations help us to do penance for our sins, to practice virtue, and above all to imitate Jesus Christ, our head, to whom it is fitting we should conform ourselves in our sufferings, if we wish to have a share in his glory.

320. **What is the meaning of *Amen* at the end of the Our Father?**
Amen means: "So be it"; "So I do desire"; "Thus do I pray the Lord"; "Thus do I hope."

321. **To obtain the graces asked in the Our Father is it enough to recite it any way at all?**
To obtain the graces asked in the Our Father we must recite it without haste and with attention; and we must put our heart into it.

322. **When should we say the Our Father?**
We should say the Our Father every day, because every day we have need of God's help.

The Hail Mary

323. **What prayer do we usually say after the Our Father?**
After the Our Father we say the Angelic Salutation, that is, the Hail Mary, through which we have recourse to the Blessed Virgin.

324. **Why is the Hail Mary called the Angelic Salutation?**
The Hail Mary is called the Angelic Salutation, because it begins with the salutation addressed by the archangel Gabriel to the Virgin Mary.

325. **Whose are the words of the Hail Mary?**
The words of the Hail Mary are partly the archangel Gabriel's, partly St. Elizabeth's, and partly the Church's.

326. **Which are the words of the archangel Gabriel?**
The words of the archangel Gabriel are these: "Hail, full of grace, the Lord is with thee; blessed art thou among women."[9]

327. **When was it that the angel said these words to Mary?**
The angel said these words to Mary when he went to announce to her, on the part of God, the mystery of the incarnation that was to be wrought in her.

328. **What is our object in saluting the Blessed Virgin with the very words of the archangel?**
In saluting the Blessed Virgin with the words of the archangel we congratulate her by recalling to mind the singular privileges and gifts which God has granted her in preference to all other creatures.

329. **Which are the words of St. Elizabeth?**
The words of St. Elizabeth are these: "Blessed art thou among women, and blessed is the fruit of thy womb."[10]

330. **When was it that St. Elizabeth said these words?**
St. Elizabeth, inspired by God, said these words when, three months before she gave birth to St. John the Baptist, she was visited by the Blessed Virgin, who then bore her divine Son in her womb.

331. **What do we intend by saying these words?**
In saying the words of St. Elizabeth we congratulate the Blessed Virgin on her high dignity as Mother of God, and we bless God and thank him for having given us Jesus Christ through Mary.

332. **Whose are the other words of the Hail Mary?**
All the other words of the Hail Mary have been added by the Church.

[9] Lk 1:28
[10] Lk 1:42

333. **What do we ask in the last part of the Hail Mary?**
In the last part of the Hail Mary we beg the protection of the Blessed Virgin during this life and especially at the hour of death, when we shall have greater need of it.

334. **Why do we say the Hail Mary, rather than any other prayer, after the Our Father?**
Because the Blessed Virgin is our most powerful advocate with Jesus Christ, and hence, after having said the prayer taught us by Jesus Christ, we pray the Blessed Virgin to obtain for us the graces we have asked therein.

335. **Why is the Blessed Virgin so powerful?**
The Blessed Virgin is so powerful, because, being the Mother of God, she cannot but be heard by him.

336. **What do the saints teach us on devotion to Mary?**
Regarding devotion to Mary the saints teach us that those who are truly devout to her are loved and protected by her with a most tender Mother's love, and that with her help they are sure to find Jesus and obtain paradise.

337. **What form of devotion to Mary does the Church recommend in a very special manner?**
The devotion to the Blessed Virgin which the Church specially recommends is the holy rosary.

SECTION III

On the Commandments of God and of the Church

The Commandments of God

The Commandments of God in General

338. **What is treated of in the third part of Christian doctrine?**
The commandments of God and of the Church are treated of in the third part of Christian doctrine.

339. **How many commandments of God's law are there?**
There are ten commandments of God's law.

I am the Lord thy God:

1. Thou shalt not have strange gods before me.
2. Thou shalt not take the name of the Lord thy God in vain.
3. Remember thou keep holy the sabbath-day.
4. Honor thy father and thy mother.
5. Thou shalt not kill.
6. Thou shalt not commit adultery.
7. Thou shalt not steal.
8. Thou shalt not bear false witness.
9. Thou shalt not covet another's wife.
10. Thou shalt not covet another's goods.

340. **Why are the commandments of God so named?**
The commandments of God are so named because God himself has stamped them on the soul of every man; promulgated them, engraved on two tables of stone, on Mount Sinai, in the old law; and Jesus Christ has confirmed them in the new law.

341. **Which are the commandments of the first table?**
The commandments of the first table are the first three, which directly regard God and our duties toward him.

342. **Which are the commandments of the second table?**
The commandments of the second table are the last seven, which regard our neighbor, and our duties toward him.

343. **Are we bound to observe the commandments?**
Yes, we are bound to observe the commandments, because we are all bound to live according to the will of God who created us, and because a serious transgression against even one of them is enough to merit hell.

344. **Are we able to observe the commandments?**
Yes, without doubt we are able to observe God's commandments, because God never commands anything that is impossible, and because he gives grace to observe them to those who ask it as they should.

345. **What, in a general way, should we consider in each of the commandments?**
In each of the commandments we should consider its positive part and its negative part, that is, what it commands and what it forbids.

The First Commandment

346. **Why is it said at the commencement of the commandments: "I am the Lord thy God"?**
It is said at the commencement of the commandments, "I am the Lord thy God," to show us that God, being our Creator and Lord, can command whatever he wills, and that we, being his creatures, are bound to obey him.

347. **In the words of the first commandment, "Thou shalt not have strange gods before me," what does God command us?**
By the words of the first commandment, "Thou shalt not have strange gods before me," he commands us to acknowledge, adore, love, and serve him alone as our sovereign Lord.

348. **How do we fulfill the first commandment?**
We fulfill the first commandment by the practice of internal and external worship.

349. **What is internal worship?**
Internal worship is the honor which is given to God with the faculties of the soul alone, that is with the intellect and will.

350. **What is external worship?**
External worship is the homage that is given to God by means of outward acts and of sensible objects.

351. **Is it not enough internally to adore God with the heart alone?**
No, it is not enough internally to adore God with the heart alone; we must also adore him externally with both soul and body, because he is the Creator and absolute Lord of both.

352. **Can there be external worship without internal worship?**

No, in no way can there be external worship without internal, because unless external worship is accompanied by internal, it is destitute of life, of merit, and of efficacy, like a body without a soul.

353. **What is forbidden by the first commandment?**

The first commandment forbids idolatry, superstition, sacrilege, heresy, and every other sin against religion.

354. **What is idolatry?**

Idolatry is the giving to any creature, for example, to a statue, to an image, or to a man, the supreme worship of adoration that belongs to God alone.

355. **How is this prohibition expressed in holy scripture?**

This prohibition is expressed in holy scripture in these words: "Thou shalt not make to thyself a graven thing, nor the likeness of anything that is in heaven above, or on the earth beneath...(and) thou shalt not adore them or serve them."[11]

356. **Do these words forbid every kind of image?**

Certainly not; but only those of false divinities, made to be adored, as idolaters adore them. So true is this, that God himself commanded Moses to make images, as, for example, the two statues of the cherubim for the ark, and the brazen serpent in the desert.

357. **What is superstition?**

Superstition is any devotion that is contrary to the teaching and practice of the Church; as also the ascribing to any action or anything whatever a supernatural virtue which it does not possess.

[11] Ex 20:4-5

358. **What is a sacrilege?**

A sacrilege is the profanation of a place, of a person, or of a thing consecrated to God and set apart for his worship.

359. **What is heresy?**

Heresy is a culpable error of the intellect by which some truth of faith is obstinately denied.

360. **What else does the first commandment forbid?**

The first commandment also forbids all dealings with the devil, and all association with anti-Christian sects.

361. **If one were to have recourse to and invoke the devil, would he commit a grave sin?**

If one were to have recourse to and invoke the devil, he would commit an enormous sin, because the devil is the most wicked enemy both of God and of man.

362. **Is it lawful to put questions to speaking or writing tables or in any way to consult the souls of the dead by means of spiritism?**

All the practices of spiritism are unlawful, because superstitious; and often they are not free from diabolical intervention; and hence they were rightly condemned by the Church.

363. **Does the first commandment forbid us to honor and invoke the angels and saints?**

No, it is not forbidden to honor and invoke the angels and saints; on the contrary, we should do so, because it is a good and useful practice highly commended by the Church; for they are God's friends and our intercessors with him.

364. **Since Jesus Christ is our only mediator with God, why have recourse also to the intercession of the Blessed Virgin and the saints?**
Jesus Christ is our mediator with God, because being true God and true man he alone in virtue of his own merits has reconciled us to God and obtains us all graces. But in virtue of the merits of Jesus Christ, and through the charity which unites them to God and to us, the Blessed Virgin and the saints help us by their intercession to obtain the graces we ask. And this is one of the great benefits of the communion of saints.

365. **May we also honor the sacred images of Jesus Christ and of the saints?**
Yes, because the honor we give the sacred images of Jesus Christ and of the saints is referred to their very persons.

366. **May the relics of the saints be honored?**
Yes, we should honor the relics of the saints, because their bodies were living members of Jesus Christ and temples of the Holy Ghost, and will rise gloriously to eternal life.

367. **What is the difference between the honor we give to God and the honor we give to the saints?**
Between the honor we give to God and the honor we give to the saints there is this difference: that we adore God because of his infinite excellence, whereas we do not adore the saints, but honor and venerate them as God's friends and our intercessors with him. The honor we give to God is called *latria*, that is, the worship of adoration; the honor we give to the saints is called *dulia*, that is, the veneration of the servants of God; while the special honor we give to the Blessed Virgin is called *hyperdulia*, that is, a special veneration of the Mother of God.

The Second Commandment

368. **What does the second commandment, "Thou shalt not take the name of God in vain," forbid?**
The second commandment, "Thou shalt not take the name of God in vain," forbids us: 1) to utter the name of God irreverently; 2) to blaspheme God, the Blessed Virgin, or the saints; 3) to take false, unnecessary, or unlawful oaths.

369. **What is meant by: "Not to utter the name of God irreverently"?**
"Not to utter the name of God irreverently" means not to mention this holy name, or any other name that in a special way refers to God himself, such as the name of Jesus, of Mary, and the saints, in anger, or in joke, or in any irreverent way whatever.

370. **What is blasphemy?**
Blasphemy is a horrible sin which consists in words or acts of contempt or malediction against God, the Blessed Virgin, the saints, or sacred things.

371. **Is there any difference between blasphemy and imprecation?**
There is a difference, because by blasphemy one wishes evil to or curses God, the Blessed Virgin, or the saints; while by imprecation one wishes evil to or curses one's self or one's neighbor.

372. **What is an oath?**
An oath is the calling on God to witness the truth of what one says or promises.

373. **Is it always forbidden to take an oath?**
It is not always forbidden to take an oath; an oath is lawful and even gives honor to God, when it is necessary, and when one swears with truth, judgment, and justice.

374. **When is an oath without truth?**
When one affirms on oath what he knows or believes to be false, or when one promises under oath to do what one has no intention of doing.

375. **When is an oath without judgment?**
When one makes oaths imprudently and without mature consideration, or in trivial matters.

376. **When is an oath without justice?**
When one makes an oath to do something unjust or unlawful, as, for example, to swear to take revenge, or to steal, and so on.

377. **Are we obliged to keep an oath to do unjust or unlawful things?**
Not only are we not obliged, but we should sin by doing such things, because they are forbidden by the laws of God and of the Church.

378. **What sin does he commit who swears falsely?**
He who swears falsely commits a mortal sin, because he grievously dishonors God, the infinite truth, by calling him to witness what is false.

379. **What does the second commandment command us to do?**
The second commandment commands us to honor the holy name of God as well as to keep our oaths and vows.

380. **What is a vow?**
A vow is a promise made to God regarding something which is good, within our power, and better than its opposite, and to the keeping of which we bind ourselves just as if it had been commanded us.

381. **If the keeping of a vow were to become very difficult, in whole or in part, what is to be done?**
Commutation or dispensation may be sought from one's bishop or from the pope, according to the character of the vow.

382. **Is it a sin to break a vow?**
It is a sin to break a vow and therefore we should not make vows without mature reflection, nor, as a rule, without the advice of our confessor or other prudent person, so as not to expose ourselves to the danger of sinning.

383. **May vows be made to our Lady and the saints?**
Vows are made to God alone; we may, however, promise God to do something in honor of our Lady or the saints.

The Third Commandment

384. **What does the third commandment, "Remember thou keep holy the sabbath-day," command us to do?**
The third commandment, "Remember thou keep holy the sabbath-day," commands us to honor God by acts of worship on festivals.

385. **What are festivals?**
In the old law they were Saturdays and certain other days regarded as specially solemn by the Jews; in the new law they are Sundays and other festivals instituted by the Church.

386. **Why is Sunday sanctified instead of Saturday in the new law?**
Sunday, which means the Lord's Day, was substituted for Saturday, because it was on that day that our Lord rose from the dead.

387. **What act of worship is commanded us on festivals?**
We are commanded to assist devoutly at the Holy Sacrifice of the Mass.

388. **With what other good works does a good Christian sanctify festivals?**
A good Christian sanctifies festivals: 1) by attending Christian doctrine, sermons, and the divine office; 2) by frequently and devoutly receiving the sacraments of penance and the Blessed Eucharist; 3) by the practice of prayer and works of Christian charity.

389. **What does the third commandment forbid?**
The third commandment forbids servile works and any other works that hinder the worship of God.

390. **What servile works are forbidden on festivals?**
The servile works forbidden on festivals are those works called manual, that is, those material works in which the body has more part than the mind, such, for instance, as are ordinarily done by servants, laborers, and artisans.

391. **What sin does one commit by working on festivals?**
One commits a mortal sin by working on festivals; brevity of time, however, will excuse from grave sin.

392. **Is no servile work at all permitted on festivals?**
On festivals those works are permitted which are necessary for life, or for the service of God; as well as those done for a grave reason, with leave, when possible, from the pastor.

393. **Why is servile work forbidden on festivals?**
Servile work is forbidden on festivals in order that we may the better attend to divine worship, and to the care of our souls; and to enable us to rest from toil. Hence innocent recreation is not forbidden.

394. **What else above all should we avoid on festivals?**
We should above all avoid sin and whatever leads to sin, such as dangerous diversions and dangerous places of amusement.

The Fourth Commandment

395. **What does the fourth commandment, "Honor thy father and thy mother," command?**

The fourth commandment, "Honor thy father and thy mother," commands us to respect our parents, obey them in all that is not sinful, and assist them in their temporal and spiritual needs.

396. **What does the fourth commandment forbid?**

The fourth commandment forbids us to offend our parents by word, or by deed, or in any other way.

397. **What other persons does this commandment include under the names of father and mother?**

Under the names of father and mother this commandment also includes all our superiors, both ecclesiastical and lay, whom we must consequently obey and respect.

398. **Whence are derived the authority of parents to command their children and the duty of children to obey their parents?**

The authority possessed by parents to command their children and the obligation children are under to obey their parents are derived from God who constituted and established family life in order that in it man might have the first helps that are necessary toward his spiritual and temporal well-being.

399. **Have parents any duties toward their children?**

Parents are bound to love, support, and maintain their children; to attend to their religious and secular education; to give them good example; to keep them from the occasions of sin; to correct their faults; and to help them to embrace the state to which God has called them.

400. **Has God given us an example of a perfect family?**
God gave us an example of a perfect family in the Holy Family in which Jesus Christ lived subject to the Blessed Virgin and St. Joseph until his thirtieth year, that is, until he began the mission of preaching the gospel entrusted to him by his eternal Father.

401. **If families were to live alone, cut off one from the other, could they provide for all their material and moral needs?**
If families lived alone, cut off one from the other, they could not provide for their individual needs, and hence it is necessary that they be united in civil society so as mutually to aid one another for the common good and happiness.

402. **What is civil society?**
Civil society is the union of many families under the authority of one head for the purpose of assisting each other in securing their mutual perfection and temporal happiness.

403. **Whence comes the authority which rules civil society?**
The authority which rules civil society comes from God, who established it for the common good.

404. **Are we under any obligation to obey the authority that governs civil society?**
Yes; all who form part of civil society are bound to respect and obey authority, because that authority comes from God, and because the common good so demands.

405. **Are all laws imposed by the civil authority to be respected?**
Yes; in accordance with the command and example of our Lord Jesus Christ, all laws imposed by the civil authority are to be respected, provided they are not contrary to the law of God.

406. **Have those who form part of civil society any other duties besides respect and obedience to the laws imposed by authority?**
Besides the obligation of respect and obedience to the laws, all those who form part of civil society are bound to live in peace, and to endeavor, each according to his means and ability, to render that society virtuous, peaceful, orderly, and prosperous.

The Fifth Commandment

407. **What does the fifth commandment, "Thou shalt not kill," forbid?**
The fifth commandment, "Thou shalt not kill," forbids us to kill, strike, wound, or do any other bodily harm to our neighbor, either of ourselves or by the agency of others; as also to wish him evil, or to offend him by injurious language. In this commandment God also forbids the taking of one's own life, or suicide.

408. **Why is it a grave sin to kill one's neighbor?**
Because the slayer unjustly invades the right which God alone has over the life of man; because he destroys the security of civil society; and because he deprives his neighbor of life, which is the greatest natural good on earth.

409. **Are there cases in which it is lawful to kill?**
It is lawful to kill when fighting in a just war; when carrying out by order of the supreme authority a sentence of death in punishment of a crime; and, finally, in cases of necessary and lawful defense of one's own life against an unjust aggressor.

410. **Does God also forbid us in the fifth commandment to do harm to the spiritual life of another?**
Yes, in the fifth commandment God also forbids us to do harm to another's spiritual life by scandal.

411. **What is scandal?**
Scandal is any word, act, or omission which is the occasion of another's committing sin.

412. **Is scandal a grave sin?**
Scandal is a grave sin because, by causing the loss of souls, it tends to destroy the greatest work of God, namely, the redemption; it effects the death of another's soul by depriving it of the life of grace, which is more precious than the life of the body; and is the source of a multitude of sins. Hence God threatens the severest chastisement to those who give scandal.

413. **Why does God, in the fifth commandment, forbid the taking of one's own life or suicide?**
In the fifth commandment God forbids suicide, because man is not the master of his own life no more than of the life of another. Hence the Church punishes suicide by deprivation of Christian burial.

414. **Is dueling also forbidden by the fifth commandment?**
Yes, dueling is also forbidden by the fifth commandment, because dueling has in it the guilt both of suicide and of homicide; and whoever voluntarily takes part in it, even as a simple onlooker, is excommunicated.

415. **Is dueling also forbidden when there is no danger of being killed?**
This sort of dueling is also forbidden, because not only are we forbidden to kill, but even voluntarily to wound ourselves or others.

416. **Is the defense of one's honor an excuse for dueling?**
No, because it is not true that the offense is repaired by dueling; and because honor cannot be repaired by an unjust, irrational, and barbarous act such as dueling.

417. **What does the fifth commandment command?**
The fifth commandment commands us to forgive our enemies and to wish well to all.

418. **What should he do who has injured another in the life of either body or soul?**
He who has injured another must not only confess his sin, but must also repair the harm by compensating his neighbor for the loss he has sustained, by retracting the errors taught, and by giving good example.

The Sixth and Ninth Commandments

419. **What does the sixth commandment, "Thou shalt not commit adultery," forbid?**
The sixth commandment, "Thou shalt not commit adultery," forbids every act, every look, and every word contrary to chastity; it also forbids infidelity in marriage.

420. **What does the ninth commandment forbid?**
The ninth commandment expressly forbids every desire contrary to that fidelity which husband and wife vowed to observe when contracting marriage; and it also forbids every guilty thought or desire of anything that is prohibited by the sixth commandment.

421. **Is impurity a great sin?**
It is a most grave and abominable sin in the sight of God and man; it lowers man to the condition of the brute; it drags him into many other sins and vices; and it provokes the most terrible chastisements both in this world and in the next.

422. **Is every thought that comes into the mind against purity a sin?**
The thoughts that come into the mind against purity are not of themselves sins, but rather temptations and incentives to sin.

423. **When is a bad thought a sin?**
Bad thoughts, even though resulting in no bad deed, are sins when we culpably entertain them, or consent to them, or expose ourselves to the proximate danger of consenting to them.

424. **What do the sixth and ninth commandments command?**
The sixth commandment commands us to be chaste and modest in act, in look, in behavior, and in speech. The ninth commandment commands us in addition to this to be chaste and pure interiorly, that is, in mind and in heart.

425. **What must we do to observe the sixth and ninth commandments?**
To be able to observe the sixth and ninth commandments, we ought to pray often and from our hearts to God; be devout to the Blessed Virgin, the Mother of purity; remember that God watches us; think on death, on the divine chastisements, and on the passion of Jesus Christ; guard the senses; practice Christian mortification; and frequent the sacraments with the proper dispositions.

426. **What must we avoid in order to preserve ourselves chaste?**
To preserve ourselves chaste we must shun idleness, bad companions, the reading of bad books and papers, intemperance, the sight of indecent statues or pictures, licentious theatres, dangerous conversations, and all other occasions of sin.

The Seventh Commandment

427. **What does the seventh commandment, "Thou shalt not steal," forbid?**
The seventh commandment, "Thou shalt not steal," forbids all unjust taking and all unjust keeping of what belongs to another, and also every other way of wronging our neighbor in his property.

428. **What is meant by stealing?**
It means taking another's goods unjustly and against the owner's will, that is to say, when he has every reason and right to be unwilling to be deprived of them.

429. **Why is it forbidden to steal?**
Because a sin is committed against justice and an injury is done to another by taking or keeping against his right and will that which belongs to him.

430. **What is meant by another's goods?**
Everything that belongs to him—everything of which he has the ownership, or the use, or the custody.

431. **In how many ways can another's goods be unjustly taken?**
In two ways: by theft and by robbery.

432. **How is theft committed?**
Theft is committed by taking another's goods secretly.

433. **How is robbery committed?**
Robbery is committed by taking another's goods openly and with violence.

434. **In what cases may another's goods be taken without sin?**
When the owner consents or even when he unjustly refuses. Thus, one in extreme necessity may take another's goods without sin, provided that he takes only so much as is absolutely necessary to relieve pressing and extreme need.

435. **Is it only by theft and robbery that another can be injured in his property?**
He can also be injured by fraud, usury, and any other act of injustice directed against his goods.

436. **How is fraud committed?**
Fraud is committed in trade by deceiving another by false weight, measure, and money, or by bad goods; by falsifying writings and documents; in short, by deceit in buying or selling, or in contracts in general, as well as by refusing to pay what is just and agreed upon.

437. **How is usury committed?**
Usury is committed by exacting, without just title, an unlawful interest for money lent, thus taking an unfair advantage of another's need or ignorance.

438. **What other sorts of injustice may be committed with regard to another's goods?**
By unjustly causing him to lose what he has; by injuring him in his possessions; by not working as in duty bound; by maliciously refusing to pay debts or wages due; by wounding or killing his stock; by damaging property held in custody; by preventing another from making just gains; by aiding thieves; and by receiving, concealing, or buying stolen goods.

439. **Is it a grave sin to steal?**
It is a grave sin against justice when the matter is grave; for it is most important for the good of individuals, of families, and of society that each one's right to his property should be respected.

440. **When is stolen matter grave?**
When that which is taken is considerable, as also when serious loss is inflicted on another by taking that which in itself is of little value.

441. **What does the seventh commandment command?**
The seventh commandment commands us to respect the property of others, to give the laborer fair wages, and to observe justice in all that concerns what belongs to others.

442. **Is it enough for one who has sinned against the seventh commandment to confess his sin?**
It is not enough for one who has sinned against the seventh commandment to confess his sin; he must also do his best to restore what belongs to others, and to repair the loss he has caused.

443. **What is meant by "repairing the losses caused"?**
"Repairing the losses caused" means the compensation which must be made to another for the goods or profits lost owing to the theft or other acts of injustice committed to his detriment.

444. **To whom must stolen property be restored?**
To him from whom it has been stolen; to his heirs, if he is dead; or if this is really impossible, the value of it ought to be devoted to the poor or to some charity.

445. **What should one do who finds something of great value?**
He should diligently seek the owner and faithfully restore it to him.

The Eighth Commandment

446. **What does the eighth commandment, "Thou shalt not bear false witness," forbid?**
The eighth commandment, "Thou shalt not bear false witness," forbids false testimony in a court of justice, and it also forbids backbiting, detraction, calumny, adulation, rash judgment and rash suspicion, and every sort of lying.

447. **What is detraction or backbiting?**
Detraction or backbiting is a sin which consists in making known another's sins and defects without sufficient reason.

448. **What is calumny?**
Calumny is a sin which consists in maliciously attributing to another faults and defects which he did not possess.

449. **What is adulation?**
Adulation is a sin which consists in deceiving another by falsely praising him or others for the purpose of profiting thereby.

450. **What is rash judgment or rash suspicion?**

Rash judgment or rash suspicion is a sin which consists in judging or suspecting evil of others without sufficient foundation.

451. **What is a lie?**

A lie is a sin which consists in asserting as true or false by word or act that which one does not believe to be really the case.

452. **How many kinds of lies are there?**

There are three kinds: the jocose lie, the officious lie, and the malicious lie.

453. **What is a jocose lie?**

A jocose lie is that which is told in jest and without injury to anyone.

454. **What is an officious lie?**

An officious lie is a false statement to benefit oneself or another without injuring anyone else.

455. **What is a malicious lie?**

A malicious lie is a false statement made to the injury of another.

456. **Is it ever lawful to tell a lie?**

It is never lawful to tell a lie, neither in joke, nor for one's own benefit, nor for the benefit of another, because a lie is always bad in itself.

457. **What kind of sin is a lie?**

A lie when jocose or officious is a venial sin; but when malicious it is a mortal sin if the harm done is grave.

458. **Is it always necessary to say all one's mind?**

It is not always necessary, especially when he who questions you has no right to know what he demands.

459. **Is it enough for him who has sinned against the eighth commandment to confess the sin?**
It is not enough for him who has sinned against the eighth commandment to confess the sin; he is also obliged to retract whatever he said when calumniating another, and to repair as far as he can the harm he has done.

460. **What does the eighth commandment command us to do?**
The eighth commandment commands us to speak the truth at the proper time and place, and, as far as we can, to put a good interpretation upon the actions of our neighbor.

The Tenth Commandment

461. **What does the tenth commandment, "Thou shalt not covet thy neighbor's goods," forbid?**
The tenth commandment, "Thou shalt not covet thy neighbor's goods," forbids the wish to deprive another of his goods and the wish to acquire goods by unjust means.

462. **Why does God forbid even the desire of another's goods?**
God forbids the unregulated desire of another's goods, because he wishes us to be just even in thought and will, and to hold ourselves completely aloof from unjust acts.

463. **What does the tenth commandment command?**
The tenth commandment commands us to be satisfied with the state in which God has placed us, and to bear poverty patiently should God have placed us in that condition.

464. **How can a Christian be content in a state of poverty?**
A Christian can be content even in a state of poverty by reflecting that our greatest good is a pure and peaceful conscience; that our true home is heaven; and that Jesus Christ made himself poor for love of us and has promised a special reward to those who bear poverty patiently.

The Precepts of the Church

The Precepts of the Church in General

465. **Besides the commandments of God, what else must we observe?**
Besides the commandments of God, we must also observe the precepts of the Church.

466. **Are we obliged to obey the Church?**
Undoubtedly we are obliged to obey the Church, because Jesus Christ himself commands us to do so, and because the precepts of the Church help us to observe the commandments of God.

467. **When does the obligation to observe the precepts of the Church begin to bind?**
As a rule, the obligation to observe the precepts of the Church begins to bind us as soon as we come to the use of reason.

468. **Is it a sin to transgress a precept of the Church?**
Knowingly to transgress a precept of the Church in grave matter is a mortal sin.

469. **Who can dispense from a precept of the Church?**
Only the pope, or one who has received from him the power to do so, can dispense from a precept of the Church.

470. **Name the precepts of the Church.**
The precepts of the Church are:

1. To hear Mass on all Sundays and on holy days of obligation.
2. To fast during Lent, on Quarter Tense, and appointed vigils, and not to eat meat on forbidden days.

3. To confess our sins at least once a year, and to receive Holy Communion at Easter, each one in his own parish.[12]
4. To contribute to the support of the Church, according to local custom.
5. Not to solemnize marriage at forbidden times, that is, from the First Sunday in Advent until the Epiphany, and from the first day of Lent until Low Sunday.

The First Precept of the Church

471. **What does the first precept of the Church, "To hear Mass on all Sundays and on holy days of obligation," order us to do?**
The first precept of the Church, "To hear Mass on all Sundays and on holy days of obligations," orders us to assist devoutly at Mass on all Sundays and on holy days of obligation.

472. **At which Mass does the Church desire us to assist on Sundays and on holy days of obligation?**
The Mass at which the Church desires us to assist, if possible, on Sundays and holy days of obligation is the parochial Mass.

473. **Why does the Church recommend the faithful to assist at the parochial Mass?**
The Church recommends the faithful to assist at the parochial Mass: 1) in order that all the parishioners of the same parish may unite in prayer together with their pastor, who is their head; 2) in order that the parishioners may participate more abundantly in the Holy Sacrifice of the Mass, which is applied principally for them; 3) in order that they may hear the truths of the gospel, which pastors are bound to explain during Mass; 4) in order that they may learn the regulations and notices which are published at that Mass.

[12] Translator's note: In the *Catechism of Pius X*, as in most Italian works of the kind, the precepts of annual confession and paschal Communion are combined, thus reducing the number to five.

474. **What is meant by the Lord's Day?**
The Lord's Day means the day of the Lord, that is, the day specially consecrated to divine service.

475. **Why in the first precept of the Church is special mention made of the Lord's Day?**
In the first precept of the Church special mention is made of the Lord's Day, because it is the principal Christian festival, as the Sabbath was the principal Jewish festival, and because it was instituted by God himself.

476. **What other festivals have been instituted by the Church?**
The Church has instituted feasts of our Lord, of the Blessed Virgin, of the angels, and of the saints.

477. **Why did the Church institute other festivals of our Lord?**
The Church instituted other festivals of our Lord in memory of his divine mysteries.

478. **And why have festivals of the Blessed Virgin and of the saints been instituted?**
Festivals of the Blessed Virgin and of the saints have been instituted: 1) in memory of the graces which God has given them, and to thank his divine goodness; 2) in order that we may honor them, imitate their example, and be aided by their prayers.

The Second Precept of the Church

479. **What is commanded by the second precept of the Church in the words: "To fast on the days prescribed"?**
By the words, "To fast on the days prescribed," the second precept of the Church commands us to observe the fast: 1) during Lent; 2) on certain days of Advent, where this is prescribed; 3) at Quarter Tense; 4) and on certain vigils.

480. **In what does fasting consist?**

Fasting consists in taking but one meal a day and in abstaining from prohibited kinds of food.

481. **On fast days may a collation be taken in the evening?**

Through the concession of the Church, a collation may be taken in the evening on fast days.

482. **What is the good of fasting?**

Fasting serves to dispose us better to prayer; to do penance for past sins; and to preserve us from sinning again.

483. **Who are bound to fast?**

Every Christian over twenty-one years of age who is not dispensed, or excused for some good reason, is bound to fast.

484. **Are those who are not bound to fast exempt from all mortification?**

Those who are not bound by the obligation of fasting are not exempt from all mortification, because all are bound to do penance.

485. **For what purpose has Lent been instituted?**

Lent has been instituted to imitate in some way the rigorous fast of forty days undergone by Jesus Christ in the desert, and to prepare us by penitential exercises to celebrate the feast of Easter devoutly.

486. **Why has the Advent fast been instituted?**

The Advent fast has been instituted to prepare us to celebrate devoutly the feast of Our Lord's Nativity.

487. **Why has the fast of Quarter Tense been instituted?**

The fast of Quarter Tense has been instituted to consecrate each of the four seasons of the year by some days' penance; to beg of God the preservation of the fruits of the earth; to thank him for those already given us;

and to beseech him to give good priests to his Church, the usual days for ordaining priests being the Saturdays of Quarter Tense.

488. **Why has fasting on vigils been instituted?**
Fasting on vigils has been instituted to prepare us to celebrate the principal feasts devoutly.

489. **What is forbidden on Fridays, and also on Saturdays where not dispensed?**
On Fridays, and also on Saturdays where not dispensed, it is forbidden to eat meat, except in case of necessity.

490. **Why does the Church wish us to abstain from eating meat on these days?**
In order that we may do penance each week, and especially on Friday, in honor of the passion, and on Saturday in memory of the burial of Jesus Christ, and in honor of the Blessed Virgin.

The Third Precept of the Church

491. **What does the Church command us in the words of the third precept: "To go to confession at least once a year"?**
By the words of the third precept, "To go to confession at least once a year," the Church obliges all Christians, who have come to the use of reason, to approach the sacrament of penance at least once a year.

492. **What is the best time to satisfy the precept of annual confession?**
The best time to satisfy the precept of annual confession is Lent, in accordance with the usage introduced and approved of by the whole Church.

493. **Why does the Church say that we are to confess at least once a year?**
The Church uses the words *at least* to let us see her desire that we should approach the sacraments more frequently.

494. **Is it useful, then, to go often to confession?**
It is most useful to go often to confession, especially as it is difficult for one who goes only rarely to make a good confession and to avoid mortal sin.

495. **What does the Church command us to do by the other words of the third precept: "To receive Holy Communion at Easter, each one in his own parish"?**
By the words of the third precept, "To receive Holy Communion at Easter, each one in his own parish," the Church obliges all Christians who have come to the age of discretion to receive the Blessed Eucharist every year at paschal time in their own parish.

496. **Are we bound to go to Holy Communion at other times besides Easter?**
We are also bound to go to Holy Communion when in danger of death.

497. **Why is it said that we are to receive Holy Communion at least at Easter?**
Because the Church earnestly desires us to approach Holy Communion which is the divine food of our souls, not only at Easter, but as often as we possibly can.

498. **Is this precept fulfilled by a sacrilegious confession or a sacrilegious Communion?**
This precept of the Church is not fulfilled by sacrilegious confession and Communion, because the intention of the Church is that we receive those sacraments for the end on account of which they were instituted, that is, for our sanctification.

The Fourth Precept of the Church

499. **How are we to observe the fourth precept: "To contribute to due support of the Church"?**
The fourth precept is satisfied by paying the dues or making the offerings which have been established in recognition of God's supreme dominion

over all things and as a means of providing for the becoming support of his ministers.

500. **How are these dues and offerings to be paid?**
They are to be paid in the way and manner customary in the place in which we live.

The Fifth Precept of the Church

501. **What does the Church forbid in the fifth precept: "Not to solemnize marriage at forbidden times"?**
In the fifth precept the Church does not forbid the celebration of the sacrament of marriage; but only the nuptial solemnities, from the First Sunday of Advent until the Epiphany, and from the first day of Lent until Low Sunday.

502. **What are the nuptial solemnities which are forbidden?**
The nuptial solemnities forbidden by this precept are the celebration of the nuptial Mass, the nuptial benediction, and marriage festivities on a large scale.

503. **Why are marriage festivities on a large scale out of place in Advent and Lent?**
Pompous displays are out of place in Advent and Lent because these seasons are specially consecrated to penance and prayer.

SECTION IV
On the Sacraments

The Sacraments in General

Nature of the Sacraments

504. **What is treated of in the fourth part of the Christian doctrine?**
In the fourth part of the Christian doctrine the sacraments are treated of.

505. **What is meant by the word *sacrament*?**
By the word *sacrament* is meant a sensible and efficacious sign of grace, instituted by Christ to sanctify our souls.

506. **Why do you call the sacraments sensible and efficacious signs of grace?**
I call the sacraments sensible and efficacious signs of grace because all the sacraments signify, by means of sensible things, the divine grace which they produce in our souls.

507. **Show by an example how the sacraments are sensible and efficacious signs of grace.**
In baptism the pouring of water on the head of the person, and the words: "I baptize thee," that is, I wash thee, "in the name of the Father, and of the Son, and of the Holy Ghost," are a sensible sign of that which baptism accomplishes in the soul; for just as water washes the body, so in like manner does the grace given in baptism cleanse the soul from sin.

508. **How many sacraments are there, and how are they called?**
The sacraments are seven: baptism, confirmation, Eucharist, penance, extreme unction, holy orders, and matrimony.

509. **What is necessary to constitute a sacrament?**
To constitute a sacrament it is necessary to have the matter, the form, and the minister, who must have the intention to do what the Church does.

510. **What is the matter of the sacraments?**
The matter of the sacraments is the sensible thing made use of in effecting the sacrament; such, for example, as natural water in baptism, oil and balsam in confirmation.

511. **What is the form of the sacraments?**
The form of the sacraments is the words which are pronounced in order to effect the sacrament.

512. **Who is the minister of the sacraments?**
The minister of the sacraments is the person who administers or confers the sacrament.

The Principal Effect of the Sacraments, i.e., Grace

513. **What is grace?**
Grace is an inward and supernatural gift given to us without any merit of our own, but through the merits of Jesus Christ in order to gain eternal life.

514. **How is grace distinguished?**
Grace is divided into sanctifying grace, which is also called habitual grace, and actual grace.

515. **What is sanctifying grace?**
Sanctifying grace is a supernatural gift inherent in our soul, and rendering us just, adopted children of God, and heirs to paradise.

516. **How many kinds of sanctifying grace are there?**
Sanctifying grace is of two kinds: first grace and second grace.

517. **What is first grace?**
First grace is that by means of which one passes from the state of mortal sin to the state of justice.

518. **And what is second grace?**
Second grace is an increase of first grace.

519. **What is actual grace?**
Actual grace is a supernatural gift which enlightens the mind, moves and strengthens the will in order to enable us to do good and avoid evil.

520. **Can we resist the grace of God?**
Yes, we can resist the grace of God, because it does not destroy our free will.

521. **By the aid of our own powers alone can we do anything available to life eternal?**
Without the help of the grace of God, and by our own powers alone, we cannot do anything helpful to life everlasting.

522. **How is grace given us by God?**
Grace is given us by God chiefly through the sacraments.

523. **Do the sacraments confer any other grace besides sanctifying grace?**
Besides sanctifying grace, the sacraments also confer sacramental grace.

524. **What is sacramental grace?**
Sacramental grace consists in the right acquired in the reception of a sacrament, to have at the proper time the actual graces necessary to fulfill the obligations arising from the sacrament received. Thus, when we were baptized, we received the right to have the grace to live a Christian life.

525. **Do the sacraments always confer grace on those who receive them?**
The sacraments always confer grace provided they are received with the necessary dispositions.

526. **Who gave to the sacraments the power of conferring grace?**
Jesus Christ by his passion and death gave to the sacraments the power of conferring grace.

527. **What sacraments confer first sanctifying grace?**
The sacraments which confer first sanctifying grace, and render us friends of God, are two: baptism and penance.

528. **How are these two sacraments called on that account?**
These two sacraments, baptism and penance, are on that account called sacraments of the dead, because they are instituted chiefly to restore to the life of grace the soul dead by sin.

529. **Which are the sacraments that increase grace in those who already possess it?**
The sacraments which increase grace in those who already possess it are the other five: confirmation, Eucharist, extreme unction, holy orders, and matrimony, all of which confer second grace.

530. **On this account how are they called?**
These five sacraments—confirmation, Eucharist, extreme unction, holy orders, and matrimony—are on that account called sacraments of the living, because those who receive them must be free from mortal sin, that is, already alive through sanctifying grace.

531. **What sin does he commit who, conscious that he is not in a state of grace, receives one of the sacraments of the living?**
He who, conscious that he is not in a state of grace, receives one of the sacraments of the living, commits a serious sacrilege.

532. **What sacraments are most necessary for salvation?**
The sacraments most necessary to salvation are two: baptism and penance. Baptism is necessary to all, and penance is necessary to all who have sinned mortally after baptism.

533. **What is the greatest of all the sacraments?**
The greatest of all the sacraments is the Eucharist, because it contains not only grace, but also Jesus Christ the author of grace and of the sacraments.

The Character Impressed by Some of the Sacraments

534. **What sacraments can be received only once?**
The sacraments that can be received only once are three: baptism, confirmation, and holy orders.

535. **Why can the three sacraments of baptism, confirmation, and holy orders be received only once?**
The three sacraments, baptism, confirmation, and holy orders, can be received only once, because each of them imprints a character.

536. **What is the character that each of the three sacraments, baptism, confirmation, and holy orders, imprints on the soul?**
The character that each of the three sacraments, baptism, confirmation, and holy orders, imprints on the soul is a spiritual mark that is never effaced.

537. **What is the purpose of the character that these three sacraments impress on the soul?**
The character that these three sacraments imprint on the soul, serves to mark us as members of Jesus Christ at baptism, as his soldiers at confirmation, and as his ministers at holy orders.

Baptism

Nature and Effects of Baptism

538. **What is the sacrament of baptism?**
Baptism is a sacrament by which we are born again to the grace of God, and become Christians.

539. **What are the effects of the sacrament of baptism?**
The sacrament of baptism confers first sanctifying grace by which original sin is washed away, as well as all actual sin if any such exists; it remits all punishment due on account of such sins; it imprints the character of a Christian; it makes us children of God, members of the Church, and heirs to paradise, and enables us to receive the other sacraments.

540. **What is the matter of baptism?**
The matter of baptism is natural water which is poured on the head of the person to be baptized in such a quantity as to flow.

541. **What is the form of baptism?**
The form of baptism is: "I baptize thee in the name of the Father and of the Son and of the Holy Ghost."

Minister of Baptism

542. **To whom does it belong to confer baptism?**
To confer baptism belongs by right to bishops and parish priests, but in case of necessity any person, whether man or woman, even a heretic or an infidel, can administer it, provided he carries out the rite of baptism, and has the intention of doing what the Church does.

543. **If it were necessary to baptize a person in danger of death, and if several people were present, who should administer the sacrament?**
If it were necessary to baptize a person in danger of death, and if several people were present, a priest, if such were at hand, should administer the sacrament, and, in his absence, one of the inferior clergy; and in the absence of such, a layman in preference to a woman, unless in the case in which the greater skill on the part of the woman, or the claims of propriety, should demand otherwise.

544. **What intention should the person baptizing have?**
The person baptizing should have the intention of doing what holy Church does in baptizing.

The Rite of Baptism and the Disposition of the Adult Who Receives It

545. **How is baptism given?**
Baptism is given by pouring water on the head of the person to be baptized—and if it cannot be poured on the head, then on some other principal part of the body—saying at the same time: "I baptize thee in the name of the Father, and of the Son, and of the Holy Ghost."

546. **If one were to pour the water and another to pronounce the words would the person be baptized?**
If one poured the water and another said the words the person would not be baptized; but it is necessary that the person who pours the water should pronounce the words.

547. **In doubt whether the person is dead, is it right to omit baptizing him?**
In doubt whether the person is dead, he should be baptized conditionally, saying: "If thou art alive, I baptize thee in the name of the Father, and of the Son, and of the Holy Ghost."

548. **When should infants be brought to the Church to be baptized?**
Infants should be brought to the Church to be baptized as soon as possible.

549. **Why such anxiety to have infants receive baptism?**
There should be the greatest anxiety to have infants baptized, because on account of their tender age, they are exposed to many dangers of death, and cannot be saved without baptism.

550. **Do parents sin, then, who, through negligence, allow their children to die without baptism, or who defer it?**
Yes, fathers and mothers who, through negligence, allow their children to die without baptism sin grievously, because they deprive their children of eternal life; and they also sin grievously by putting off baptism for a long time, because they expose them to danger of dying without having received it.

551. **When the person who is being baptized is an adult, what dispositions should he have?**
An adult who is being baptized, besides faith, should have at least imperfect contrition for the mortal sins he may have committed.

552. **If an adult in mortal sin was baptized without such sorrow, what would he receive?**
If an adult was baptized in mortal sin without such sorrow, he would receive the character of baptism, but not the remission of his sins nor sanctifying grace. And these two effects would be suspended, until the obstacle is removed by perfect contrition or by the sacrament of penance.

Necessity of Baptism and Obligations of the Baptized

553. **Is baptism necessary to salvation?**

Baptism is absolutely necessary to salvation, for our Lord has expressly said: "Unless a man be born again of water and the Holy Ghost, he cannot enter into the kingdom of God."[13]

554. **Can the absence of baptism be supplied in any other way?**

The absence of baptism can be supplied by martyrdom, which is called baptism of blood; or by an act of perfect love of God, or of contrition, along with the desire, at least implicit, of baptism, and this is called baptism of desire.

555. **To what is the person baptized bound?**

The person baptized is bound to always profess the faith and observe the law of Jesus Christ and of his Church.

556. **In receiving holy baptism what do we renounce?**

In receiving holy baptism we renounce forever the devil, his works and pomps.

557. **What is meant by "the works and pomps of the devil"?**

By "the works and pomps of the devil" we mean sin and the maxims of the world that are contrary to the maxims of the gospel.

Names and Sponsors

558. **Why is the name of a saint given to him who is being baptized?**

To him who is being baptized is given the name of a saint in order to put him under the protection of a heavenly patron, and to animate him to imitate that saint's example.

[13] Jn 3:5

559. **Who are the godfathers and godmothers in baptism?**
The godfathers and godmothers in baptism are those persons who, in accordance with the decree of the Church, hold the infants at the font, answer for them, and become guarantees in the sight of God for their Christian education, especially in the absence of the parents.

560. **Are we obliged to keep the promises and renunciations made for us by our sponsors?**
We are certainly obliged to observe the promises and renunciations made for us by our sponsors, because it is only on this condition that God has received us into his grace.

561. **What sort of persons should be chosen as godfathers and godmothers?**
There should be chosen as godfathers and godmothers Catholics of good life, and obedient to the laws of the Church.

562. **What are the obligations of godfathers and godmothers?**
Godfathers and godmothers are bound to see that their spiritual children are instructed in the truths of faith, and live as good Christians; and they should edify them by their good example.

563. **What tie do sponsors contract in baptism?**
Sponsors contract a spiritual relationship with the baptized and with the parents of the baptized, which causes an impediment to marriage with these persons.

Chrism or Confirmation

564. **What is the sacrament of confirmation?**
Confirmation is a sacrament which gives us the Holy Ghost, imprints on our souls the mark of a soldier of Jesus Christ, and makes us perfect Christians.

565. **How does the sacrament of confirmation make us perfect Christians?**
The sacrament of confirmation makes us perfect Christians by confirming us in the faith and perfecting the other virtues and gifts received in baptism; hence it is called confirmation.

566. **What gifts of the Holy Ghost are received in confirmation?**
The gifts of the Holy Ghost received in confirmation are these seven: wisdom, understanding, counsel, fortitude, knowledge, piety, and the fear of the Lord.

567. **What is the matter of this sacrament?**
The matter of this sacrament, besides the imposition of hands by the bishop, is the anointing of the forehead of the baptized with sacred chrism; and for this reason it is also called the sacrament of chrism, that is, anointing.

568. **What is sacred chrism?**
Sacred chrism is oil of olives mingled with balsam, and consecrated by the bishop on Holy Thursday.

569. **What do the oil and balsam in this sacrament signify?**
In this sacrament the oil, which is unctuous and strengthening, signifies the abounding grace which is diffused over the soul of the Christian to confirm him in his faith; and the balsam, which is fragrant and prevents corruption, signifies that the Christian, strengthened by this grace, is enabled to

give forth a good odor of Christian virtue and preserve himself from the corruption of vice.

570. **What is the form of the sacrament of confirmation?**
The form of the sacrament of confirmation is this: "I sign thee with the sign of the cross, and I confirm thee with the chrism of salvation, in the name of the Father, and of the Son, and of the Holy Ghost. Amen."

571. **Who is the minister of the sacrament of confirmation?**
The ordinary minister of the sacrament of confirmation is the bishop alone.

572. **How does the bishop administer confirmation?**
In administering the sacrament of confirmation, the bishop first stretches his hands over those to be confirmed, and invokes the Holy Ghost upon them; next, he anoints the forehead of each one with sacred chrism in the form of a cross, saying the words of the form; then he gives each one confirmed a light stroke on the cheek with his right hand, saying: "Peace be with you"; finally, he solemnly blesses all those he has confirmed.

573. **Why is the anointing made on the forehead?**
The anointing is made on the forehead, where signs of fear and shame appear, in order that he who is confirmed may understand that he should not blush at the name and profession of a Christian, nor fear the enemies of his faith.

574. **Why is a light stroke given to the person confirmed?**
A light stroke is given to the person confirmed to show him that he should be ready to bear all insults and endure all sufferings for the faith of Jesus Christ.

575. **Should all endeavor to receive the sacrament of confirmation?**
Yes, all should endeavor to receive the sacrament of confirmation and to have those under them receive it.

576. **At what age is it advisable to receive the sacrament of confirmation?**
The age at which it is advisable to receive the sacrament of confirmation is about the seventh year, because it is then that temptations usually begin, and the grace of the sacrament can be sufficiently discerned and a recollection be had of having received it.

577. **What dispositions are required to receive worthily the sacrament of confirmation?**
To receive worthily the sacrament of confirmation it is necessary to be in the grace of God; know the principal mysteries of our holy faith; and approach it with reverence and devotion.

578. **Would he who received confirmation a second time be guilty of sin?**
He would commit a sacrilege; because confirmation is one of the sacraments that imprint a character on the soul and hence may be received only once.

579. **What should a Christian do to preserve the grace of confirmation?**
To preserve the grace of confirmation a Christian should pray often, do good works, and live according to the laws of Jesus Christ, in spite of human respect.

580. **Why also are there godfathers and godmothers in confirmation?**
In order that they by word and example may show the confirmed the way to eternal life and help him in the spiritual combat.

581. **What qualifications are required in sponsors?**
They should be of proper age, Catholics, confirmed, instructed in the necessary truths of religion, and persons of good life.

582. **Does a sponsor in confirmation contract any relationship with the confirmed and the parents of the confirmed?**
The sponsor in confirmation contracts the same spiritual relationship as is contracted in baptism.

The Blessed Eucharist

The Nature of This Sacrament—The Real Presence

583. **What is the sacrament of the Eucharist?**
The Eucharist is a sacrament in which, by the marvelous conversion of the whole substance of bread into the body of Jesus Christ, and of that of wine into his precious blood, is contained truly, really, and substantially, the body, the blood, the soul, and divinity of the same Lord Jesus Christ, under the appearance of bread and wine as our spiritual food.

584. **In the Eucharist is there the same Jesus Christ who is in heaven, and who was born on earth of the Blessed Virgin?**
Yes, in the Eucharist there is truly the same Jesus Christ who is in heaven, and who was born on earth of the Blessed Virgin.

585. **Why do you believe that in the Eucharist Jesus Christ is really present?**
I believe that in the Eucharist Jesus Christ is truly present, because he himself has said it, and holy Church teaches it.

586. **What is the matter of the sacrament of the Eucharist?**
The matter of the sacrament of the Eucharist is that which was used by Jesus Christ himself, that is, wheaten bread and wine of the vine.

587. **What is the form of the sacrament of the Eucharist?**
The form of the sacrament of the Eucharist consists of the words used by Jesus Christ himself: "This is my body";[14] "This is my blood."[15]

[14] Mt 26:26; Mk 14:22
[15] Mt 26:28; Mk 14:24

588. **What is the host before consecration?**
The host before consecration is bread.

589. **After consecration what is the host?**
After consecration the host is the true body of our Lord Jesus Christ, under the species of bread.

590. **What is in the chalice before consecration?**
In the chalice before consecration there is wine with a few drops of water.

591. **After consecration what is in the chalice?**
After consecration there is in the chalice the true blood of our Lord Jesus Christ, under the species of wine.

592. **When does the change of the bread into the body and of the wine into the blood of Jesus Christ take place?**
The change of the bread into the body and of the wine into the blood of Jesus Christ is made in the very moment in which the priest pronounces the words of consecration during Holy Mass.

593. **What is the consecration?**
The consecration is the renewal, by means of the priest, of the miracle wrought by Jesus Christ at the last supper, of changing bread and wine into his adorable body and blood by saying: "This is my body…This is my blood."

594. **What does the Church call the miraculous change of bread and of wine into the body and blood of Jesus Christ?**
The Church calls the miraculous change which is daily wrought upon our altars transubstantiation.

595. **Who gave this great power to the words of consecration?**
Our Lord Jesus Christ himself, who is Almighty God, gave this great power to the words of consecration.

596. **Is there nothing left of the bread and of the wine after consecration?**
After consecration, the species of the bread and of the wine alone are left.

597. **What are the species of the bread and of the wine?**
The species of the bread and of the wine are the quantity and sensible qualities of the bread and of the wine, such as the form, the color, and the taste.

598. **How can the species of the bread and of the wine remain without their substance?**
The species of the bread and of the wine remain without their substance in a wonderful way by the power of God Almighty.

599. **Under the species of the bread is there only the body of Jesus Christ, and under the species of the wine only his blood?**
Both under the species of the bread and under the species of the wine the living Jesus Christ is all present, with his body, his blood, his soul, and his divinity.

600. **Can you tell me why Jesus Christ is whole and entire both in the host and in the chalice?**
Both in the host and in the chalice Jesus Christ is whole and entire, because he is living and immortal in the Eucharist as he is in heaven; hence where his body is, there also are his blood, his soul, and his divinity; and where his blood is, there also are his body, his soul, and his divinity, all these being inseparable in Jesus Christ.

601. **When Jesus Christ is in the host does he cease to be in heaven?**
When Jesus Christ is in the host he does not cease to be in heaven, but is at one and the same time in heaven and in the Blessed Sacrament.

602. **Is Jesus Christ present in all the consecrated hosts in the world?**
Yes, Jesus Christ is present in all consecrated hosts in the world.

603. **How can Jesus Christ be present in all the consecrated hosts in the world?**
Jesus Christ is present in all the consecrated hosts in the world by the omnipotence of God, to whom nothing is impossible.

604. **When the host is broken is the body of Jesus Christ broken also?**
When the host is broken, the body of Jesus Christ is not broken, but only the species of the bread are broken.

605. **In which part of the host is the body of Jesus Christ?**
The body of Jesus Christ is entire in all the parts into which the host is broken.

606. **Is Jesus Christ just as much in a particle of a host as in a large host?**
Just as much in a particle of a host as in a large host there is the same Jesus Christ.

607. **Why is the most Blessed Eucharist preserved in our churches?**
The most Blessed Eucharist is preserved in our churches that it may be adored by the faithful, and brought to the sick when necessary.

608. **Ought the Eucharist to be adored?**
The Eucharist ought to be adored by all, because it contains really, truly, and substantially our Lord Jesus Christ himself.

The Institution and Effects of the Sacrament of the Eucharist

609. **When did Jesus Christ institute the sacrament of the Eucharist?**
Jesus Christ instituted the sacrament of the Eucharist at the last supper, which he took with his disciples, the evening before his passion.

610. **Why did Jesus Christ institute the most Holy Eucharist?**
Jesus Christ instituted the most Holy Eucharist for three principal reasons: 1) to be the sacrifice of the new law; 2) to be the food of our souls; 3) to be

a perpetual memorial of his passion and death, and a precious pledge both of his love for us and of eternal life.

611. **Why did Jesus Christ institute this sacrament under the appearances of bread and wine?**
Jesus Christ instituted this sacrament under the appearances of bread and wine, because, the Eucharist being intended to be our spiritual nourishment, it was therefore fitting that it should be given to us under the form of food and drink.

612. **What are the effects which the most Holy Eucharist produces in us?**
The principal effects which the most Holy Eucharist produces in those who worthily receive it are these: 1) it preserves and increases the life of the soul, which is grace, just as natural food sustains and increases the life of the body; 2) it remits venial sins and preserves us from mortal sin; 3) it produces spiritual consolation.

613. **Does not the most Holy Eucharist produce other effects in us?**
Yes; the most Holy Eucharist produces three other effects in us: 1) it weakens our passions, and in particular it allays in us the fires of concupiscence; 2) it increases in us the fervor of charity toward God and our neighbor, and aids us to act in conformity with the will of Jesus Christ; 3) it gives us a pledge of future glory and of the resurrection of our body.

The Dispositions Necessary to Receive Holy Communion Worthily

614. **Does the sacrament of the Eucharist always produce its marvelous effects in us?**
The sacrament of the Eucharist produces its marvelous effects in us when it is received with the requisite dispositions.

615. **What conditions are necessary to make a good Communion?**
To make a good Communion, three conditions are necessary: 1) to be in the grace of God; 2) to be fasting from midnight until the moment of Holy

Communion; 3) to know what we are about to receive, and to approach Holy Communion devoutly.

616. **What is meant by being "in the grace of God"?**
To be "in the grace of God" means to have a pure conscience, and to be free from every mortal sin.

617. **What should one who knows that he is in mortal sin do before receiving Communion?**
One who knows that he is in mortal sin must make a good confession before going to Holy Communion, for even an act of perfect contrition is not enough without confession to enable one who is in mortal sin to receive Holy Communion properly.

618. **Why does not even an act of perfect contrition suffice to enable one who knows he is in mortal sin to go to Communion?**
Because the Church, out of respect for this sacrament, has ordained that no one in mortal sin should dare to go to Communion without first going to confession.

619. **Does he who goes to Communion in mortal sin receive Jesus Christ?**
He who goes to Communion in mortal sin receives Jesus Christ, but not his grace; moreover, he commits a sacrilege and renders himself deserving of sentence of damnation.

620. **What sort of fast is required before Communion?**
Before Communion there is required a natural fast which is broken by taking the least thing by way of food or drink.

621. **If one were to swallow a particle that had remained between the teeth, or a drop of water while washing, might he still go to Communion?**
If one were to swallow a particle that had remained between the teeth, or a drop of water while washing, he might still go to Communion, because

in both cases these things would either not be taken as food or drink, or they would have already lost the nature of either.

622. **Is it ever allowed to go to Communion after having broken the fast?**
To go to Communion after having broken the fast is permitted to the sick who are in danger of death, and to those who on account of prolonged illness have received a special dispensation from the pope. Communion given to the sick in danger of death is called viaticum, because it supports them on their way from this life to eternity.

623. **What is meant by the words: "to know what we are about to receive"?**
"To know what we are about to receive" means to know and firmly believe what is taught in Christian doctrine concerning this sacrament.

624. **What do the words, "to receive Holy Communion with devotion," mean?**
"To receive Holy Communion with devotion" means to approach Holy Communion with humility and modesty in person and dress; and to make a preparation before, and an act of thanksgiving after, Holy Communion.

625. **In what does the preparation before Communion consist?**
Preparation before Communion consists in meditating for some time on whom we are about to receive, and on who we are; and in making acts of faith, hope, charity, contrition, adoration, humility, and desire to receive Jesus Christ.

626. **In what does the thanksgiving after Communion consist?**
Thanksgiving after Communion consists in keeping ourselves recollected in order to honor the Lord who is within us; renewing our acts of faith, of hope, of charity, of adoration, of thanksgiving, of offerings, and of requests, especially for those graces which are most necessary for ourselves and for those for whom we are bound to pray.

627. **What should we do during the day on which we have received Communion?**
During the day on which we have received Communion we should remain as recollected as possible, occupy ourselves in works of piety, and discharge the duties of our state with greater diligence.

628. **How long does Jesus Christ abide within us after Holy Communion?**
After Holy Communion Jesus Christ abides within us by his grace as long as we commit no mortal sin; and he abides within us by his real presence until the sacramental species are consumed.

The Way to Go to Communion

629. **How should we act while receiving Holy Communion?**
In the act of receiving Holy Communion we should be kneeling, hold our head slightly raised, our eyes modest and fixed on the sacred host, our mouth sufficiently open, and the tongue slightly out over the lips.

630. **How should the Communion cloth be held?**
The Communion cloth should be held in such a way as to receive the sacred host in case it should fall.

631. **When should the sacred host be swallowed?**
We should try to swallow the sacred host as soon as possible, and we should avoid spitting for some time.

632. **If the sacred host should cling to the palate, what should be done?**
If the sacred host should cling to the palate, it should be removed with the tongue, but never with the finger.

The Precept of Holy Communion

633. **When are we bound to receive Communion?**
We are bound to go to Communion once a year, at Easter, each one in his own parish; and also when in danger of death.

634. **At what age does the precept of paschal Communion begin to bind?**
The precept of paschal Communion begins to bind as soon as a child is capable of receiving with the requisite dispositions.

635. **Do they sin who are old enough to receive Communion and do not?**
They who are old enough to receive Communion and do not either because they are unwilling, or because, through their own fault, they are not instructed, undoubtedly sin. Their parents or guardians also sin if the delay of Communion is owing to their fault, and they shall have to render a strict account to God for it.

636. **Is it a good and useful thing to go often to Communion?**
It is an excellent thing to go to Communion often, and even daily in accordance with the desire of the Church, provided we do so with the requisite dispositions.

637. **How often may we go to Holy Communion?**
We may go to Holy Communion as often as we are advised to do so by a pious and learned confessor.

The Holy Sacrifice of the Mass

The Essence, Institution, and Ends of the Holy Sacrifice of the Mass

638. **Should the Holy Eucharist be considered only as a sacrament?**
The Holy Eucharist, besides being a sacrament, is also the permanent sacrifice of the new law, which Jesus Christ left to his Church to be offered to God by the hands of his priests.

639. **In what, in general, does a sacrifice consist?**
In general, a sacrifice consists in the offering of some sensible thing to God, and in some way destroying it as an acknowledgment of his supreme dominion over us and over all things.

640. **What is this sacrifice of the new law called?**
This sacrifice of the new law is called the Holy Mass.

641. **What, then, is the Holy Mass?**
The Holy Mass is the sacrifice of the body and blood of Jesus Christ offered on our altars under the appearances of bread and wine, in commemoration of the sacrifice of the cross.

642. **Is the Sacrifice of the Mass the same as that of the cross?**
The Sacrifice of the Mass is substantially the same as that of the cross, for the same Jesus Christ, who offered himself on the cross, it is who offers himself by the hands of the priests, his ministers, on our altars; but as regards the way in which he is offered, the Sacrifice of the Mass differs from the sacrifice of the cross, though retaining the most intimate and essential relation to it.

643. **What difference and relation then is there between the Sacrifice of the Mass and that of the cross?**
Between the Sacrifice of the Mass and that of the cross there is this difference and relation: that on the cross Jesus Christ offered himself by shedding his blood and meriting for us; whereas on our altars he sacrifices himself without the shedding of his blood, and applies to us the fruits of his passion and death.

644. **What other relation has the Sacrifice of the Mass to that of the cross?**
Another relation of the Sacrifice of the Mass to that of the cross is that the Sacrifice of the Mass represents, in a sensible way, the shedding of the blood of Jesus Christ on the cross; because, in virtue of the words of consecration, only the body of our Savior is made present under the species

of the bread, and only his blood under the species of the wine; although by natural concomitance and by the hypostatic union, the living and real Jesus Christ is present under each of the species.

645. **Is not the sacrifice of the cross the one only sacrifice of the new law?**
The sacrifice of the cross is the one only sacrifice of the new law, inasmuch as through it our Lord satisfied divine justice, acquired all the merits necessary to save us, and thus, on his part, fully accomplished our redemption. These merits, however, he applies to us through the means instituted by him in his Church, among which is the Holy Sacrifice of the Mass.

646. **For what ends then is the Holy Sacrifice of the Mass offered?**
The Sacrifice of the Mass is offered to God for four ends: 1) to honor him properly, and hence it is called *latreutical*; 2) to thank him for his favors, and hence it is called *eucharistical*; 3) to appease him, make him due satisfaction for our sins, and to help the souls in purgatory, and hence it is called *propitiatory*; 4) to obtain all the graces necessary for us, and hence it is called *impetratory*.

647. **Who is it that offers to God the Sacrifice of the Holy Mass?**
The first and principal offerer of the Sacrifice of the Holy Mass is Jesus Christ, while the priest is the minister who in the name of Jesus Christ offers the same sacrifice to the eternal Father.

648. **Who instituted the Sacrifice of the Holy Mass?**
Jesus Christ himself instituted the Sacrifice of the Holy Mass when he instituted the sacrament of the Blessed Eucharist and said that this should be done in memory of his passion.

649. **To whom is the Holy Mass offered?**
The Holy Mass is offered to God alone.

650. **If the Holy Mass is offered to God alone, why are so many Masses celebrated in honor of the Blessed Virgin and the saints?**
Mass celebrated in honor of the Blessed Virgin and the saints is always a sacrifice offered to God alone; it is said to be celebrated in honor of the Blessed Virgin and the saints to thank God for the gifts he has given them, and through their intercession to obtain from him more abundantly the graces of which we have need.

651. **Who shares in the fruits of the Mass?**
The entire Church shares in the fruits of the Mass, but more particularly: 1) the priest and those who assist at Mass, the latter being united with the priest; 2) those for whom the Mass is applied, both living and dead.

The Way to Assist at Holy Mass

652. **What is required in order to assist at Holy Mass well and profitably?**
To assist at Holy Mass well and profitably two things are necessary: 1) modesty of person; 2) devotion of heart.

653. **In what does modesty of person consist?**
Modesty of person consists especially in being modestly dressed, in observing silence and recollection, and, as far as possible, in remaining kneeling, except during the time of the two gospels which are heard standing.

654. **In hearing Holy Mass, which is the best way to practice true devotion?**
In hearing Holy Mass, the best way to practice true devotion is the following: 1) from the very beginning, to unite our intention with that of the priest, offering the holy sacrifice to God for the ends for which it was instituted; 2) to accompany the priest in each prayer and action of the sacrifice; 3) to meditate on the passion and death of Jesus Christ and to heartily detest our sins, which have been the cause of them; 4) to go to Communion, or at least to make a spiritual Communion while the priest communicates.

655. **What is spiritual Communion?**

Spiritual Communion is a great desire to be united sacramentally with Jesus Christ, saying, for example: "My Lord Jesus Christ, I desire with my whole heart to be united with thee now and forever"; and then make the same acts that are to be made before and after sacramental Communion.

656. **Does the recitation of the rosary or other prayers during Mass prevent us from hearing it with profit?**

The recitation of the rosary and other prayers during Mass does not prevent us from hearing it with profit, provided we try as far as possible to follow the parts of the holy sacrifice.

657. **Is it advisable to pray for others while assisting at Mass?**

Yes, it is advisable to pray for others while assisting at Mass; nay, more, the time of Holy Mass is the most suitable of all times to pray for the living and the dead.

658. **What should we do after Mass?**

After Mass, we should give God thanks for having allowed us to assist at this great sacrifice, and we should ask pardon for all the faults we may have committed while assisting at it.

The Sacrament of Penance

Penance in General

659. **What is the sacrament of penance?**

The sacrament of penance, also called confession, is a sacrament instituted by Jesus Christ to remit the sins committed after baptism.

660. **Why is the name of penance given to this sacrament?**
The name of penance is given to this sacrament, because to obtain pardon for sins it is necessary to detest them penitently; and because he who has committed a fault must submit to the penance which the priest imposes.

661. **Why is this sacrament also called confession?**
This sacrament is also called confession, because to obtain pardon for sins it is not enough to detest them, but it is necessary also to accuse oneself of them to the priest, that is, to make a confession of them.

662. **When did Jesus Christ institute the sacrament of penance?**
Jesus Christ instituted the sacrament of penance on the day of his resurrection, when, entering the supper room, he solemnly gave his apostles the power of remitting sin.

663. **How did Jesus Christ give his apostles the power of remitting sin?**
Jesus Christ gave his apostles the power of remitting sin thus: "Breathing upon them he said: 'Receive ye the Holy Ghost; whose sins you shall forgive they are forgiven; and whose sins you shall retain they are retained.'"[16]

664. **What is the matter of the sacrament of penance?**
The matter of the sacrament of penance is divided into remote and proximate. The remote matter consists of the sins committed by the penitent after baptism; and the proximate matter are the acts of the penitent himself, that is, contrition, confession, and satisfaction.

665. **What is the form of the sacrament of penance?**
The form of the sacrament of penance is this: "I absolve thee from thy sins."

666. **Who is the minister of the sacrament of penance?**
The minister of the sacrament of penance is a priest authorized by the bishop to hear confessions.

[16] Jn 20:22-23

667. **Why do you say that a priest must be authorized by the bishop?**

A priest must be authorized by the bishop to hear confessions, because to administer this sacrament validly the power of orders is not enough, but there is also necessary the power of jurisdiction, that is, the power to judge, which must be given by the bishop.

668. **Which are the parts of the sacrament of penance?**

The parts of the sacrament of penance are contrition, confession, and satisfaction on the part of the penitent, and absolution on the part of the priest.

669. **What is contrition or sorrow for sin?**

Contrition or sorrow for sin is a grief of the soul leading us to detest sins committed and to resolve not to commit them anymore.

670. **What does the word *contrition* mean?**

Contrition means a crushing or breaking up into pieces as when a stone is hammered and reduced to dust.

671. **Why is the name of contrition given to sorrow for sin?**

The name of contrition is given to sorrow for sin to signify that the hard heart of the sinner is in a certain way crushed by sorrow for having offended God.

672. **In what does confession of sins consist?**

Confession of sins consists in a distinct accusation of our sins made to the confessor in order to obtain absolution and receive penance for them.

673. **Why is confession called an accusation?**

Confession is called an accusation, because it must not be a careless recital, but a true and sorrowful manifestation of our sins.

674. **What is satisfaction or penance?**

Satisfaction or penance is that prayer or other good work which the confessor enjoins on the penitent in expiation of his sins.

675. **What is absolution?**
Absolution is the sentence which the priest pronounces in the name of Jesus Christ when remitting the penitent's sins.

676. **Of all the parts of the sacrament of penance which is the most necessary?**
Of all the parts of the sacrament of penance the most necessary is contrition, because without it no pardon for sins is obtainable, while with it alone, perfect pardon can be obtained, provided that along with it there is the desire, at least implicit, of going to confession.

The Effects and the Necessity of the Sacrament of Penance and the Dispositions to Receive It Properly

677. **Which are the effects of the sacrament of penance?**
The sacrament of penance confers sanctifying grace by which are remitted the mortal sins and also the venial sins which we confess and for which we are sorry; it changes eternal punishment into temporal punishment, of which it even remits more or less according to our dispositions; it revives the merits of the good works done before committing mortal sin; it gives the soul seasonable aid against falling into sin again; and it restores peace of conscience.

678. **Is the sacrament of penance necessary to all for salvation?**
The sacrament of penance is necessary for salvation to all who have committed a mortal sin after baptism.

679. **Is it a good thing to go to confession often?**
Yes, it is an excellent thing to go to confession often, because the sacrament of penance, besides taking away sin, gives the graces necessary to avoid sin in the future.

680. **Has the sacrament of penance the power of remitting all sins, no matter how numerous or how great they are?**
The sacrament of penance has the power of remitting all sins, no matter how numerous and great they are, provided it is received with the requisite dispositions.

681. **How many conditions are necessary to make a good confession?**
To make a good confession, five things are necessary: 1) examination of conscience; 2) sorrow for having offended God; 3) a resolution of sinning no more; 4) confession of our sins; 5) satisfaction or penance.

682. **What should we do first of all to make a good confession?**
To make a good confession, we should first of all earnestly beseech God to give us light to know all our sins and strength to detest them.

Examination of Conscience

683. **What is the examination of conscience?**
The examination of conscience is a diligent search for the sins committed since the last good confession.

684. **How is the examination of conscience made?**
The examination of conscience is made by carefully calling to mind before God all the sins committed but not confessed, in thought, word, deed, and omission, against the commandments of God and the Church, and against the duties of our state.

685. **On what else should we examine ourselves?**
We should also examine ourselves on our bad habits and on the occasions of sin.

686. **In our examination, should we also try to discover the number of our sins?**
In our examinations, we should also try to discover the number of our mortal sins.

687. **What is required for a sin to be mortal?**
For a sin to be mortal, three things are required: grave matter, full advertence, and perfect consent of the will.

688. **When is the matter to be considered grave?**
The matter is grave when the thing under examination is seriously contrary to the laws of God and his Church.

689. **When is there full advertence in sinning?**
Full advertence in sinning is had when we know perfectly well that we are doing a serious evil.

690. **When is perfect consent of the will verified in sinning?**
Perfect consent of the will is verified in sinning when we deliberately determine to do a thing although we know that thing to be sinful.

691. **What diligence should be used in the examination of conscience?**
In the examination of conscience, the same diligence is demanded as is used in a matter of great importance.

692. **How much time should be spent in the examination of conscience?**
More or less time should be spent in the examination of conscience according to the needs of each case, that is, according to the number or kind of sins that burden the conscience, and according to the time that has elapsed since the last good confession.

693. **How may the examination of conscience be rendered easy?**
The examination of conscience is rendered easy by making an examination of conscience every evening upon the actions of the day.

Sorrow

694. **What is sorrow for sin?**
Sorrow for sin consists in grief of soul and in a sincere detestation of the offense offered to God.

695. **How many kinds of sorrow are there?**
Sorrow is of two kinds: perfect sorrow or contrition, and imperfect sorrow or attrition.

696. **What is perfect sorrow or contrition?**
Perfect sorrow is a grief of soul for having offended God because he is infinitely good and worthy of being loved for his own sake.

697. **Why do you call the sorrow of contrition perfect sorrow?**
I call the sorrow of contrition perfect sorrow for two reasons: 1) because it considers the goodness of God alone and not our own advantage or loss; 2) because it enables us at once to obtain pardon for sins, even though the obligation to confess them still remains.

698. **Perfect sorrow, then, obtains us pardon of our sins independently of confession?**
Perfect sorrow does not obtain us pardon of our sins independently of confession, because it always includes the intention to confess them.

699. **Why does perfect sorrow or contrition produce the effect of restoring us to the grace of God?**
Perfect sorrow or contrition produces this effect, because it proceeds from charity which cannot exist in the soul together with sin.

700. **What is imperfect sorrow or attrition?**
Imperfect sorrow or attrition is that by which we repent of having offended God because he is our supreme judge, that is, for fear of the chastisement

deserved in this life or in the life to come, or because of the very foulness of sin itself.

701. **What qualities must sorrow have to be true sorrow?**
Sorrow, in order to be true, must have four qualities: it must be internal, supernatural, supreme, and universal.

702. **What is meant by saying that sorrow must be internal?**
It means that it must exist in the heart and will, and not in words alone.

703. **Why must sorrow be internal?**
Sorrow must be internal because the will, which has been alienated from God by sin, must return to God by detesting the sin committed.

704. **What is meant by saying that sorrow must be supernatural?**
It means that it must be excited in us by the grace of God and conceived through motives of faith.

705. **Why must sorrow be supernatural?**
Sorrow must be supernatural because the end to which it is directed is supernatural, namely, God's pardon, the acquisition of sanctifying grace, and the right to eternal glory.

706. **Explain more clearly the difference between natural and supernatural sorrow.**
He who repents of having offended God because God is infinitely good and worthy of being loved for his own sake; of having lost heaven and merited hell; or because of the intrinsic malice of sin, has supernatural sorrow, since all these are motives of faith. On the contrary, he who repents only because of the dishonor or chastisement inflicted by men, or because of some purely temporal loss, has a natural sorrow, since he repents from human motives alone.

707. **Why must sorrow be supreme?**
Sorrow must be supreme because we must look upon and hate sin as the greatest of all evils, being as it is an offense against God.

708. **To have sorrow for sin, is it necessary to weep, as we sometimes do, in consequence of the misfortunes of this life?**
It is not necessary to shed tears of sorrow for our sins; it is enough if in our heart we make more of having offended God than of any other misfortune whatsoever.

709. **What is meant by saying that sorrow must be universal?**
It means that it must extend to every mortal sin committed.

710. **Why should sorrow extend to every mortal sin committed?**
Because he who does not repent of even one mortal sin still remains an enemy to God.

711. **What should we do to have sorrow for our sins?**
To have sorrow for our sins, we should ask it of God with our whole heart, and excite it in ourselves by the thought of the great evil we have done by sinning.

712. **What should you do to excite yourself to detest your sins?**
To excite myself to detest my sins: 1) I will consider the rigor of the infinite justice of God, and the foulness of sin which has defiled my soul and made me worthy of the eternal punishment of hell; 2) I will consider that by sin I have lost the grace, friendship, and sonship of God and the inheritance of heaven; 3) that I have offended my Redeemer who died for me, and that my sins caused his death; 4) that I have despised my Creator and my God, that I have turned my back upon him who is my supreme good, and worthy of being loved above everything else, and of being faithfully served.

713. **In going to confession, should we be extremely solicitous to have a true sorrow for our sins?**
In going to confession, we should certainly be very solicitous to have a true sorrow for our sins, because this is of all things the most important; and if sorrow is wanting, the confession is no good.

714. **If one has only venial sins to confess, must he be sorry for all of them?**
If one has only venial sins to confess, it is enough to repent of some of them for his confession to be valid; but to obtain pardon of all of them it is necessary to repent of all he remembers having committed.

715. **If one has only venial sins to confess and if he does not repent of even one of them, does he make a good confession?**
If one confesses only venial sins without having sorrow for at least one of them, his confession is in vain; moreover, it would be sacrilegious if the absence of sorrow was conscious.

716. **What should be done to render the confession of only venial sins more secure?**
To render the confession of venial sins more secure it is prudent also to confess with true sorrow some grave sin of the past, even though it has been already confessed.

717. **Is it well to make an act of contrition often?**
It is well and most useful to make an act of contrition often, especially before going to sleep or when we know we have or fear we have fallen into mortal sin, in order to recover God's grace as soon as possible; and this practice will make it easier for us to obtain from God the grace of making a like act at time of our greatest need, that is, when in danger of death.

Resolution of Sinning No More

718. **In what does a good resolution consist?**

A good resolution consists in a determined will not to commit sin for the future and to use all necessary means to avoid it.

719. **What conditions should a resolution have in order to be good?**

A resolution, in order to be good, should have three principal conditions: it ought to be absolute, universal, and efficacious.

720. **What is meant by an "absolute resolution"?**

It means that the resolution ought to be without any restrictions of time, place, or person.

721. **What is meant by a "universal resolution"?**

It means that we should avoid all mortal sins, both those already committed as well as those which we can possibly commit.

722. **What is meant by an "efficacious resolution"?**

It means that there must be a determined will to lose everything rather than commit another sin; to avoid the dangerous occasions of sin; to stamp out our bad habits; and to discharge the obligations that may have been contracted in consequence of our sins.

723. **What is meant by a "bad habit"?**

By a "bad habit" is meant an acquired disposition to fall easily into those sins to which we have become accustomed.

724. **What must be done to correct bad habits?**

To correct bad habits, we must watch over ourselves, pray much, go often to confession, have one good director, and put into practice the counsels and remedies which he gives us.

725. **What is meant by "dangerous occasions of sin"?**
By "dangerous occasions of sin" are meant all those circumstances of time, place, person, or things, which, of their very nature or because of our frailty, lead us to commit sin.

726. **Are we strictly bound to shun dangerous occasions?**
We are strictly bound to shun those dangerous occasions which ordinarily lead us to commit mortal sin, and which are called the proximate occasions of sin.

727. **What should a person do who cannot avoid a certain occasion of sin?**
A person who cannot avoid a certain occasion of sin should lay the matter before his confessor and follow his advice.

728. **What considerations will help us to make a good resolution?**
The same considerations help us to make a good resolution as are efficacious in exciting sorrow; that is, a consideration of the motives we have to fear God's justice and to love his infinite goodness.

The Accusation of Sins to the Confessor

729. **Having prepared properly for confession by an examination of conscience, by exciting sorrow, and by forming a good resolution, what do you do next?**
Having prepared properly for confession by an examination of conscience, by sorrow, and by a purpose of amendment, I will go and make an accusation of my sins to the confessor in order to get absolution.

730. **What sins are we bound to confess?**
We are bound to confess all our mortal sins; it is well, however, to confess our venial sins also.

731. **Which are the qualities the accusation of sins, or confession, ought to have?**
The principal qualities which the accusation of our sins ought to have are five: it ought to be humble, entire, sincere, prudent, and brief.

732. **What is meant by saying that the accusation ought to be humble?**
That the accusation ought to be humble means that the penitent should accuse himself to his confessor without pride or boasting; but with the feelings of one who is guilty, who confesses his guilt, and who appears before his judge.

733. **What is meant by saying that the accusation ought to be entire?**
That the accusation ought to be entire means that all mortal sins we are conscious of having committed since our last good confession must be made known, together with their circumstances and number.

734. **What circumstances must be made known for the accusation to be entire?**
For the accusation to be entire, the circumstances which change the species of the sin must be made known.

735. **Which are the circumstances which change the species of a sin?**
The circumstances which change the species of a sin are: 1) those by which a sinful action from being venial becomes mortal; 2) those by means of which a sinful action contains the malice of two or more mortal sins.

736. **Give an example of a circumstance making a venial sin mortal.**
If, to excuse himself, a man were to tell a lie and by doing so occasion serious harm to another, he would be bound to make known this circumstance, which changes the lie from an officious lie to a seriously harmful lie.

737. **Give an example of a circumstance on account of which a single sinful action contains the malice of two or more sins.**
If a man were to steal a sacred object, he would be bound to accuse himself of this circumstance which adds to the theft the malice of sacrilege.

738. **If a penitent is not certain of having committed a sin, must he confess it?**
If a penitent is not certain of having committed a sin, he is not bound to confess it; and if he does confess it, he should add that he is not certain of having committed it.

739. **What should he do who does not remember the exact number of his sins?**
He who does not distinctly remember the number of his sins must mention the number as nearly as he can.

740. **Does he who through forgetfulness does not confess a mortal sin, or a necessary circumstance, make a good confession?**
He who through pure forgetfulness does not confess a mortal sin, or a necessary circumstance, makes a good confession, provided he has been duly diligent in trying to remember it.

741. **If a mortal sin forgotten in confession is afterward remembered, are we bound to confess it in another confession?**
If a mortal sin forgotten in confession is afterward remembered, we are certainly bound to confess it the next time we go to confession.

742. **What does he commit who, through shame or some other motive, willfully conceals a mortal sin in confession?**
He who, through shame or some other motive, willfully conceals a mortal sin in confession profanes the sacrament and is consequently guilty of a very great sacrilege.

743. **In what way must he relieve his conscience who has willfully concealed a mortal sin in confession?**
He who has willfully concealed a mortal sin in confession must reveal to his confessor the sin concealed, say in how many confessions he has concealed it, and make all these confessions over again from the last good confession.

744. **What reflection should a penitent make who is tempted to conceal a sin in confession?**
He who is tempted to conceal a mortal sin in confession should reflect: 1) that he was not ashamed to sin in the presence of God who sees all; 2) that it is better to manifest his sin secretly to the confessor than to live tormented by sin, die an unhappy death, and be covered with shame before

the whole world on the day of general judgment; 3) that the confessor is bound by the seal of confession under the gravest sin and under threat of the severest punishments, both temporal and eternal.

745. **What is meant by saying that the accusation ought to be sincere?**
By saying that the accusation ought to be sincere is meant that we must unfold our sins as they are, without excusing them, lessening them, or increasing them.

746. **What is meant by saying that the confession ought to be prudent?**
That the confession ought to be prudent means that in confessing our sins we should use the most careful words possible, and be on our guard against revealing the sins of others.

747. **What is meant by saying that the confession ought to be short?**
That the confession ought to be short means that we should say nothing that is useless for the purpose of confession.

748. **Is it not a heavy burden to be obliged to confess one's sins to another, especially when these are shameful sins?**
Although it may be a heavy burden to confess one's sins to another, still it must be done, because it is of divine precept, and because pardon can be obtained in no other way; and, moreover, because the difficulty is compensated by many advantages and great consolations.

How to Make a Good Confession

749. **How do you present yourself to the confessor?**
I kneel at the feet of the confessor and I say: "Bless me, Father, for I have sinned."

750. **What do you do while the confessor blesses you?**
I humbly bow my head to receive the blessing and I make the sign of the cross.

751. **Having made the sign of the cross what should you say?**
Having made the sign of the cross, I say: "I confess to Almighty God, to Blessed Mary ever Virgin, to all the saints, and to you, my spiritual Father, that I have sinned."

752. **And then what must you say?**
Then I must say: "I was at confession such a time; by the grace of God, I received absolution, performed my penance, and went to Holy Communion." Then I accuse myself of my sins.

753. **When you have finished the accusation of your sins, what do you do?**
When I have finished the accusation of my sins I say: "I accuse myself also of all the sins of my past life, especially of those against such or such a virtue"—for example, against purity or against the fourth commandment, etc.

754. **After this accusation what should you say?**
I should say: "For all these sins and for those I do not remember, I ask pardon of God with my whole heart, and penance and absolution of you, my ghostly Father."

755. **Having thus finished the accusation of your sins what remains to be done?**
Having finished the accusation of my sins, I should listen respectfully to what the confessor says, accept the penance with a sincere intention of performing it; and, from my heart, renew my act of contrition while he gives me absolution.

756. **Having received absolution, what remains to be done?**
Having received absolution, I should thank the Lord, perform my penance as soon as possible, and put in practice the advice of the confessor.

Absolution

757. **Must confessors always give absolution to those who go to confession to them?**
Confessors should give absolution to those only whom they judge properly disposed to receive it.

758. **May confessors sometimes defer or refuse absolution?**
Confessors not only may, but must defer or refuse absolution in certain cases so as not to profane the sacrament.

759. **Who are those penitents who are to be accounted badly disposed and to whom absolution must as a rule be refused or deferred?**
Penitents who are to be accounted badly disposed are chiefly the following: 1) those who do not know the principal mysteries of their faith, or who neglect to learn those other truths of Christian doctrine which they are bound to know according to their state; 2) those who are gravely negligent in examining their conscience, or who show no signs of sorrow or repentance; 3) those who are able but not willing to restore the goods of others, or the reputations they have injured; 4) those who do not from their heart forgive their enemies; 5) those who will not practice the means necessary to correct their bad habits; 6) those who will not abandon the proximate occasions of sin.

760. **Is not a confessor too severe who defers absolution because he does not believe the penitent is well enough disposed?**
A confessor who defers absolution because he does not believe the penitent well enough disposed is not too severe; on the contrary, he is very charitable and acts as a good physician who tries all remedies, even those that are disagreeable and painful, to save the life of his patient.

761. **Should the sinner to whom absolution is deferred or refused despair, or leave off going to confession altogether?**
A sinner to whom absolution is deferred or refused should not despair or leave off going to confession altogether; he should, on the contrary, humble himself, acknowledge his deplorable state, profit by the good advice his confessor gives him, and thus put himself as soon as possible in a state deserving of absolution.

762. **What should a penitent do with regard to selecting a confessor?**
A genuine penitent should earnestly recommend himself to God for help to enable him to select a pious, learned, and prudent confessor, into whose hands he should put himself, obeying him as his judge and physician.

Satisfaction or Penance

763. **What is satisfaction?**
Satisfaction, which is also called sacramental penance, is one of the acts of the penitent by which he makes a certain reparation to the justice of God for his sins, by performing the works the confessor imposes on him.

764. **Is the penitent bound to accept the penance imposed on him by the confessor?**
Yes, the penitent is bound to accept the penance imposed on him by the confessor if he can perform it; and if he cannot, he should humbly say so, and ask some other penance.

765. **When should the penance be performed?**
If the confessor has fixed no time, the penance should be performed as soon as convenient, and as far as possible while in the state of grace.

766. **How should the penance be performed?**
The penance should be performed entirely and devoutly.

767. **Why is a penance imposed in confession?**
A penance is imposed because, after sacramental absolution which remits sin and its eternal punishment, there generally remains a temporal punishment to be undergone, either in this world or in purgatory.

768. **Why has our Lord willed to remit all the punishment due to sin in the sacrament of baptism, and not in the sacrament of penance?**
Our Lord has willed to remit all the punishment due to sin in the sacrament of baptism, and not in the sacrament of penance, because the sins after baptism are much more grievous, being committed with fuller knowledge and greater ingratitude for God's benefits, and also in order that the obligation of satisfying for them may restrain us from falling into sin again.

769. **Can we of ourselves make satisfaction to God?**
Of ourselves we cannot make satisfaction to God, but we certainly can do so by uniting ourselves to Jesus Christ, who gives value to our actions by the merits of his passion and death.

770. **Does the penance which the confessor imposes always suffice to discharge the punishment which remains due to our sins?**
The penance which the confessor imposes does not ordinarily suffice to discharge the punishment remaining due to our sins; and hence we must try to supply it by other voluntary penances.

771. **Which are the works of penance?**
The works of penance may be reduced to three kinds: prayer, fasting, and almsdeeds.

772. **What is meant by prayer?**
By prayer is meant every kind of pious exercise.

773. **What is meant by fasting?**
By fasting is meant every kind of mortification.

774. **What is meant by almsgiving?**
By almsgiving is meant every spiritual or corporal work of mercy.

775. **Which penance is the more meritorious: that which the confessor gives, or that which we do of our own choice?**
The penance which the confessor imposes is the most meritorious, because being part of the sacrament it receives greater virtue from the merits of the passion of Jesus Christ.

776. **Do those who die after having received absolution, but before they have fully satisfied the justice of God, go straight to heaven?**
No, they go to purgatory; there to satisfy the justice of God and be perfectly purified.

777. **Can the souls in purgatory be relieved of their pains by us?**
Yes, the souls in purgatory can be relieved by our prayers, almsdeeds, all our other good works, and by indulgences, but above all by the Holy Sacrifice of the Mass.

778. **Besides his penance, what else must the penitent do after confession?**
Besides performing his penance after confession, the penitent, if he has justly injured another in his goods or reputation, or if he has given him scandal, must as soon as possible, and as far as he is able, restore him his goods, repair his honor, and remedy the scandal.

779. **How can the scandal given be remedied?**
The scandal given can be remedied by removing the occasion of it and by edifying by word and example those whom we have scandalized.

780. **How should we make satisfaction to one whom we have offended?**
We should make satisfaction to one whom we have offended by asking his pardon, or by some other suitable reparation.

781. **What fruits does a good confession produce in us?**
A good confession: 1) remits the sins we have committed and gives us the grace of God; 2) restores us peace and quiet of conscience; 3) reopens the gates of heaven and changes the eternal punishment of hell into a temporal punishment; 4) preserves us from falling again, and renders us capable of partaking of the treasury of indulgences.

Indulgences

782. **What is an indulgence?**
An indulgence is the remission of the temporal punishment due on account of our sins which have been already pardoned as far as their guilt is concerned—a remission accorded by the Church outside the sacrament of penance.

783. **From whom has the Church received the power to grant indulgences?**
The Church has received the power to grant indulgences from Jesus Christ.

784. **In what way does the Church by means of indulgences remit this temporal punishment?**
The Church by means of indulgences remits this temporal punishment by applying to us the superabundant merits of Jesus Christ, of the Blessed Virgin, and of the saints, which constitute what is known as the treasure of the Church.

785. **Who has the power to grant indulgences?**
The pope alone has the power to grant indulgences in the whole Church, and the bishop in his own diocese, according to the faculty given him by the pope.

786. **How many kinds of indulgences are there?**
Indulgences are of two kinds: plenary and partial.

787. **What is a plenary indulgence?**

A plenary indulgence is that by which the whole temporal punishment due to our sins is remitted. Hence, if one were to die after having gained such an indulgence, he would go straight to heaven, being, as he is, perfectly exempt from the pains of purgatory.

788. **What is a partial indulgence?**

A partial indulgence is that by which is remitted only a part of the temporal punishment due to our sins.

789. **Why does the Church grant indulgences?**

In granting indulgences, the Church intends to aid our incapacity to expiate all the temporal punishment in this world, by enabling us to obtain by means of works of piety and Christian charity that which in the first ages Christians gained by the rigor of canonical penances.

790. **What is meant by an indulgence of forty or a hundred days, or of seven years and the like?**

By an indulgence of forty or a hundred days, or of seven years and the like, is meant the remission of so much of the temporal punishment as would have been paid by penances of forty or a hundred days, or seven years, anciently prescribed in the Church.

791. **What value should we set on indulgences?**

We should set the greatest value on indulgences because by them we satisfy the justice of God and obtain possession of heaven sooner and more easily.

792. **Which are the conditions necessary to gain indulgences?**

The conditions necessary to gain indulgences are: 1) the state of grace (at least at the final completion of the work), and freedom from those venial faults, the punishment of which we wish to cancel; 2) the fulfillment of all the works the Church enjoins in order to gain the indulgence; 3) the intention to gain it.

793. **Can indulgences be applied also to the souls in purgatory?**
Yes, indulgences can be applied also to the souls in purgatory, when he who grants them says that they may be so applied.

794. **What is a jubilee?**
A jubilee, which as a rule is granted every twenty-five years, is a plenary indulgence to which are attached many privileges and special concessions, such as that of being able to obtain absolution from certain reserved sins and from censures, and the commutation of certain vows.

The Sacrament of Extreme Unction

795. **What is extreme unction?**
Extreme unction is a sacrament instituted for the spiritual as well as for the temporal comfort of the sick in danger of death.

796. **What are the effects of the sacrament of extreme unction?**
The sacrament of extreme unction produces the following effects: 1) it increases sanctifying grace; 2) it remits venial sins, and also the mortal sins which the sick person, if contrite, is unable to confess; 3) it takes away weakness and sloth which remain even after pardon has been obtained; 4) it gives strength to bear illness patiently, to withstand temptation, and to die holily; 5) it aids in restoring us to health of body if it is for the good of the soul.

797. **When should extreme unction be received?**
Extreme unction should be received when the illness is dangerous, and after the sick person has received, if possible, the sacraments of penance and the Blessed Eucharist; it is even well to receive it while he has the use of his senses, and has still some hope of recovery.

798. **Why is it well to receive extreme unction when the sick person has still the use of his senses, and has still some hope of recovery?**
It is well to receive extreme unction while the sick person retains the use of his senses, and while there remains some hope of his recovery, for he thus receives it with better dispositions, and is hence able to derive greater fruit from it; and also, because this sacrament restores health of body (should it be for the good of the soul) by assisting the powers of nature; and hence it should not be deferred until recovery is despaired of.

799. **With what dispositions should the sacrament of extreme unction be received?**
The principal dispositions for receiving extreme unction are: to be in the state of grace; to have confidence in the power of this sacrament and in the mercy of God; and to be resigned to the will of the Lord.

800. **What should be the sick person's feelings on seeing the priest?**
On seeing the priest, the sick person should feel thankful to God for having sent him; and should gladly receive the comforts of religion, which, if he is able, he should request himself.

The Sacrament of Holy Orders

801. **What is the sacrament of holy orders?**
Holy orders is a sacrament which gives power to exercise the sacred duties connected with the worship of God and the salvation of souls, and which imprints the character of minister of God on the soul of him who receives it.

802. **Why is it called orders?**
It is called orders because it comprises various grades, the one subordinate to the other, from which the sacred hierarchy is composed.

803. **Which are these grades?**
The highest is the episcopate, which contains the fullness of the priesthood; then comes the priesthood; then the diaconate, the subdiaconate, and the orders called minor.

804. **When did Jesus Christ institute the sacerdotal order?**
Jesus Christ instituted the sacerdotal order at the last supper when he conferred on the apostles and their successors the power of consecrating the Blessed Eucharist. Then on the day of his resurrection he conferred on them the power of remitting and retaining sin, thus constituting them the first priests of the new law in all the fullness of their power.

805. **Who is the minister of this sacrament?**
The bishop is the minister of this sacrament.

806. **Is the dignity of the Christian priesthood a great dignity?**
The dignity of the Christian priesthood is great indeed, because of the twofold power which Jesus Christ has conferred upon it—that over his real body and that over his mystical body, or the Church; and because of the divine mission committed to priests to lead men to eternal life.

807. **Is the Catholic priesthood necessary in the Church?**
The Catholic priesthood is necessary in the Church, because without it the faithful would be deprived of the Holy Sacrifice of the Mass and of the greater part of the sacraments; they would have no one to instruct them in the faith; and they would be as sheep without a shepherd, a prey to wolves; in short, the Church, such as Christ instituted it, would no longer exist.

808. **Will the Catholic priesthood therefore never cease on this earth?**
In spite of the war that hell wages against it, the Catholic priesthood will last until the end of time, because Jesus Christ has promised that the powers of hell shall never prevail against his Church.

809. **Is it a sin to despise priests?**
It is a very grave sin, because the scorn and insults cast on priests fall upon Jesus Christ himself, who said to his apostles: "He who despises you, despises me."[17]

810. **What motive should he have who embraces the ecclesiastical state?**
The motive of one who embraces the ecclesiastical state should be the glory of God and the salvation of souls alone.

811. **What is necessary to enter the ecclesiastical state?**
To enter the ecclesiastical state a divine vocation is necessary before all else.

812. **What should be done to find out whether God calls us to the ecclesiastical state?**
To find out if God calls us to the ecclesiastical state, we should: 1) fervently pray the Lord to make known his will to us; 2) consult our bishop or a learned and prudent director; 3) diligently examine whether we have the capacity necessary for the studies, the duties, and the obligations of this state.

813. **If one were to enter the ecclesiastical state without a divine vocation would he do wrong?**
If one were to enter the ecclesiastical state without a divine vocation, he would commit a great wrong and run the risk of being lost.

814. **Do those parents sin who, from worldly motives, impel their sons to embrace the ecclesiastical state without any vocation?**
Those parents who, for worldly motives, impel their sons to embrace the ecclesiastical state without any vocation commit a very grave sin, because by thus acting they usurp the right God has reserved to himself alone of choosing his own ministers; and they expose their children to the danger of eternal damnation.

[17] Lk 10:16

815. **Which are the duties of the faithful toward those who are called to holy orders?**
The faithful should: 1) give their children and dependents full liberty to follow the call of God; 2) pray God to deign to grant good pastors and zealous ministers to his Church—it is precisely for this end that the fasts of Quarter Tense have been instituted; 3) have special respect for all who are consecrated by holy orders to God's service.

The Sacrament of Matrimony

Nature of the Sacrament of Matrimony

816. **What is the sacrament of matrimony?**
Matrimony is a sacrament, instituted by our Lord Jesus Christ, which creates a holy and indissoluble union between a man and woman, and gives them grace to love one another holily and to bring up their children as Christians.

817. **By whom was matrimony instituted?**
Matrimony was instituted by God himself in the garden of paradise, and was raised to the dignity of a sacrament by Jesus Christ in the new law.

818. **Has the sacrament of matrimony any special signification?**
The sacrament of matrimony signifies the indissoluble union of Jesus Christ with the Church, his spouse, and our holy mother.

819. **Why do we say that the bond of marriage is indissoluble?**
We say that the bond of marriage is indissoluble or that it cannot be dissolved except by the death of either husband or wife, because God so ordained from the beginning and so Jesus Christ our Lord solemnly proclaimed.

820. **Can the contract be separated from the sacrament in Christian marriage?**
No, in marriage among Christians the contract cannot be separated from the sacrament, because, for Christians, marriage is nothing else than the natural contract itself, raised by Jesus Christ to the dignity of a sacrament.

821. **Among Christians, then, there can be no true marriage that is not a sacrament?**
Among Christians, there can be no true marriage that is not a sacrament.

822. **What effects does the sacrament of matrimony produce?**
The sacrament of matrimony: 1) gives an increase of sanctifying grace; and 2) gives a special grace for the faithful discharge of all the duties of the married state.

Minister, Rite, Dispositions

823. **Who are the ministers of this sacrament?**
The ministers of this sacrament are the couple themselves, who together confer and receive the sacrament.

824. **How is this sacrament administered?**
This sacrament, preserving, as it does, the nature of a contract, is administered by the contracting parties themselves, who declare, in the presence of the parish priest, or another priest delegated by him, and of two witnesses, that they take each other in marriage.

825. **What use, then, is the blessing which the parish priest gives to the married couple?**
The blessing which the parish priest gives to the married couple is not necessary to constitute the sacrament, but it is given to sanction their union in the name of the Church and to invoke on them more abundantly the blessing of God.

826. **What intention should those have who contract marriage?**
Those who contract marriage should have the intention: 1) of doing the will of God, who calls them to that state; 2) of working out in that state the salvation of their souls; 3) of bringing up their children as Christians, if God should bless them with any.

827. **How should those about to be married prepare themselves to receive this sacrament with fruit?**
In order to receive this sacrament with fruit, those about to be married should: 1) earnestly recommend themselves to God, so as to know his will and obtain the graces necessary for that state; 2) consult their parents before making any promise, because obedience and the respect due to them demand this; 3) prepare themselves by a good confession, or, if necessary, a general confession of their whole life; 4) avoid all dangerous familiarity in word or act while in each other's company.

828. **Which are the principal obligations of married persons?**
Married persons should: 1) guard inviolably their conjugal fidelity and behave always and in all things as Christians; 2) love one another, bear patiently with one another, and live in peace and concord; 3) think seriously of providing for their children, if they have any, according to their needs; bring them up as Christians, and leave them free to choose the state of life to which they are called by God.

Conditions and Impediments

829. **What is necessary to contract Christian marriage validly?**
To contract Christian marriage validly, it is necessary to be free from every diriment impediment to marriage; and to give consent freely to the marriage contract in the presence of the parish priest (or a priest delegated by him) and of two witnesses.

830. **What is necessary to contract marriage lawfully?**
To contract marriage lawfully, it is necessary to be free from every impeding impediment to marriage; to be instructed in the principal truths of religion; and, finally, to be in a state of grace; otherwise, a sacrilege would be committed.

831. **What are impediments to marriage?**
Impediments to marriage are certain circumstances which render marriage either invalid or unlawful. The former are called diriment impediments and the latter impeding impediments.

832. **Give examples of diriment impediments.**
Diriment impediments are, for example, relationship to the fourth degree, spiritual relationship, a solemn vow of chastity, or difference in religion, that is, when one party is baptized and the other is not.

833. **Give examples of impeding impediments.**
Impeding impediments are, for example, the forbidden times, a simple vow of chastity, and the like.

834. **Are the faithful obliged to make known to ecclesiastical authority impediments of which they have a knowledge?**
The faithful are obliged to make known to ecclesiastical authority impediments of which they have knowledge; and for this reason, the names of those who intend to get married are published in the Church.

835. **Who has the power to regulate impediments to marriage, to dispense from them, and to judge of the validity of Christian marriage?**
The Church alone has power to regulate impediments to marriage, to judge of the validity of marriage among Christians, and to dispense from the impediments which she has placed.

836. **Why has the Church alone power to place impediments and to judge of the validity of marriage?**
The Church alone has power to place impediments, to judge of the validity of marriage, and to dispense from the impediments which she has placed, because the contract, being inseparable from the sacrament in a Christian marriage, also comes under the power of the Church, to which alone Jesus Christ gave the right to make laws and give decisions in sacred things.

837. **Can the civil authority dissolve the bonds of Christian marriage by divorce?**
No, the bond of Christian marriage cannot be dissolved by the civil authority, because the civil authority cannot interfere with the matter of the sacrament, nor can it put asunder what God has joined together.[18]

Appendix

ON THE VIRTUES, VICES, AND BEATITUDES

The Theological Virtues in General

838. **What is a supernatural virtue?**
A supernatural virtue is a quality infused by God into the soul by which the latter acquires inclination, facility, and promptness to know good and do it toward eternal life.

839. **How many principal supernatural virtues are there?**
The principal supernatural virtues are seven: three theological, and four cardinal virtues.

[18] Translator's note: In the text of the *Catechism of Pius X* certain questions are given, dealing with civil marriage, which, however, do not as a rule concern English-speaking countries, and are consequently omitted here.

840. **Which are the theological virtues?**
The theological virtues are: faith, hope, and charity.

841. **Why are faith, hope, and charity called theological virtues?**
Faith, hope, and charity are called theological virtues, because they have God as their immediate and principal object, and are infused by him.

842. **How can the theological virtues have God for their immediate object?**
The theological virtues have God for their immediate object in this way: that by faith, we believe in God, and believe all he has revealed; by hope, we hope to possess God; and by charity, we love God, and in him we love ourselves and our neighbor.

843. **When does God infuse the theological virtues into the soul?**
God in his goodness infuses the theological virtues into the soul when adorning us with his sanctifying grace; and hence, when receiving baptism, we were enriched with these virtues and, along with them, with the gifts of the Holy Ghost.

844. **Is it enough toward salvation to have received the theological virtues in baptism?**
For one who has come to the use of reason, it is not enough to have received the theological virtues in baptism; it is also necessary to make frequent acts of faith, hope, and charity.

845. **When are we obliged to make acts of faith, hope, and charity?**
We are obliged to make acts of faith, hope, and charity when we come to the use of reason; often during life; and when in danger of death.

Faith

846. **What is faith?**
Faith is a supernatural virtue, which God infuses into our souls, and by which, relying on the authority of God himself, we believe everything

which he has revealed and which through his Church he proposes for our belief.

847. **How do we know the truths God has revealed?**
We know the revealed truths by means of the Church, which is infallible; that is, by means of the pope, the successor of St. Peter, and by means of the bishops, the successors to the apostles, who were taught by Jesus Christ himself.

848. **Are we certain of the truths the Church teaches us?**
We are most certain of the truths the Church teaches, because Jesus Christ pledged his word that the Church should never be led into error.

849. **By what sin is the faith lost?**
Faith is lost by denying or voluntarily doubting even a single article proposed for our belief.

850. **How is lost faith recovered?**
Lost faith is recovered by repenting of the sin committed and by believing anew all the Church believes.

851. **Can we comprehend all the truths of faith?**
No, we cannot comprehend all the truths of faith, because some of these truths are mysteries.

852. **What are mysteries?**
Mysteries are truths above reason and which we are to believe even though we cannot comprehend them.

853. **Why must we believe mysteries?**
We must believe mysteries because they are revealed to us by God, who, being infinite truth and goodness, can neither deceive nor be deceived.

854. **Are mysteries contrary to reason?**
Mysteries are above, not contrary to, reason; and even reason itself persuades us to accept the mysteries.

855. **Why cannot the mysteries be contrary to reason?**
The mysteries cannot be contrary to reason, because the same God who has given us the light of reason has also revealed the mysteries, and he cannot contradict himself.

856. **Where are the truths which God has revealed contained?**
The truths which God has revealed are contained in sacred scripture and in tradition.

Hope

857. **What is hope?**
Hope is a supernatural virtue, infused by God into our soul, by which we desire and expect that eternal life that God has promised to his servants, as well as the means necessary to attain it.

858. **What grounds have we to hope that God will give us heaven and the means necessary to secure it?**
We hope that God will give us heaven and the necessary means to attain it, because the all-merciful God, through the merits of our Lord Jesus Christ, has promised it to those who faithfully serve him; and, being both faithful and omnipotent, he never fails in his promises.

859. **What are the conditions necessary to obtain heaven?**
The conditions necessary to obtain heaven are the grace of God, the practice of good works, and perseverance until death in his holy love.

860. **How is hope lost?**
Hope is lost as often as faith is lost; and it is also lost by the sin of despair and presumption.

861. **How is lost hope regained?**

Lost hope is regained by repenting of the sin committed, and by exciting anew confidence in the divine goodness.

Charity

862. **What is charity?**

Charity is a supernatural virtue, infused into our soul by God, by which we love God above all for his own sake, and our neighbor as ourselves for love of God.

863. **Why should we love God?**

We should love God because he is the supreme good, infinitely good and perfect; and also, because he commands us to do so, and because of the many benefits we receive from him.

864. **How are we to love God?**

We are to love God above all things else, with our whole heart, with our whole mind, with our whole soul, and with all our strength.

865. **What is meant by loving God "above all other things"?**

To love God "above all other things" means to prefer him to all creatures, even the dearest and most perfect, and to be willing to lose everything rather than offend him or cease to love him.

866. **What is meant by loving God "with our whole heart"?**

To love God "with our whole heart" means consecrating all our affections to him.

867. **What is meant by loving God "with our whole mind"?**

To love God "with our whole mind" means directing all our thoughts to him.

868. **What is meant by loving God "with our whole soul"?**
To love God "with our whole soul" means consecrating to him the use of all the powers of our soul.

869. **What is meant by loving God "with all our strength"?**
To love God "with all our strength" means striving to grow ever more and more in his love, and so to act that all our actions should have as their one motive and end the love of him and the desire of pleasing him.

870. **Why should we love our neighbor?**
We should love our neighbor for the love of God, because God commands it, and because every man is made to God's image.

871. **Are we obliged to love even our enemies?**
We are obliged to love even our enemies, because even they are our neighbors and because Jesus Christ has made this love the object of an express command.

872. **What is meant by "loving our neighbor as ourselves"?**
To "love our neighbor as ourselves" means to wish him and do him, as far as possible, the good which we ought to wish for ourselves, and not to wish or to do him any evil.

873. **When do we love ourselves as we ought?**
We love ourselves as we ought when we endeavor to serve God and to place all our happiness in him.

874. **How is charity lost?**
Charity is lost by each and every mortal sin.

875. **How is charity regained?**
Charity is regained by making acts of the love of God, by duly repenting, and making a good confession.

On Actual Sins

876. **How many kinds of sin are there?**
There are two kinds of sin: original sin and actual sin.

877. **What is original sin?**
Original sin is the sin in which we are all born, and which we contracted by the disobedience of our first parent, Adam.

878. **What evil effects has the sin of Adam brought upon us?**
The evil effects of the sin of Adam are: the privation of grace, the loss of paradise, together with ignorance, inclination to evil, death, and all our other miseries.

879. **How is original sin canceled?**
Original sin is canceled by holy baptism.

880. **What is actual sin?**
Actual sin is that which man, after coming to the use of reason, commits of his own free will.

881. **How many kinds of actual sin are there?**
There are two kinds of actual sin: mortal and venial.

882. **What is mortal sin?**
Mortal sin is a transgression of the divine law by which we seriously fail in our duties toward God, toward our neighbor, or toward ourselves.

883. **Why is it called mortal?**
It is called mortal because it brings death on the soul by making it lose sanctifying grace which is the life of the soul, just as the soul itself is the life of the body.

884. **What injury does mortal sin do the soul?**
1) Mortal sin deprives the soul of grace and of the friendship of God. 2) It makes it lose heaven. 3) It deprives it of merits already acquired, and renders it incapable of acquiring new merits. 4) It makes it the slave of the devil. 5) It makes it deserve hell as well as the chastisements of this life.

885. **Besides grave matter, what is required to constitute a mortal sin?**
To constitute a mortal sin, besides grave matter there is also required full consciousness of the gravity of the matter, along with the deliberate will to commit the sin.

886. **What is venial sin?**
Venial sin is a lesser transgression of the divine law, by which we slightly fail in some duty toward God, toward our neighbor, or toward ourselves.

887. **Why is it called venial?**
Because it is light compared with mortal sin; because it does not deprive us of divine grace; and because God more readily pardons it.

888. **Then little account need be made of venial sin?**
That would be a very great mistake, not only because venial sin is always an offense against God; but also because it does no little harm to the soul.

889. **What harm does venial sin do the soul?**
Venial sin: 1) weakens and chills charity in us; 2) disposes us to mortal sin; and 3) renders us deserving of great temporal punishments both in this world and in the next.

The Vices

890. **What is a vice?**
A vice is an evil disposition of the mind to shirk good and do evil, arising from the frequent repetition of evil acts.

891. **What difference is there between a sin and a vice?**
Between sin and vice there is this difference: that sin is a passing act, whereas a vice is a bad habit, contracted by continually falling into some sin.

892. **Which are the vices called capital?**
The vices called capital are seven: pride, covetousness, lust, anger, gluttony, envy, and sloth.

893. **How are the capital vices conquered?**
The capital vices are conquered by the exercise of the opposite virtues: Thus pride is conquered by humility; covetousness by liberality; lust by chastity; anger by patience; gluttony by abstinence; envy by brotherly love; sloth by diligence and fervor in the service of God.

894. **Why are these vices called capital?**
They are called capital because they are the head and fount of many other vices and sins.

895. **How many are the sins against the Holy Ghost?**
The sins against the Holy Ghost are six: 1) despairing of being saved; 2) presuming on being saved without merit; 3) opposing the known truth; 4) envying another's graces; 5) obstinately remaining in sin; and 6) final impenitence.

896. **Why are these sins specially said to be against the Holy Ghost?**
These sins are specially said to be against the Holy Ghost, because they are committed through pure malice, which is contrary to goodness, the special attribute of the Holy Ghost.

897. **Which are the sins that are said to cry to God for vengeance?**
The sins that are said to cry to God for vengeance are these four: 1) voluntary homicide; 2) sins against nature; 3) oppression of the poor; 4) defrauding the laborer of his hire.

898. **Why are these sins said to cry to God for vengeance?**
These sins are said to cry to God for vengeance because the Holy Ghost says so, and because their iniquity is so great and so manifest that it provokes God to punish them with the severest chastisements.

On the Beatitudes

899. **Name the beatitudes.**
The beatitudes are eight:

1. Blessed are the poor in spirit, for theirs is the kingdom of heaven.
2. Blessed are the meek, for they shall possess the land.
3. Blessed are they that mourn, for they shall be comforted.
4. Blessed are they that hunger and thirst after justice, for they shall be filled.
5. Blessed are the merciful, for they shall obtain mercy.
6. Blessed are the clean of heart, for they shall see God.
7. Blessed are the peacemakers, for they shall be called the children of God.
8. Blessed are they that suffer persecution for justice' sake, for of such is the kingdom of heaven.

900. **Why did Jesus Christ propose the beatitudes to us?**
Jesus Christ proposed the beatitudes to us to make us detest the maxims of the world, and to invite us to love and practice the maxims of the gospel.

901. **Who are they whom the world calls happy?**
The world calls those happy who abound in riches and honors, who lead a pleasant life, and who meet with no occasions of suffering.

902. **Who are the poor in spirit whom Jesus Christ calls blessed?**
The poor in spirit are, according to the gospel, those whose hearts are detached from riches; who make good use of riches should they have any; who do not seek them too eagerly, if they have none; and who suffer the loss of such things with resignation when deprived of them.

903. **Who are the meek?**

The meek are those who act tenderly toward their neighbor, bear patiently with his defects, and accept the offenses and injuries they receive from him without contention, resentment, or vengeance.

904. **Who are they that mourn, yet are called happy?**

They that mourn, yet are called happy, are they who suffer tribulations with resignation, and who mourn over sins committed, over the evils and scandals that prevail in the world, over paradise because it is so distant, and over the danger there is of losing it.

905. **Who are they that hunger and thirst after justice?**

They that hunger and thirst after justice, are those who ardently desire to increase daily more and more in divine grace and in the exercise of good and virtuous works.

906. **Who are the merciful?**

The merciful are those who love their neighbor in God and for God's sake, compassionate his miseries, spiritual as well as corporal, and endeavor to succor him according to their means and position.

907. **Who are the clean of heart?**

The clean of heart are those who retain no affection for sin and keep aloof from it, and who above all else avoid every sort of impurity.

908. **Who are the peacemakers?**

The peacemakers are those who preserve peace with their neighbor and with themselves, and who endeavor to bring about peace and concord between those who are at variance.

909. **Who are they that suffer persecution for justice' sake?**

They that suffer persecution for justice' sake are those who patiently bear derision, reproof, and persecution for the sake of the faith and of the law of Jesus Christ.

910. **What do the various rewards promised by Jesus Christ in the beatitudes denote?**
The various rewards promised by Jesus Christ in the beatitudes all denote under different names the eternal glory of paradise.

911. **Do the beatitudes procure us the glory of paradise alone?**
The beatitudes not only procure us the glory of paradise, but are also the means of leading a happy life, as far as this is possible here on earth.

912. **Do those who follow the path of the beatitudes receive any reward in this life?**
Yes, certainly; those who follow the path of the beatitudes do receive a reward even in this life, inasmuch as they enjoy interior peace and contentment, which is the beginning, even though an imperfect one, of the happiness of heaven.

913. **Can those that follow the maxims of the world be called truly happy?**
No, because they have no true peace of soul, and are in danger of being lost eternally.

Oath against Modernism

I . . . . firmly embrace and accept all and singly those articles which have been defined, set forth, and declared by the Church's inerrant teaching-authority and especially those heads of doctrines which directly conflict with the errors of this age. And,

I confess that God, the beginning and end of all things, can with certainty be known and proved to be by the natural light of reason from those things which are made, that is, by the visible works of creation, even as a cause may be certainly proved from its effects.

I accept and acknowledge the external arguments of revelation, that is, the divine facts, especially miracles and prophecy, and I also accept the most sure proofs of the divine origin of the Christian religion and hold that they are preeminently adapted to the intelligence of all ages and men and, in particular, of this age.

And with firm faith, I equally believe that the Church, the guardian and teacher of the revealed word, was directly founded by the real and historical Christ himself, as he dwelt with us, and that she was built upon Peter, the prince of the apostolic hierarchy and his successors forever.

I sincerely receive the teaching of the faith as it has been handed down to us from the apostles and orthodox fathers, and handed down in the same sense and meaning; and furthermore, I utterly reject the heretical fiction of the evolution of dogmas, according to which they change from one meaning to another and a meaning contradictory to that meaning which the Church before had given; and equally do I condemn that entire error according to which philosophical discovery suffices, although the divine deposit was given to Christ's bride and given to be faithfully guarded by her, or according to which it [the teaching] is little by little transformed in meaning by the creations of the human consciousness and man's effort, and brought to perfection in the future by an indefinite progression.

I most surely hold and sincerely declare that faith is not a blind realization of religion drawn out of the darkness of the subconscience, morally enlightened by the influence of the heart and the inflexions of the will, but that it is an honest assent by the intellect given to truth accepted, through hearing of the ear, by the which we believe as true those things which have been revealed and confirmed by a personal God, our Creator and Lord, and on the basis of the authority of God, who in the highest sense is trustworthy.

Likewise—and this is equally important—I submit myself reverently and with my whole mind to all the condemnations, declarations, and commands contained in the encyclical *Pascendi* and the decree *Lamentabili*, especially in regard to that which they call the history of dogmas. I also reprobate the error of those who assert that the faith offered by the Church may, by any possibility, conflict with history; and the error that it is not possible to harmonize, in the sense in which they are now understood, the Catholic dogmas with the origins of the Christian religion, which are the more trustworthy.

I condemn and reject the opinions of those who say that the more learned Christians may represent at one and the same time two persons, the one a believer, the other a historian, as if it were possible to hold on as a historian to things which are contradictory to the faith of the believer, or lay down premises according to which it follows that dogmas are either false or dubious, just so they be not openly set aside.

Equally do I reprobate that principle of judging the holy scriptures and interpreting them, which, in defiance of the Church's tradition, the analogy of faith, and the rules of the apostolic see, suits itself to the comments of rationalists, and, scarcely less lawlessly than rashly, accepts textual criticism as the one only and supreme rule.

Further, I reject the theory of those who hold that the teacher in the department of historic theology, as well as the writer on its subjects, must place opinion above the principle of the supernatural origin of Catholic tradition and the promise of divine aid in the preservation of all truth, and further, that the writings of the individual fathers must be explained by the principles of science alone, apart from any sacred authority and by the same free judgment that any profane document is studied or investigated.

Finally, I profess myself most averse to the error of the Modernists who hold that in sacred tradition there is not a divine element; or—what is far worse—who reason in a pantheistic sense, so that nothing is left but the bare and naked historic occurrence like unto other occurrences of history, which are left to men to carry on in subsequent periods by their industry, shrewdness, and genius the teaching begun by Christ and his apostles.

And I do most firmly hold to the faith of the fathers and will continue so to do to the last breath of life, the faith concerning the unfailing charism of the truth which now inheres, has inhered, and will always continue to inhere in the episcopal succession from the apostles; that nothing is to be regarded as better or more opportune which the culture of this age or that age can suggest, and that nothing is at any time to be otherwise believed or otherwise understood as the absolute and immutable truth preached from the beginning by the apostles.

To all these things I promise to hold faithfully, sincerely, and wholly, and I promise to keep them inviolably, never departing from them in teaching or by any words or writings. Thus I promise and swear, so help me God and these holy gospels of God.[1]

[1] English translation is from Volume 2 of the 1919 edition of Philip Schaff's *Bibliotheca Symbolica Ecclesiæ Universalis* (New York: Harper & Brothers).

ABOUT THIS SERIES

Tradivox was first conceived as an international research endeavor to recover lost and otherwise little-known Catholic catechetical texts. As the research progressed over several years, the vision began to grow, along with the number of project contributors and a general desire to share these works with a broader audience.

Legally incorporated in 2019, Tradivox has begun the work of carefully remastering and republishing dozens of these catechisms which were once in common and official use in the Church around the world. That effort is embodied in this *Tradivox Catholic Catechism Index*, a multi-volume series restoring artifacts of traditional faith and praxis for a contemporary readership. More about this series and the work of Tradivox can be learned at www.Tradivox.com.

SOPHIA INSTITUTE

Sophia Institute is a nonprofit institution that seeks to nurture the spiritual, moral, and cultural life of souls and to spread the Gospel of Christ in conformity with the authentic teachings of the Roman Catholic Church.

Sophia Institute Press fulfills this mission by offering translations, reprints, and new publications that afford readers a rich source of the enduring wisdom of mankind.

Sophia Institute also operates the popular online resource CatholicExchange.com. *Catholic Exchange* provides world news from a Catholic perspective as well as daily devotionals and articles that will help readers to grow in holiness and live a life consistent with the teachings of the Church.

In 2013, Sophia Institute launched Sophia Institute for Teachers to renew and rebuild Catholic culture through service to Catholic education. With the goal of nurturing the spiritual, moral, and cultural life of souls, and an abiding respect for the role and work of teachers, we strive to provide materials and programs that are at once enlightening to the mind and ennobling to the heart; faithful and complete, as well as useful and practical.

Sophia Institute gratefully recognizes the Solidarity Association for preserving and encouraging the growth of our apostolate over the course of many years. Without their generous and timely support, this book would not be in your hands.

www.SophiaInstitute.com
www.CatholicExchange.com
www.SophiaInstituteforTeachers.org